The Resume Kit

THE RESUME KIT

FIFTH EDITION

RICHARD H. BEATTY

WILEY

JOHN WILEY & SONS, INC.

Published by John Wiley & Sons, Inc., Hoboken, New Jersey.
Published simultaneously in Canada.

For general information on our other products and services please contact our Customer Care Department within the United States at (800) 762-2974, outside the United States at (317) 572-3993 or fax (317) 572-4002.

Wiley also publishes its books in a variety of electronic formats. Some content that appears in print may not be available in electronic books. For more information about Wiley products, visit our Web site at www.wiley.com.

Library of Congress Cataloging-in-Publication Data:

Beatty, Richard H., 1939–
  The resume kit / Richard H. Beatty.—5th ed.
     p. cm.
  Includes index.
  ISBN 0-471-44926-1 (pbk.)
    1. Resumes (Employment). I. Title.
HF5383.B33   2003
650.14′2—dc21

                       2003045076

Printed in the United States of America.

10 9 8 7 6 5 4 3 2 1

To my wife, Carolyn,
and my sons, Chris and Scott,
who have added great joy and much fullness to my life

PREFACE

Welcome to the new, Fifth Edition of *The Resume Kit*, a best-seller since 1983.

Since its inception, hundreds of thousands of readers have benefited from this book and found it to be an indispensable guide and companion in conducting a successful job search.

This, the Fifth Edition, is even better than the last. It is loaded with great new information that will help you write a dynamite resume—one that grabs an employer's attention and gets your job search off to a flying start.

Writing an effective resume is at the heart of a successful job-hunting campaign. Think about the many important roles this document plays! First, as a communications and marketing document, you must count on it to get you in the door. Then it becomes the focal point or road map during the job interview. If well written, it focuses attention on your strengths and contributions—the things that get you a job offer. If poorly designed, it does just the opposite! And finally, it is the document often used to compare you with other candidates, when it's time for the employer to make that all-important employment decision. You have much to gain (or lose) when preparing this document, so you need to give it your best shot.

There are tons of books out there on resume preparation, so why should you choose this one? That's a reasonable question.

First, there is the matter of the author's experience and credentials. There are so many differing opinions about what a "good" resume is, how do you know whom and what to believe? You have to consider the author's background and experience. What hands-on resume experience has the author had that qualifies him or her as an expert—one who can credibly distinguish between a resume that is effective and one that is not? My hands-on experience with resumes is considerable.

As a former Fortune 200 corporate employment executive and the previous vice president of a major, international executive search firm, I have personally read an estimated 200,000+ resumes and, on the basis of resume quality, made decisions on whom to interview. Reading this kind of resume volume allows me to fully understand and appreciate the fine points that distinguish between those effective resumes and those that are not. I've "earned my spurs" in this category.

Additionally, over the past 15 years, my firm, Brandywine Consulting Group, has run large outplacement projects for several major corporations. In doing so, we have written thousands of resumes for separated employees going through the job search process. Over the years, we have experimented with slight variations in resume format and content to discover what really works best.

Our continuous refinement of this process has resulted in a recommended resume format that has proven enormously effective. In following this book's advice, therefore, you will be the beneficiary of solid recommendations, proven to work in the marketplace. This is the "acid test," so to speak.

Another good reason to consider this book is my approach to teaching resume writing. Here you will find a systematic, easy-to-follow, step-by-step approach supported by many examples. If you follow these steps, I guarantee they will turn a sometimes arduous and frustrating task into a simple and painless process. Best of all, you will end up with a powerful resume that will serve you well as you venture out into this competitive labor market.

This Fifth Edition of *The Resume Kit* has been completely updated to capture the latest thinking and concepts in modern resume writing. Further, the newly added Chapter 1 (*The Resume—What Employers Say They Want*) not only reflects my own observations on good resume preparation, but is also supported by the results of a large resume survey of human resource professionals, conducted by the Society for Human Resource Management (SHRM).* This survey reflects the resume preferences of nearly 600 professionals who read resumes for a living. These are the very persons your resume needs to impress—a good reason to listen to what they have to say.

Since the Internet is playing an ever-increasing role in the employment process, you need to take full advantage. (Some 95 percent of Fortune 500 companies now use their own Web site for recruiting.) Here you have an excellent opportunity to use modern, computer technology to mass-market your resume and credentials to the hundreds-of-thousands of employers, who now use the Internet as a primary recruiting source. Chapter 13, *The Electronic Resume*, and Chapter 18, *The Top 20 Internet Career Sites*, are loaded with good information on how to fully exploit and take advantage of this excellent job-hunting resource.

The 20 Internet sites (highlighted in Chapter 18) alone can help you automatically search over four million current job openings and instantly get your resume in front of those employers in whom you have interest. This book tells you which (out of an estimated 25,000 such sites) are the leading job boards—the ones most likely to get you the best results.

Additionally, whether you are seeking an international position or one located here in the United States, Chapter 17 (*The Top 50 Executive Search Firms*), is intended to help you

---

*For those readers interested in securing the full SHRM Cover Letters and Resumes Survey, it can be ordered online from the SHRM bookstore (www.SHRM.org) at a cost of $39.95.

identify and send your resume to the top 50 executive search firms in the world. BlueStep, the shared, online resume database from which these firms draw candidates, is highlighted in Chapter 18. Getting your resume into this database should be a high priority for anyone seeking either a middle or senior management position.

Regardless of whether you are an experienced pro or a neophyte in job search, there is much you will gain from this book.

My best to you in your quest for a successful job search and rewarding career. I trust you will keep this book handy as a helpful companion and guide as you travel into an exciting future.

RICHARD H. BEATTY

West Chester, Pennsylvania

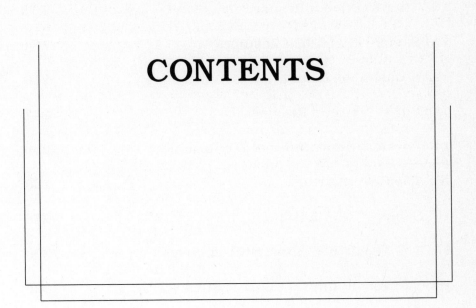

CONTENTS

1

THE RESUME—WHAT EMPLOYERS SAY THEY WANT

The employment resume—its form and content—has long been a topic of much debate. Like politics and religion, this subject has been the center of much discussion, and there are numerous so-called "experts" with a wide range of divergent opinions. Many would have you believe they know all the answers—if only you would lend them your ear.

Should you wish to put this observation to the test, let me suggest that the next time you are at lunch with a group of friends or coworkers ask them the following questions about proper resume construction and compare the consistency of answers:

- What is the proper resume length (single page, two pages, three pages, etc.)?
- What is the best resume format?

- Should you include an objective or not? How is it best worded?
- Where is education best positioned—near the beginning or end?
- Should the resume include hobbies and extracurricular activities?
- How about personal data such as height, weight, marital status?
- Should salary history be shown on the resume?
- What is the best format for facilitating Internet job search or employer scanning?

These questions are bound to generate some lively discussion and a wide range of diverse opinions. For example, some will say, "Everyone knows a resume should never be longer than a single page." Others will convincingly state, "I understand a two-page document is quite acceptable." Still, others will emphatically exclaim, "A two-page resume can never possibly do justice to 10 years or more experience." All of these comments may sound logical and provide equally persuasive arguments, but who is right? Who should you believe? What really works? What are the facts?

If you want to compound this confusion, go to your local bookstore, pick up a half-dozen or so best-selling resume books, and compare what the authors have to say. Once again, you'll find much disagreement, with each offering his or her own "magic bullet" answer. So, whom can you believe? Where do you go for credible advice? Who can you trust as a reliable authority, and how do you know if they are truly an "expert" on the subject?

Since you are looking for employment advice, I would strongly suggest you start by seeking the advice of an employment expert—someone who makes his or her full-time living by screening resumes, interviewing candidates, and hiring people. The simple logic behind this answer is that these are the very persons who will be reading your resume, screening your credentials, conducting the phone screen, and/or deciding to extend an invitation to interview with their company. These are the "front line of defense," the persons whom your resume must influence if you are going to get a shot at a given job opportunity. They need to be your ultimate guide for creating an effective resume that successfully promotes your candidacy in today's job market.

Although this seems such a simple, logical answer, many job seekers make the mistake of picking up a book on resume writing without the slightest notion of the author's background or expertise on the subject. This can be a fatal error and provide no more reliable advice than that proffered by those well-meaning friends with whom I earlier suggested you might have lunch.

When looking for legitimate resume advice, another common pitfall is to ask a human resources professional, assuming they are experts in this field. The mere fact that someone works in human resources does not necessarily mean they are an "employment expert." I know a number of human resource professionals, for instance, who have little or no real employment experience. This can be especially true in large companies where a separate department, manned by staffing specialists, handles all employment. In such cases, the human resources manager may have little or no real staffing background and may, therefore, not be qualified to offer quality resume advice.

Additionally, in smaller companies, where growth has stagnated for a number of years, the human resources function may have little or no real employment experience. Don't assume the human resources manager is an expert on resume preparation. This might not be the case, and you may end up getting less than professional, credible advice on the subject.

I have extensive (30+ years) employment experience. My background includes over seven years as a Fortune 100 corporate employment executive as well as over 18 years as an executive search consultant, providing staffing services across a wide range of companies and industries. On the practical side, I have conducted thousands of interviews, hired hundreds of persons, and, over the years, estimate that I have read well over 200,000 resumes.

Although most persons in the human resources field would readily classify me as an "employment expert," you need to know that the resume advice offered in this book is not mine alone. It is well-backed and documented through discussions with numerous other employment professionals, as well as surveys on the subject. Additionally, it is well-supported by some 15 years of live, hands-on research, during which time my company, Brandywine Consulting Group, Inc., has provided career consulting and resume writing support to thousands of persons. This research, both formal and informal, has significantly contributed to my knowledge of resume preparation, and thus serves as the basis for the advice and recommendations contained throughout this book.

Of particular note on the topic of effective resume writing is the August 1999 resume and cover letter survey, conducted by the Society of Human Resource Management (SHRM). Despite the survey date, it is the single largest known study of its kind (582 respondents—all human resource professionals) and has further validated what many of us who have spent a number of years reading resumes have already known about effective resume writing for quite some time. Nonetheless, it is good to have some hard, independent data on which to hang our hats.

Drawing from the SHRM survey, discussions with other employment professionals, as well as our own research and hands-on career consulting experience, the following represents some common, universal findings that should give you a solid understanding of what employers prefer in an employment resume. With few exceptions, these findings should serve as a reliable guide for resume construction.

KEY FINDINGS—WHAT EMPLOYERS WANT IN A RESUME

- The majority of employers (i.e., 74 percent by SHRM survey) prefer the "reverse chronological" format over other resume styles.

- Almost all employers (i.e., 99 percent of SHRM respondents) consider a "detailed job history" important to resume effectiveness.

- With the exception of recent graduates (those having little or no work experience), most employers (91 percent by SHRM survey) find a two-page resume quite acceptable, with some preferring it to a single-page format.
- Most employers (i.e., 62 percent by SHRM survey) prefer a resume be no longer than two pages in length.
- A large percentage of employers prefer that the job seeker provide a stated job objective (89 percent according to the SHRM survey).

With few exceptions, the data suggest employers strongly prefer job seekers to adhere to the following universal criteria when designing their resumes:

- Use a reverse chronological format.
- Include a job objective statement.
- Provide a detailed job history.
- Utilize a two-page format.

Although these are the preferred standards, and the great majority of job seekers should definitely adhere to these guidelines, there are some exceptions. These exceptions, and appropriate alternatives, will be thoroughly discussed throughout this book.

2

FACT VERSUS FICTION—EXPLODING COMMON RESUME MYTHS

The world of resume writing abounds with a number of common myths. Several of these are carryovers from a decade or two ago, when the job market was less sophisticated than today. Others are monuments to time itself and have doggedly persisted throughout the ages despite evidence to the contrary.

With myths, the more they are repeated, the more credible they become. Soon it becomes difficult for the general populous to distinguish illusion from reality—to judge "what is real and what is Memorex," as a popular advertisement used to say.

In this chapter, we will deal with 12 of these common myths. We will examine them, one-by-one, and dispel the underlying logic that has caused them to stubbornly persist as eternal truths among unknowing and unsuspecting job seekers.

Myth 1. Resumes should be kept to a single page in length.

We have already noted, in Chapter 1, that most employers find a double-page resume quite acceptable, with some actually preferring it. So why, then, does the single-page myth continue to survive?

Advocates of this myth have long declared that, no matter how many years experience a job seeker has nor how extensive the candidate's list of skills and competencies, all pertinent information required for the skilled employment professional to make an informed judgment can be condensed to a single-page resume document. To support this position, some proponents argue that a candidate's inability to comply with the one-page rule may suggest to the employer that he or she is wordy, disorganized, lacks critical thinking ability, or some other such unflattering descriptors.

A common theme that underlies this position is the unfounded belief that most employment professionals are pressed for time and simply will not take the time to read a multipage document. Thus, the argument goes, "Resumes of two pages or longer seldom receive more than a cursory glance, and are prone to be the ready recipient of the dreaded "no-interest" stamp."

Although, in most business quarters, brevity is considered a virtue, there can be such a thing as "too brief." In reality, most staffing professionals are strongly motivated to serve their clients well and fill positions promptly. They are also charged with bringing quality candidates to the fore, and take this responsibility seriously. Thus, assuming they are kept to a reasonable length (typically two, but sometimes three pages), employment professionals will generally read multipage resumes with the same interest and intensity as single-page documents. And, for more senior level positions, many actually prefer the multipage document— but don't overdo it.

Candidates with a long job history will have considerable difficulty squeezing their extensive experience onto a single page, and shouldn't! Forcing this information onto one page will often require omitting key accomplishments or significant achievements that are career highlights, and are critically important catching the eye and interest of an employer. This is the resume equivalent of being pennywise and pound-foolish.

When deciding whether or not to spill onto second page, I generally recommend doing so if you have held three or more positions or have worked for more than two employers. Although it is not strongly encouraged, should you be a senior level executive with considerable experience, spilling over on to a third page is not considered totally inappropriate.

It should be pointed out, with the Internet becoming a key resume delivery vehicle, many employers are now using keyword searches to electronically screen resumes and quickly identify candidates with the credentials they seek. Thus, having a two-page, and in some cases a three-page resume, does not represent the obstacle it once did when a busy staffing executive was processing all resumes manually.

Myth 2. Lengthy resumes (greater than three pages) are essential to fully describe one's credentials and should be used if you have considerable experience.

Proponents of this myth typically claim that adequately describing 15 or 20 years of work experience is impossible when using a two- or three-page resume format. In restricting yourself in this way, they argue, you are unnecessarily depriving yourself of the opportunity to present your full and complete credentials.

Although it's true that longer resumes do a better job of fully describing one's credentials, the problem is they will seldom be read. This is confirmed by the SHRM resume survey that showed that 62 percent of human resources professionals dislike resumes greater than two pages in length.

Put yourself in the employment manager's shoes. Assume you are actively attempting to fill more than 100 positions, and typically screen more than 1,000 resumes per week. How many four-, five-, or six-page resumes would you like to read? Not very many, right? I think you have gotten the point.

Besides the obvious "reader resistance" created by a lengthy resume, such resumes also take more time for the staffing professional to ferret-out key information critical to determine level of interest in the candidate. If not easy to quickly pinpoint these key qualifications, the reader is likely to give up in disgust and rapidly move on to the next candidate's resume.

Don't make the mistake of thinking that the use of resume screening technology, such as key word search, now makes it more feasible to submit lengthy resumes to employers. The fact is, unlike a local newspaper, Internet job listings can reach a global audience. Thus, a single Internet job posting can sometimes produce literally thousands of resume responses, versus the 50 or so resumes typically produced by an ad in the local rag.

Keyword search, combined with computer resume scanning, can process thousands of resumes within a few short minutes. However, the practical matter is there will still be hundreds of resumes that land on the "possible interest" pile. At this point, someone is now going to have to process these manually, and we are back to the same old problem. Lengthy resumes just won't be read!

It's best to keep resumes to no more than two to two-and-a-half pages in length. Do yourself a favor, keep them to this maximum standard!

Myth 3. Unique or unusual resumes attract attention and will therefore be read more readily.

Defenders of this myth would clearly make better marketers than they would employment professionals. Such gimmicks do far better selling peanut butter and cosmetics than they do qualified employment candidates. And, in many cases, such antics can actually backfire! A short story of one such resume may help to make the point. Hard to believe, but the following is a true story.

A few years back, while technical employment manager for a major corporation, I received a resume from a young lady, who I will call Holly Hobbie. Holly clearly wanted her resume and qualifications to be seen, so in addition to her resume (which, I recall, was about 6 or 7 pages long), she also sent an 8½ by 11 inch black-and-white photograph of herself in a bikini. As if this wasn't enough, she also included a cover letter advising us that she had recently separated from her husband and went on to explain, in detail, the reasons for this separation. A little bazaar, don't you think?

Now. I must admit, this particular resume did attract some attention! In fact, I will go so far as to say it probably set an all-time record for resume readership. Additionally, several managers asked that Holly be scheduled in for interviews, but we had no approved employment requisitions for her specific qualifications, and thus sent her a "no interest" letter. Can you believe it?

Over the years, while working in employment, I have received almost every conceivable gimmick resume that you can imagine. I have received resumes where things jumped up or popped out, red resumes, pink resumes, chartreuse resumes, resumes on toilet paper (I worked for a paper company), resumes on construction paper, resumes jotted on the back of an envelope, resumes written on the backs of postcards, several bound in book form, resumes that enclosed a dollar bill (to buy a cup of coffee while I read the resume, of course), and one from an injection-molded design engineer who had enclosed his resume (folded into a small wad) inside an injection-molded pill box, which he had designed. Did we hire any of these candidates? The answer is "no"!

Gimmick resumes, designed to attract attention, are often a distraction instead. They tend to draw attention away from the legitimate qualifications of the candidate, and focus instead on the novelty of the resume presentation. Because they do not follow a conventional format, with which employment professionals are familiar, they are more difficult to read quickly and make it harder for the employer to rapidly identify important selection criteria. Thus, although they do attract attention, they do not focus the reader's attention on the right things.

For more conservative companies, use of a gimmick resume can, in fact, cause a candidate to be eliminated from consideration immediately. Such companies may prejudge the candidate as exhibiting odd, or unusual behavior—a person who subscribes to unconventional wisdom, lacks business sophistication, and demonstrates a degree of immaturity.

I would strictly limit the use of gimmick resumes to certain entertainment, amusement, or creative industries— if even then. My best recommendation is to forget them entirely.

Myth 4.   Resume content is far more important than format (i.e., layout).

Proponents of this myth argue that if a person has excellent credentials, the resume format chosen to present these credentials is irrelevant. Such individuals would propose that staffing professionals will know a good candidate when they see one. They proffer that any good employment professional, worth their weight in salt, is quite willing to wade through a labyrinth of words and disorganization to find that one true diamond—the one the company is dying to hire.

I don't think so! Few things turn an experienced employment professional off faster than a poorly written, disorganized resume! Such resumes require an inordinate amount of time to sift through, and can severely test the patience of an otherwise easy-going staffing manager. To some, such resume presentation may suggest the candidate lacks common sense, is poorly organized, is undisciplined, lacks basic understanding of business protocol, is sloppy, careless, or worse.

It is widely known that a high percentage of employers will instantly eliminate an employment candidate on the basis of poorly organized resume alone—regardless of qualifications or content! The bottom-line message is, "Format is every bit as important as content, so best pay careful attention to both."

Myth 5.   Feel free to exaggerate accomplishments, employers never check.

I've always said, the resume should be used to blow your own horn—but not to the extent of being an outright prevaricator. I've seen surveys that say better than a third of all resumes contain blatant distortions of the facts, if not outright lies. Employers are becoming more sensitized to this possibility and, consequently, have become far more skilled at ferreting out the "bull" than they used to be. So, if you are going to "throw the bull," you had better be darn good at it.

The advent of more sophisticated interviewing techniques, such as situational and behavior-based interviewing, have made it far more difficult to conceal the facts and sugarcoat the truth. If your resume claims that you were solely responsible for solving a critical problem and achieving a certain result, but you were not, a good behavioral interview question such as, "Tell me, in some detail, exactly what you did to achieve this," will probably flush out the truth and cause you to be a bit red-faced in the process. Situational-based follow-up questions, such as asking you to solve a similar problem to the one you claimed to have solved on your resume, are going to cause still further embarrassment, as it becomes clearly evident to the interview team that you don't know what you are talking about.

Additionally, you might like to know that skilled interviewers often use an interviewing technique known as *patterning.* When employing this tactic, the interviewer will ask the same question, slightly disguised, at different points throughout the interview, and compare the consistency of your answers with what is on your resume. If answers are inconsistent or don't agree with resume facts, they will pounce on this inconsistently immediately, confronting you with the discrepancy. For example, they might say, "John, your resume states that you were project manager on this project, but now you are describing your role as that of a sole project engineer, help me understand this." Obviously, this interview is headed south at warp speed!

Further, in filling key positions, most employers are going to be very thorough in checking references. They will request at least three to four business references, persons with whom you have closely worked and can attest to the quality and thoroughness of your work. Additionally, the employer will take this opportunity to carefully verify key information, such as important accomplishments, stated on your resume.

So, my best advice is—"Feel free to use the resume to toot your own horn, but make sure you stick to only those notes you know you can reproduce, when asked to do so."

Myth 6. Always list references on your resume.

Persons who recommend listing references on the resume often do so on the basis they feel it suggests to the employer that they are well qualified, are of solid character, and would welcome employers to verify this through a discussion with those who know them well. The quaint notion here is that the employer, seeing the listed reference, will get "warm feelings" that they are dealing with someone who is solid and reliable.

The truth is references are excluded from the modern resume. This quaint notion went out a few decades ago. The immediate purpose of the resume is to solicit sufficient employer interest in your qualifications to warrant an interview. References are unimportant at this stage of the process, and only take up valuable resume space. You are far better off using this same space to further describe your job-relevant qualifications rather than to prematurely offer up personal or businesses references.

Another thing you might want to know about premature reference presentation is that it can sometimes be used against you and, if checked in advance by an overzealous employer, could result in cancellation of the job interview. I have actually seen this happen. A slightly questionable reference, checked in advance, can sometimes cause an employer to feel uncomfortable and not want to waste time interviewing. So, you may not even get in the door to offset this initial negative impression, let alone make the sale.

In reality, most employers will not ask you for references until they have established you are a strong candidate for the position, and they wish to make you a job offer. At this point they will ask you for references, but not before! So, keep a typed list of references handy in case you are asked for them, but don't provide them until you are asked to do so.

Myth 7. Hobbies and extracurricular activities should be included on the resume, since they testify to the author's diversification and well-roundness.

Those who support this position would argue that inclusion of hobbies and extracurricular activities on the resume presents the image of one who is diverse, interesting, active, involved and other such adjectives thought to be positive attributes—the "total Renaissance person," so to speak.

What some advocates fail to realize is, in some cases, listing such items on the resume can have an adverse effect. Take, for instance, a workaholic hiring manager, who is totally dedicated to his or her job. An extensive listing of hobbies and extracurricular activities may suggest, to such an individual, that you are not equally dedicated to getting the work done. How could you possibly have time for all these extraneous activities if you are strongly committed to turning in outstanding performance in your job?

Additionally, unless specifically job-related, employers have absolutely no idea why you have included a healthy list of hobbies or extracurricular activities on your resume. How does this relate to your work? Could it be that you are unhappy in your current job, and need an emotional outlet? Could it be your marriage is on the rocks, and these activities afford you a convenient opportunity to get away from your spouse? Who knows? Certainly these activities do nothing to support your qualifications for the job opening currently at hand.

As with references, hobbies and extracurricular activities take up valuable resume space that could otherwise be used to promote job-relevant qualifications in which the employer has interest. Why then clutter the resume with irrelevant data that has no real bearing on your job search objective?

The bottom line: "Avoid listing these items on your resume."

Myth 8. Personal data—age, height, weight, health status—belong on the resume.

We won't waste much time on this one! The practice of listing personal data, such as the above, on an employment resume went out the window about 30+ years ago. With the advent of civil rights legislation in 1964, and numerous subsequent state and federal and state laws designed to protect members of "protected classes," employers simply don't want to see such personal data on the resume. They simply don't want to be presented with nonrelevant data that might potentially be used to discriminate against you in favor of other candidates. I don't think you want to risk this possibility either. Do you?

Do not present personal data, of any kind, on your resume. It is not relevant to your qualifications, and should be excluded.

Myth 9.   The use of personal photos on the resume provides a personal touch and adds to your marketability.

It's hard to believe, but we are still receiving an occasional resume containing a personal photo of the job seeker. This idea is truly ancient and went out of fashion a good 50 or so years ago—but we still see them!

As with personal data, the use of a personal photo on the resume is totally inappropriate in this day and age. Unless you are applying for a position as a model or a type-cast actor, employers are not at all interested in knowing what you look like. Your appearance has absolutely no relevance to your employment qualifications, and raises the specter of possible employment discrimination. It is a resume "no-no."

In nine simple words: "Do not include a personal photo with your resume!"—even if you are breathtakingly gorgeous!

Myth 10.   It is a good idea to include salary history on your resume, especially if you have been well compensated.

Those who subscribe to this myth feel, in those cases where an individual can use the resume to demonstrate generous salary treatment and rapid progression, they convey the image of one who is a highly valued, solid contributor. From their prospective, so doing serves to paint a picture of a highly desirable candidate and creates a competitive advantage over others who may be applying for the same position.

Although this argument is not totally without merit, the reality is that the modern resume does not include salary history. There must be good reasons for this. Here are a few of the standard counter arguments:

1. Employers are more interested in your accomplishments and contributions, not your cost.
2. If perceived to be too highly compensated, the employer may decide to "pass" on your candidacy, thereby

forfeiting the opportunity for you to convince them of your value.

3. Inclusion of salary history, since this is an unusual practice, may suggest you are more interested in money than you are in the work that you do.

4. Revealing cost, before establishing value, has never been a sound marketing strategy—whether selling products or yourself.

5. Highlighting your compensation could eliminate you from a lateral move opportunity that could lead to significant short-term career progression. (You may even have considered a salary reduction, just for the opportunity to interview for such a position.)

The general recommendation made by most employment and career experts is, "Don't volunteer salary information of any kind in either your resume or accompanying cover letter, unless specifically asked to do so by the employer." Additionally, if asked to provide your compensation requirements, try to avoid being too specific. In such cases, provide a fairly broad range, so as not to automatically screen you from an otherwise interesting opportunity. Keep your options open! Final salary negotiations can come later.

Myth 11. The cover letter is more important than the resume.

Some people would have you believe that the cover letter is far more important than the resume. The argument here is that the resume can be a somewhat sterile and boring document—lacking energy and excitement. On the other hand, the cover letter is a living, breathing document that reflects the "real you." By writing a dynamic, convincing cover letter, so the story goes, the employer may not even need to read your resume—they will bring you in for interviews based on the cover letter alone.

Although I will readily grant you that a well-written cover letter can be a dynamite marketing tool (when accompanied by a great resume), the idea that it can actually replace the resume is the stuff of which pipedreams are made. No way!

Seasoned employment pros realize that being a talented cover letter writer does not necessarily guarantee you are also the ideal candidate for the job. Too many times, we have seen candidates describe themselves as Don Johnson in the cover letter, but in the door walks Don Knox! You know the old adage, "Don't believe everything you read."

Because a candidate describes himself or herself as "dynamic, through, conscientious, hard-working, and the like, doesn't mean that's what you're going to get. I've been known to read just a few a puffery-filled resumes with the proverbial "tongue in cheek."

What people, who exaggerate the importance of the cover letter, don't realize is that most experienced staffing pros invariably skip the cover letter and go straight to the resume. The reason is that, after reading a few hundred resumes, they quickly realize that much of the information provided in the typical cover letter is redundant to that contained in the cover letter. They are thus reading the same information twice.

By reading both the cover letter and the resume, in effect, they are increasing their reading workload by a third. Imagine what this means, if you have a couple of thousand resumes to read! Do you think you would continue to read cover letters, under these circumstances? I doubt it.

So, the message is, "Don't skimp on the resume, thinking the cover letter will save the day." It won't. In fact, if the resume is poor, the chances are good that the cover letter will never be read!

Don't think, however, that the cover letter has no value whatsoever. It does! Although not typically read until the employment manager has scanned the resume and determined there is interest in the candidate, the cover letter can serve to heighten (or retard) that interest. In addition to providing some limited supplemental information about the candidate's technical qualifications, the cover letter can also provide strong clues about the candidate's broader qualifications.

For example, the cover letter provides "real time" measurement of your written communication skills and can leave some definite impressions about your organizational skills as well. The staffing professional may also use the cover letter to make other observations (good or bad) about certain other of your competencies, such as creativity, critical thinking skills, and overall personality. It is important, therefore, that it be well written. If skillfully written, and combined with an equally well designed resume, the two documents, together, can prove to be the "dynamic duo" in helping to make the sale.

Myth 12.   Always choose the "functional" resume over the "reverse chronological" resume. It does a far better job of marketing your skills to employers right up front—so they will see them.

Although we are getting a little ahead of ourselves, and you may want to review Chapters 6 and 10 to gain a full appreciation for these two resume styles, the functional resume (with few exceptions) should clearly not be the resume style of choice for the great majority of job seekers. There are valid reasons for this.

To begin with, employment professionals have a strong preference for the reverse chronological, rather than the functional resume. The SHRM cover letter and resume survey shows that 74 percent of survey respondents have a distinct preference for this style resume, and with good reason:

- *The ping-pong effect:* Since the functional resume highlights key skills and competencies on page 1, but doesn't show job history and dates until page 2, it creates the "ping-pong effect." The recruiter keeps jumping back and forth between page 1 and page 2 in an attempt to connect specific accomplishments and results with the employers and jobs listed on the second page of the resume. This can become tiresome and frustrating, causing the staffing professional to simply give up and move on to the next resume.
- *The "negative halo" effect:* Over the years, the functional resume has become the resume of choice for those who have had a weak employment history. Persons who have had a number of jobs in a short time-span, individuals

with poor career progression, persons with frequent, unexplained employment gaps, and so on, invariably choose the functional resume to attempt to disguise these facts. The logic is, that by citing strong skills and accomplishments on page 1 of the resume, the employment professional will have a tendency to somehow overlook the spotty employment history on page 2.

Staffing managers have long been attuned to this practice and are automatically conditioned to view the functional resume with suspicion, right from the start. I know, in my case, I always went to page 2 immediately to see what the problem was. Thus, there is a "negative halo effect," when one uses the functional resume. It can cause employment professionals to initiate an immediate witch-hunt—trying to ascertain what is wrong (rather than right) with the candidate's qualifications.

- *Less familiarity:* The functional resume is used infrequently and is therefore a less familiar format than the traditional reverse chronological style resume. I would estimate that less than 2 percent to 3 percent of resumes I see utilize this format. Because of its infrequent use, employment managers can find the functional resume more difficult to read and zero in on the key information they are seeking. This can cause them to automatically jump over candidates employing this style of resume in favor of those using the popular and familiar reverse chronological approach.

As you can see, there are many false prophets out there—continuing to perpetuate these myths. So, when you hear them and they sound convincing, just remember this chapter. Don't allow yourself to be captured by their logic and mystic allure, because as with the Greek sirens of old, you could find yourself crashing upon the rocks.

3

THROUGH THE EYES OF THE EMPLOYMENT MANAGER

In large companies, it is not uncommon for the corporate employment function to receive well over 100,000 resumes a year. With the explosion of the Internet, where a single job posting now reaches a global, rather than a limited local audience, the volume of resumes received by these companies is expanding exponentially.

Where, in the past, you responded to a newspaper ad and were among a few dozen persons responding, now a single Internet ad may put your resume in a pool of thousands of respondents. The competition has become increasingly more intense just by virtue of the shear numbers of candidates competing for the same position.

On the employer's side, things haven't gotten any easier either. This means that the staffing professional must now process considerably more resumes just to get the same result. This has compelled employers to look to technology for answers.

Today, a rapidly growing number of companies have purchased resume and candidate management software to help them deal with the increase resume flow. This software makes use of a keyword search as the basis for electronically scanning resumes to identify qualified candidates, although some of these products also allow employers to make use of limited online interviewing or testing as the basis for candidate identification. By loading certain keywords into the software's search engine, the computer can now scan thousands of resumes in a matter of minutes, quickly identifying those containing the keywords sought.

Although, on the surface, this seems to provide an answer to handling large volumes of resumes efficiently, in reality it has provided only a partial solution. Candidates have learned how important it is to load up their resumes with a bunch of keywords to increase the probability that their resumes will be identified. Consequently, the technology doesn't provide as good an answer as employers might like, still leaving hiring managers with the need to process huge volumes of resumes manually.

When we consider the daily work schedule of the employment professional, we come to realize that many times resume reading is done at night. Daytime schedules are hectic and are full of activities such as interviewing candidates, coordinating postinterview feedback from interview teams, recommending and securing approvals on job offers, phone-screening prospective candidates, setting up and coordinating interview schedules of new candidates, coordinating candidate travel and lodging reservations, arranging for candidate expense reimbursement, making and negotiating job offers, processing new employment requisitions, writing and placing employment ads on Internet job boards and newspapers, coordinating college interview schedules at target schools, debriefing campus recruiters after college interviews, providing interview training, and on and on.

As the former employment manager of a major corporation, I can tell you that it is next to impossible to get it all done during the day. As a result, much of the work spills into the evening hours. Early evenings are often consumed by phone-screening candidates and making job offers by phone. Then, if a parent, it's time to spend some quality time with the kids before they go to bed. Finally, about 9:00 P.M. or so, you finally have time to settle in and read a couple of hundred resumes before "lights out."

In reviewing this schedule, you can readily imagine the limited attention your individual resume is bound to get, if it's 10:00 P.M. or so, and the corporate recruiter still has another 100 or 150 resumes to go. According to the SHRM survey, 19 percent of companies average less than one minute scanning a resume, with some 73 percent spending less than three minutes with this activity. Larger companies, who process large volumes of resumes, are known to average less than a minute per resume. I know, in my case, resume scanning typically took less than 30 seconds on an initial scan. The bottom line is—"Your resume may have less than one minute to grab the recruiter's interest, so it needs to be good"!

HOW RESUMES ARE SCREENED AND READ

For most employment professionals, resume reading is a two-step process. First comes a quick scan, as the recruiter looks for key qualifications. If these are missing, the resume is immediately eliminated. If key qualifications are present, the initial scan is then followed by a more concentrated reading, as the recruiter determines whether the candidate's overall qualifications and interests align well with the requirements of current job openings. Bear in mind, a single recruiter may be attempting to fill 50, 100 or more openings and must perform the mental gymnastics of not just scanning your resume for your core qualifications, but also mentally comparing this core set with the requirements of dozens of job openings he or she must fill. This is not an easy task.

You don't want to make the staffing professional's work even more difficult by presenting a poorly prepared resume that is sloppy, difficult to read, or otherwise complicates the

matter. If the resume is poorly prepared, sloppy, badly organized, or in any way difficult to read, the probabilities are
quite high it will be immediately rejected, with the recruiter moving quickly to the next resume without even a
second's thought.

It should be obvious from the foregoing discussion that
having a well-designed, easy-to-read resume is absolutely
critical to "making the cut." Anything short of this is sure
to get your resume relegated to the no interest pile in less
than a New York minute.

HOW RESUMES ARE PROCESSED

In larger companies, the staffing department is typically
subdivided into functional specialties, each having its own
employment manager. For example, there may be an Administrative Employment Manager, responsible for hiring for the
company's administrative areas (i.e., accounting, finance,
law, information technology, human resources). Technical
functions (i.e., research and development, central engineering, quality control, technical services) may be serviced by a
Technical Employment Manager. Still another employment
specialist, the Marketing and Sales Employment Manager,
may be designated to handle employment for the company's
marketing and sales functions. In smaller companies, a single employment manager may handle all employment, or you
may find this function handled entirely by the company's
human resources manager.

As resumes are received, whether via the Internet or by
snail mail, there is often one individual who screens and
sorts them for either manual or electronic distribution to
the appropriate employment manager. In the case of more
sophisticated companies, employing online screening technology, the resumes may be electronically screened and automatically distributed directly to the employment manager
or hiring manager in direct response to a specific Internet
job posting. In some cases, all resumes (especially those
that were unsolicited by the company) are automatically
entered into a single resume database to which authorized

managers have access through the use of electronic search engines and keyword search.

Where the resume is unsolicited, and there is no appropriate opening identified for the candidate, the candidate may or may not receive a no-interest letter. This is more prone to happen when the resume is electronically submitted and the company employs resume-screening software. In such cases, the process is automated, so generating no-interest letter or e-mail is automatic. Where a hard copy resume is submitted by regular mail, however, don't be surprised if you hear nothing at all. Many companies, in the interest of cutting staffing expenses, in recent years have adopted a policy of not responding at all to persons submitting their resumes on an unsolicited basis. Don't be discouraged by this since it likely has nothing to do with your overall qualifications, but is simply a reflection that the company does not currently have an appropriate opening that matches your qualifications or interests.

In companies where resume processing is still manual, the typical process for handling resumes is as follows: As resumes are received, they are first visually scanned against the current slate of job openings and sorted accordingly. Often an administrative assistant or staffing associate performs this initial screening. Those resumes matching current requirements are forwarded to the appropriate employment manager, while the balance are typically sorted into two separate piles: (1) future possible or (2) permanent no-interest.

The term *future possible* means, although there is no suitable current opening, the candidate's profile may be of future possible interest to the employer, and the resume is thus manually stored for review against future openings. The term *permanent no-interest* means the candidate's profile is unlikely to be of interest to future openings that might develop. Such candidates usually have background and experience totally unrelated to the employer's business or related occupational requirements.

In both cases, the candidate may or may not receive a no-interest letter. If a letter is sent, the candidate fitting the future possible category is likely to get a letter stating that, although there is no appropriate opening immediately available, their resume will be retained for a specified period of time (usually a year) in the event a suitable opportunity should develop in the future. In the case of the permanent no-interest group, the letter is likely to simply say there are no appropriate openings available for which the candidate is a fit. In such cases, there is usually no further commitment on the company's part to further review the resume.

When, after initial review, the employment professional determines there is a probable match for a given opening, the resume is typically forwarded directly to the hiring manager (i.e., the manager having the opening) for further consideration. Where interested, the hiring manager, upon review, returns the resume to the employment department with a request to either phone-screen the candidate or to simply schedule the candidate for an interview. On the other hand, where the hiring manager determines the candidate is not a match for the opening, the resume is returned to the employment department with instructions to so notify the candidate via a no-interest letter.

As we review this process, it is important for you to note that the resume must pass three distinct screening steps as follow:

1. *Initial screen.* This is done either manually or electronically. If electronically, keyword search is used to identify resumes containing the selected key words. If manually screened, the screener (normally an administrative assistant) is screening out those candidates not appearing to meet bare minimum requirements or whose job interests are incompatible with current needs. Additionally, at this stage, sloppy, incomplete, or otherwise poorly organized resumes are also likely to "get the axe."

2. *Employment manager screen.* If passing the initial screen, this second screen, typically performed by an employment professional, is a little more through and is designed to ferret out those candidates who appear best qualified for a given position, based on overall qualifications and compatibility of job interest.

3. *Hiring manager screen.* Since employment professionals usually lack the ability to judge a candidate's technical competence, the hiring manager makes this assessment. At this stage of the screening process, the resume is carefully scrutinized to be sure the candidate has the depth and breath of specialized knowledge and skills needed for job success.

The competitive nature of the job market, combined with the thoroughness of employer screening, makes preparation of a high-impact, professional resume an absolute must, if you plan to be one of the candidates selected for interviewing. Resume preparation cannot be left to chance, if you hope to survive this rigorous selection process.

Let's now take a closer look at the screening process normally employed by the staffing manager. How does this person read a resume? What is he or she typically seeking? What factors determine whether your resume will get screened in or screened out?

THE CANDIDATE SPECIFICATION

The employment process invariably begins with preparation of an employment requisition. This document, originated by the hiring manager, is designed to accomplish three things:

1. Provide management authorization to hire.
2. Define and communicate core job data (e.g., title, job level, salary range, reporting relationship, key job responsibilities, desired hiring salary).
3. Define and communicate desired candidate qualifications (e.g., educational requirements [level and type of degree], experience requirements [length, level, and specific type], skills, behavioral competencies).

Seasoned employment professionals realize the employment requisition, alone, seldom provides sufficient detail to do a though, professional job of candidate identification and screening. Often, the staffing manager will follow receipt of the approved employment requisition with a meeting with the hiring manager. Such meetings are designed to flush out additional selection criteria such as desired personal traits and characteristics, specific selection preferences/priorities, and other relevant data enabling the employment manager to more accurately perform the candidate screening process.

The following are two examples of a candidate specification, as extracted from the typical employment requisition. They should provide some insight on what an employment professional is typically working with when screening your resume and/or conducting a telephone screening interview.

Example A—Chief Project Engineer

Job Title: Chief Project Engineer

Job Level: 600 Hay Points

Salary Range: $80,000—$100,000

Department: Central Engineering

Report To: Director of Project Engineering

Education:

  Preferred: MS Mechanical Engineering

  Acceptable: BS Mechanical Engineering

Experience:

Eight plus years experience in the design, development, installation, start-up, and debugging of Herrington winders and auxiliary equipment. Demonstrated project leadership ($8 to $10 million range), including management of teams of 5 or more engineers and technicians.

Maximum Offer: $90,000

Example B—Director of Human Resources

Job Title: Director of Human Resources

Job Level: Level 14

Salary Range: $100,000 to $120,000

Estimated Bonus: 20 percent to 30 percent

Department: Corporate Human Resources

Report to: Chief Administrative Officer

Education: MS in Human Resources

Experience:

Requires 15+ years senior HR management experience in 20,000+ employee manufacturing company. Broad-based experience must include: staffing, compensation and benefits, management development, training, and employee relations. Requires up-to-date expertise in HR planning, organization effectiveness, and executive assessment. Must demonstrate leadership in providing corporate staff direction and guidance to autonomous HR functions in a multidivision, highly diversified company environment. Must be experienced in development of corporate-wide labor strategy in a multiunction setting. Candidate must have managed a large staff (20+) of midmanagement and professional level HR employees.

Maximum Offer: $110,000 Base Salary

HOW RESUMES ARE READ

As you see from these examples, candidate specifications are pretty specific, not leaving much latitude for interpretation if you were a staffing professional. In such a case, it would be your job to find candidates who most closely fit your client's requirements. If you forwarded a lot of resumes that didn't closely match the client's requirements, you would be in trouble rather quickly. The last thing hiring managers want to do is to unnecessarily review a bunch of resumes not fitting their requirements.

It is the employment manager's job to rapidly scan resumes against the core criteria contained in the candidate specification. The key question constantly asked during this process is: "Does the candidate meet all the essential criteria shown on the specification?"

The staffing professional rarely bothers to read a resume in any degree of detail, unless the initial scan reveals the presence of at least some of the core criteria sought. In such cases, as keywords and headings suggest a possible match, the recruiter will slow down and begin to read with a more critical eye. If several criteria appear to match position requirements, it is not uncommon for the staffing professional to return to the beginning of the document and then proceed with a far more thorough review. Contrarily, if key qualifications appear to be missing, no time is lost moving on to the next resume.

QUICK "KNOCKOUT FACTORS"

During initial screening, the employment professional is alert for key factors that will serve to immediately eliminate a candidate from further consideration. These so-called "knockout factors" invariably mean sure death to a person's candidacy. These typically include:

1. Job objective incompatible with current openings.
2. Inappropriate or insufficient educational credentials.
3. Incompatible salary level or compensation requirements.
4. Poorly organized, sloppy, or hard-to-read resume.
5. Geographic restrictions incompatible with current openings.
6. Job hopper—too many employers in a short period of time.

7. Lengthy resume—a book rather than a resume.

8. Lacking U.S. Citizen or Permanent Resident status.

Presence of any of these common knockout factors signals the employment manager that it would be a waste of time to read further, thus compelling immediate use of the reader's no-interest stamp. It is a good idea, therefore, to sanitize your resume document—making sure to avoid these fatal pitfalls.

CRITICAL READING

Having survived the initial screening, your resume will then frequently undergo a more thorough, critical reading. Concentration is now centered on the "Work Experience" section, and the employment manager begins to mentally ask the following common questions:

1. Are there sufficient years and level of experience?

2. Is experience in the appropriate areas?

3. Is any critical experience missing?

4. Does there appear to be sufficient breath and depth of technical knowledge?

5. Is there evidence of sufficient managerial or leadership skills?

6. Do any critical skills—technical or leadership—appear to be missing?

7. Is there a reasonable history of contributions and achievement?

8. How does this candidate stack up against others already identified?

9. Based on what I am seeing, coupled with past experience with this client, is there a reasonable probability that a job offer could be made?

There is little advice that can be provided to the job seeker in this area. You are what you are, and the facts cannot be changed. You either have the desired core qualifications, or you don't. The best you can hope for is that through thought-ful, diligent resume design, you have clearly presented your overall skills and credentials in a highly effective, convinc-ing manner that will grab the employer's attention. This book is intended to provide you with the expert guidance and advice to do just that.

There is nothing mysterious about the resume reading process. It is both logical and straightforward. It is simply a comparison process by which the staffing professional and/or hiring manager compares your qualifications to those contained in the candidate specification, for the pur-pose of screening you in or out of the running. Neatness, clarity, organization, style, and format are the key ingredi-ents essential to overall resume impact and effectiveness. These topics are thoroughly covered in the subsequent chap-ters of this book.

4

PREPARING
TO WRITE

If you are feeling a little apprehensive by the challenge of writing an effective resume, relax—you have a lot of company. Resume writing is not a process that comes easily to most. On the contrary, the great majority of people find this exercise a difficult one. I have seen very bright, talented, and highly successful people rendered almost helpless when it came to reducing their outstanding credentials to a concise, forceful, and effective resume document. Additionally, I have read the resumes of thousands of highly qualified individuals in which it was painfully clear that the author had experienced considerable difficulty in developing this all-important summary.

This chapter will help you overcome this initial anxiety and provide you with the structure and techniques needed to approach this task with confidence. If you carefully follow the advice and instructions contained in this chapter, you should be fully prepared to construct an effective resume that does full justice to your background and professional qualifications.

RESUME ANXIETY

When dealing with the feelings of apprehension or uneasiness associated with resume writing, a little careful analysis can go a long way. Generally speaking, fear or uneasiness is normally associated with the unknown or unexpected. People feel least uncomfortable with those things with which they are most familiar. In fact, where the individual has firsthand, intimate knowledge of the subject, there is a strong sense of security and self-confidence. To the contrary, when the individual has little or no experience, there is a lack of security and confidence. Applying this logic to the subject of resume writing, it is easy to see why so many people have a feeling of uneasiness. Few have had much experience in this important undertaking.

Generally, anxiety over resume preparation falls into one or more of the following three categories:

1. Content (What do I say/not say?)
2. Format (How should it be organized?)
3. Style (How should I say it?)

If you know what to say, how to organize it, and how to say it, there should be little reason to feel uncomfortable about this process. In addition, the more you have prepared, organized, and rehearsed, the more comfortable and confident you will feel in your skill and ability to write an effective employment resume. This chapter is designed to help you develop these resume-preparation skills and the confidence necessary to move on to the actual writing process.

More specifically, this chapter is intended to assist you in two areas. The first is the area of advance preparation. Basic guidelines for collecting and organizing all of the advance data that you will need for resume preparation are provided. Second, assistance in developing the writing skills and style necessary for an effective and forceful resume is offered. Our focus will thus be on content and style. The subject of resume format or structure is dealt with in depth in Chapters 6, 8, and 10 and is not covered here.

ADVANCE PREPARATION

With most difficult tasks, the need for organization and advance preparation is paramount. Resume writing is no exception! Before you can proceed with the actual writing, you will need to have a number of facts and details at your fingertips. Further, these facts will have to be organized in such a way that they may be found when you need them. This advance-preparation step then is essential to an efficient and orderly process. It will save you considerable time and frustration as you proceed with the writing process.

The following forms are designed to organize these data in an orderly manner that will allow you to locate information quickly and efficiently.

Education

In the spaces provided, fill in all the information requested, starting with most recent degree first.

Degree: _____

School: _____   Date Graduated: _____

Major: _____   Grade Point Average: _____

Honoraries: _____

_____

Scholarships: _____

_____

Offices Held: _____

_____

Degree: _____

School: _____   Date Graduated: _____

Major: _____   Grade Point Average: _____

Honoraries: _____

_____

Scholarships: _____

_____

Offices Held: _____

_____

Degree: _____

School: _____   Date Graduated: _____

Major: _____   Grade Point Average: _____

Honoraries: _____

_____

Scholarships: _____

_____

Offices Held: _____

_____

Professional Designation: _____

Date Certified: _____

Certifying Organization: _____

Professional Designation: _____

Date Certified: _____

Certifying Organization: _____

Work Experience

Starting with your most recent employer first, list all employers for whom you have worked, including dates of employment, title of position held, and key job accountabilities. In those cases where you have held more than one position with a given employer, indicate this by writing "Same" in the space provided for the employer's name. List such positions in reverse chronological order (starting with the most recent position first), again showing dates that positions were held and key job responsibilities.

1. Dates Employed: From: _____ To: _____

Employer: _____

Division: _____

Position Title: _____

Key Responsibilities: _____

_____

_____

----

2. Dates Employed: From: _____ To: _____

Employer: _____

Division: _____

Position Title: _____

Key Responsibilities: _____

_____

_____

_____

_____

3. Dates Employed: From: _____ To: _____

Employer: _____

Division: _____

Position Title: _____

Key Responsibilities: _____

_____

_____

_____

_____

_____

4. Dates Employed: From: _____ To: _____

Employer: _____

Division: _____

Position Title: _____

Key Responsibilities: _____

_____

_____

_____

_____

5. Dates Employed: From: _____ To: _____

Employer: _____

Division: _____

Position Title: _____

Key Responsibilities: _____

_____

_____

_____

_____

6. Dates Employed: From: _____ To: _____

Employer: _____

Division: _____

Position Title: _____

Key Responsibilities: _____

_____

_____

_____

_____

If you have worked for more than six employers or held more than six positions with a number of different employers, continue this exercise on a separate piece of paper. Continue to list the information in the same format until you have accounted for all the employers and positions you have held since beginning your full-time, professional career. If you are a recent graduate, list this information for part-time and summer jobs as well.

Go back over the work that you have just completed. Take a few minutes to research your accomplishments and, at the end of the key responsibilities section for each of the positions that you have described, jot down any kind of quantitative information that will be helpful later on in describing the size and scope of your job accountabilities. Include such things as the number of persons managed or supervised, annual budget, sales volume (if in sales or marketing), amount and/or value of goods manufactured (if in manufacturing), capital project costs (if in engineering), and so on. Being able to find this quantitative information quickly during the actual writing of your resume will prove extremely valuable and will save you considerable time.

You now have the basic facts that you will be needing as you begin the writing process. At this point, let's discuss some other things you need to do before you move on to the actual preparation process.

WINNING ATTITUDE

If you don't believe and feel that you are a winner, no one else will! Feelings of uneasiness, apprehension, and insecurity are bound to be reflected in the way you express yourself in the resume. A seasoned employment professional will sense this from the tone and style of your writing. Conversely, if you are confident in your skills and knowledge and feel that you have something of value to contribute to a prospective employer, this positive attitude and enthusiasm is bound to be sensed by the person who reads your resume. It should not surprise you that being in a positive frame of mind is critical to the writing of a good resume. If you are not feeling positive and good about yourself, don't even start!

There are, however, some things that you can do to affect your attitude and self-confidence in a very positive way. The next section should help you considerably.

Developing a Positive Attitude

The key to establishing a positive attitude and improved self-confidence is to take the time to be reflective—to look within yourself for a sense of value. All employers are eager to hire someone who can add value to their organization's bottom-line results! Such "added value" can take many different forms, including the following:

1. Ability to solve key, long-standing problems.
2. Ability to bring new, fresh ideas—to bring change and improvement.

3. Ability to lead and motivate others to achieve high levels of productivity.

4. Ability to spot and realize key cost-reduction opportunities.

5. Ability to identify and bring about expansion and substantially improved profits through identification and procurement of key acquisitions.

6. Ability to design new, innovative, and profit-generating equipment.

These are but a few of the numerous ways that an individual can add value to a prospective employer's organization.

The employment resume and the accompanying cover letter are your only opportunities to prove that you are a valuable commodity, that you have something of great or unique value to contribute to the prospective employer. This is the time to "toot your own horn" in an effective yet inoffensive and tasteful way. This can best be done by citing specific achievements and contributions that you have made to past as well as current employers.

Employment managers are instinctively looking for value in the resume. They are looking for evidence that suggests that the candidate will make a good addition to their company: for example, that they have the capability to make valuable contributions to their employers. Most of these managers believe that the best predictor of future behavior and accomplishment is the behavior and accomplishment of the past. What other evidence does an employment professional have for predicting the candidate's future value?

Thus, in addition to combing the resume for specific education, knowledge, and experience, the professional employment manager is also carefully looking for indications and hard evidence that the candidate will prove to be a good performer—that he or she will get important things done.

One of the biggest mistakes that people make in writing resumes is that they neglect to cite their accomplishments. Frequently the Work Experience section of the resume reads like a job description. It describes what the candidate is responsible for doing but fails to describe what he or she has actually done. Thus many resume writers completely miss the mark. They fail to focus in on their major achievements, leaving the reader guessing how effective they have been in their past positions.

DEFINING YOUR VALUE

It's now time to think about your value to prospective employers. Listed below are several questions followed by blanks to be filled in. Take some time to carefully consider each of these questions and fill in a well-thought-out answer in the space provided. Some of these questions may sound redundant, but the purpose of these exercises is to help you define your value. Asking some of the same questions in a slightly different way may help to stimulate your thinking. One question may not provide much stimulus, but asked in a slightly different way it could serve to trigger a host of ideas and responses.

If you asked a group of five or six of your friends or peers to describe your greatest attributes, what adjectives would they use to describe you? (Use single words only.)

Go back and rank these adjectives from 1 to 12 based upon how you feel these friends would rank them: Number 1 would represent the adjective that your friends would choose to best describe you, with 12 representing the adjective that least describes you.

What positive things are there about your behavior and/or achievements that cause these individuals to describe you in this fashion?

Positive Behavior/Achievements: _____

_____

_____

_____

_____

What are your greatest strengths? Describe these strengths in terms of specific skills and knowledge.

Strongest Skills: _____

_____

_____

_____

_____

Greatest Knowledge: _____

_____

_____

_____

_____

Rank these in order from greatest strength to least strength.

In a business sense, what are those things that you do with greatest proficiency?

Do Best: _____

_____

_____

Reviewing the above list, what is there about you or your skills and abilities that enables you to do these things well? Describe below.

_____

_____

_____

_____

_____

_____

_____

_____

In reviewing your life to date, what do you consider to be your most significant accomplishments and achievements? Of which achievements are you most proud? List three achievements in each of the categories shown.

Education: 1. _____

_____

2. _____

_____

3. _____

_____

Business: 1. _____

_____

2. _____

_____

3. _____

_____

Personal: 1. _____

_____

2. _____

_____

3. _____

_____

Taking each of the employers and jobs that you listed earlier in this chapter, list the three most significant contributions that you made for each position shown.

1. Employer: _____ Job Title: _____

Achievements:

1. _____

_____

2. _____

_____

3. _____

_____

2. Employer: _____ Job Title: _____

Achievements:

1. _____

_____

2. _____

_____

3. _____

_____

3. Employer: _____ Job Title: _____

Achievements:

1. _____

_____

2. _____

_____

3. _____

_____

4. Employer: _____ Job Title: _____

Achievements:

1. _____

_____

2. _____

_____

3. _____

_____

5. Employer: _____ Job Title: _____

Achievements:

1. _____

_____

2. _____

_____

3. _____

_____

6. Employer: _____ Job Title: _____

Achievements:

1. _____

_____

2. _____

_____

3. _____

_____

Take a few minutes to reflect upon the information that you provided in each of the preceding exercises. You have probably been successful in identifying quite a few strengths and accomplishments—things that will be of value to a prospective employer. Having done this, take a minute to answer the following important questions:

Why do I deserve the type of position for which I am applying? Which of my overall strengths and accomplishments best qualifies me for such a position?

You should now be convinced that you have a lot to offer a prospective employer, and you should be confident in your skills and knowledge. The previous exercises should have enabled you to cite a number of key attributes and accomplishments that will add strength and credibility to your resume and your job-hunting campaign as well.

So far in this chapter we dealt with two components of advance preparation. The first was resume content, that is, those dates and facts that you will need at your fingertips as you begin the actual resume-writing process. Second, we developed a series of exercises designed to build a positive, confident attitude. Finally, we deal with the subject of writing style.

WRITING STYLE

Writing style is an extremely important element of the resume-writing process. It is an important aspect from two standpoints. First, style is important in conveying a maximum amount of information in a clear, precise manner that leaves little or no room for misinterpretation or misunderstanding. Second, writing style is critical to the conciseness necessary to condense several years of experience on to a two-page format. If you are going to compete effectively with the thousands of other employment resumes that the employment manager will be reading, your resume must be written in a concise, precise, and forceful way. A sloppy, uninteresting style could cost you interviews! How you say it is as important as what you say.

So that you have a better appreciation for the importance of writing style, take a few moments to consider the following examples. These examples describe identical work experience.

Example A

I worked five years as Manager of Marketing. I was responsible for nationwide sales of all plumbing supplies and managed 15 other sales representatives. I also prepared all marketing plans and strategies. I was responsible for planning all product advertising, including some sizable campaigns. We were very successful and increased sales quite a bit in the second year.

Example B

Marketing Manager. Corporate-wide accountability for marketing and sales for this manufacturer of quality pumps and valves (annual sales $85 million). Developed key marketing plans and strategies which led to a 53% increase in sales in second year. Managed sales force of 15 area representatives.

In reviewing these two examples, I am sure that you would agree that Example B is far more dynamic and interesting than Example A. What makes this difference? What is there about the writing style used in Example B that makes it more effective than Example A? How is this accomplished? Let's take a few moments to examine these two examples more closely. This exercise should give you some pretty strong clues on how to write effectively. Consider the following points:

1. *Job Title.* It is not necessary to repeat the position title in describing job responsibilities. The position title has been listed previously as part of the heading. Listing it again is redundant and adds no new information or increased understanding.
2. *Pronouns.* Note that the pronoun "I" is conspicuously missing from Example B. Since the resume reader is already aware that this is your resume, the "I" is understood.

3. *Complete Sentences.* Since the pronoun "I" is under-stood, it is not necessary to use complete sentences in writing a resume. Descriptive phrases or clauses are sufficient as long as they convey a complete thought and are clearly understandable.

4. *Brevity.* Note that Example B starts two out of three sentences with a verb followed by a noun or adjective. The practice of starting sentences with a verb will force you to be more concise and precise. This practice will help you to improve your resume-writing style.

5. *Condense and Consolidate.* Where possible, you should attempt to condense related information into a single statement rather than make two separate statements. Note that Example B has combined the "development of marketing plans and strategies" with the "increase in sales in the second year." In Example A, these were treated as two unrelated statements. Where possible, condense and consolidate, eliminating all nonessential information that adds little or no meaning to your employment qualifications.

6. *Quantitative Descriptions.* Where possible, use quanti-tative terms or descriptions to convey greater under-standing of the magnitude or scope of your respon-sibilities and accomplishments. Example B has made use of this technique—citing $85 million to quantify annual sales volume and 53% to communicate the size of the sales increase. In addition to providing the reader with a more thorough understanding of your qualifica-tions, quantitative terms make the resume consider-ably more interesting.

The writing style used in the resume is also important from another standpoint. This style is thought by most em-ployment professionals to be reflective of the personal style of the candidate. Thus, if resume style is rambling and ver-bose, the candidate's personal style is thought to be ranbling and verbose. To the contrary, if the resume is brief, concise, and interesting, it would not be unreasonable to envision an employment candidate who is concise, efficient, and interest-ing. Thus resume style can sometimes be as important as content and format, if not more so. It is an element that will prove extremely important to the overall effectiveness of your resume.

We have now covered three of the four major elements necessary to preparing you for the actual resume-writing process. These have included positive attitude, resume content, and writing style. The remaining key element is the format, the organization or structure that the resume should take. Chapter 6, The Chronological Resume; Chapter 8, The Linear Resume; and Chapter 10, The Functional Resume, will provide you with step-by-step processes for preparing these three most popular and commonly used resume formats.

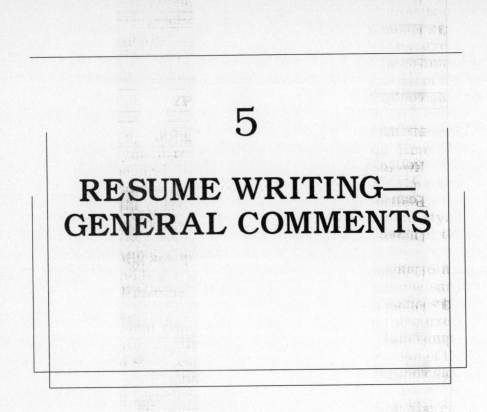

5

RESUME WRITING—
GENERAL COMMENTS

TYPES OF RESUMES

Generally speaking, there are three conventional styles of employment resumes: the chronological resume, the linear resume, and the functional resume.

Sample resumes A, B, and C at the end of Chapter 6 are examples of the chronological resume. In these resume samples, note that the Experience sections of these resumes list jobs in reverse chronological order, starting with the current or most recently held position. The linear resume (see sample resumes D and E at the end of Chapter 8) is a variation of the chronological resume and follows the reverse chronological order as well.

The functional resume (see sample resume F at the end of Chapter 10), on the other hand, is different from the chronological style resume and is organized to give primary emphasis to functional areas in which the candidate has significant experience or particular strengths. Although the functional resume focuses on results or accomplishments, it is somewhat confusing when you attempt to determine in which positions (or with which employer) specific results where achieved. The employment professional is therefore frequently at a loss to effectively evaluate the specifics of the candidate's qualifications with this type of resume.

Thus the functional resume immediately raises some red flags in the mind of the employment professional. For this reason alone, I strongly suggest in most cases that you avoid using this format. Additionally, as mentioned previously, it is difficult for the employment manager to fully understand and evaluate the specific nature of your past positions and accomplishments and relate these to the positions you have held. Many won't even try before they move on to the next resume.

Both the chronological and the linear resumes, by contrast with the functional resume, represent a very straightforward, direct approach to presenting your employment credentials. They leave little doubt in the mind of the employment professional as to where you have been and what you have accomplished. As an employment professional, I can assure you that in almost all cases your chances of securing an employment interview are substantially increased by using these chronological formats as opposed to the functional approach.

I estimate that from 97 to 98 percent of all resumes now use either the chronological or linear format. Choosing these formats, therefore, assures you that your resume will be well understood and well accepted by the majority of employment professionals who will be scrutinizing this document.

PURPOSE OF RESUME

Before proceeding to the actual preparation of your employment resume, it is important to have a clear understanding of the purpose of the resume. Unfortunately, many employment candidates have a rather narrow understanding of the purposes this document serves.

The primary purpose of the employment resume is to convince a prospective employer that you are an outstanding candidate for employment and that it would be well worth his or her time to interview you in person. It must convince the employer that you have something of value to contribute to his or her company—that somehow the company's performance and profitability will be improved by hiring you.

The focus or emphasis of the employment resume must therefore be on your major results, contributions, and accomplishments. It cannot simply state the names of past employers and provide the job titles and descriptions of your past positions. These alone cannot be expected to convince the employer of your value. Your resume must suggest to the employer that you are someone who will bring improvements and make major contributions to the solution of key business problems. Only past contributions and accomplishments will serve to "make the sale."

Although the primary objective of the resume is to help you secure an employment interview, it often serves two additional and very important purposes:

1. It is the road map for your employment interview. The interviewer will frequently use it to structure the employment interview and to focus on the information that you have chosen to emphasize or highlight.

2. After the interview has taken place, the employer will often use the resume as a reference source for recalling and evaluating your specific qualifications and strengths in the light of the credentials of other candidates.

Keeping in mind the several important roles that the resume must play, it should be evident to you by now that you will need to pay particular attention to its sales appeal. If it is to convince a prospective employer to hire you, it must present your qualifications in the most favorable light and must focus on past results and major accomplishments. Additionally, it must continue to remind the prospective employer of your excellent qualifications.

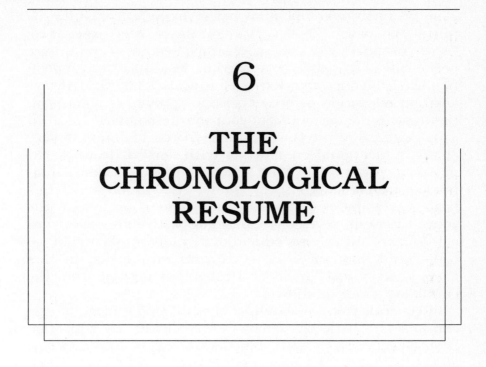

6

THE CHRONOLOGICAL RESUME

A review of the sample chronological resumes provided at the end of this chapter (as well as Chapter 7) reveals that the resume is divided into the following components:

1. Heading.
2. Objective.
3. Education.
4. Experience.

Although the order in which these components are arranged on the resume may vary, the sequence presented above is the most commonly used, accepted, and recommended format. The most frequent deviation from this recommended sequence, however, is the positioning of the education and experience components. You will note that the resume on page 65 positions education before experience, while the resume on pages 66–69, lists education after experience. Close examination of these two sample resumes reveals why.

The rule of thumb to be applied in deciding where to position the Education and Experience sections is this: Always position education before experience providing such positioning will not detract from your marketability.

In the case of the first resume, the candidate has very strong educational credentials with very little work experience. Additionally, the schools that the candidate attended are considered prestigious. The candidate is thus best served by placing education first. Conversely, the second resume reveals a candidate with extensive work experience but whose educational credentials might be considered light by some employers' standards. In this case, positioning education first might detract from the candidate's marketability.

In general, younger candidates with good education credentials and little work experience should list education first. Older workers with considerable experience and persons who do not have strong education credentials are generally best served by placing education after experience.

For the older worker, placing education first can often draw attention to his or her age, something that should be avoided. Unfortunately, even though age discrimination is illegal, there are still many companies that practice it. Why then attract attention to your age by placing education first? If you can get the employer to review your work experience and major accomplishments first, and thereby convince him or her that you have something to contribute, perhaps the employer will pay less attention, or, even better, disregard the age issue entirely.

We are now ready to begin the step-by-step process of resume preparation. Our approach will be to examine each component of the employment resume in some detail and provide you with practical exercises that will assist you to expertly develop each of these components. When finished with this section, you will have prepared a logical, professional resume that will effectively portray and market your qualifications to prospective employers.

HEADING

The resume heading consists of three items: your full name, complete address, and home telephone number. Some sample resume headings follow.

JOHN C. SMITH
325 Blue Street
Cleveland Heights
Cleveland, Ohio 39820
Phone: (315) 472-8975

DAVID B. MARKS
126 Lake Road
Windsor, New York 17530
Phone: Home—(212) 744-1965
Office—(212) 658-9712

You may also want to add your cell phone number and e-mail address to the same line now listing your phone number(s). See resume samples in later chapters which illustrate how this can be done. Today, showing an e-mail address is critical, since so much of the employment process is now moving to the Web.

Your name should be typed in capital letters and set in bold type so it stands out from the rest of the heading. Address and telephone number are typed in lower case. Although there are acceptable alternatives, generally the heading should be centered on the page.

It is usually not advisable to include your office telephone number on the resume unless you feel confident that you can accept employment-related phone calls with adequate privacy. Additionally, if the office number is listed on the resume, it may serve to raise some suspicion on the part of prospective employers that your current employer is aware that you are job hunting and may even be eager to have you depart. The rule of thumb is to avoid listing your office phone number on the resume unless prospective employers will otherwise have difficulty in reaching you. Having an answering machine on your home phone provides an effective solution, and allows you to easily access calls at will with the assurance of absolute privacy.

Most employment managers are willing to call you at home in the evening if you ask them to do so in your cover letter. In the absence of an answering machine, another way to get around the telephone-contact hurdle is to include a statement similar to the following in the cover letter that accompanies your resume:

I can normally be reached at my home telephone number after 7:00 P.M. In the event that you find it necessary to contact me during business hours, my wife, Sally, will be pleased to relay your message. Sally can be reached at (212) 947-3015.

Today, it is strongly recommended that you also include your e-mail address in the resume heading. This is particularly important, since e-mail is rapidly becoming the primary communication link between employers and Job Seekers.

Keeping in mind the above instructions for developing your resume heading, try to write your own heading.

OBJECTIVE

In developing the Objective section of your resume, take care that your objective is neither too narrow nor too broad. Consider the following statements of job objective:

1. *Objective.* Senior level Accounting or Financial position with broad responsibility for achievement of company's financial objectives.
2. *Objective.* Overall direction of the Financial Planning function with advancement opportunities to senior level management position.

You will note Objective 1 is worded very broadly and suggests that the candidate is receptive to a wide range of financial and accounting positions (including Financial Planning). By contrast, Objective 2 is very specific and suggests to the prospective employer that the candidate will only consider positions in Financial Planning.

Unless by specific intent, care should be taken not to word your objective too narrowly or it could cause the employer to screen you out from positions that could be of real interest to you. As a case in point, in our example above, the narrow statement of Objective 2 could easily cause a prospective employer to screen you from consideration for such positions as:

Director of Corporate Accounting

Director of Manufacturing Accounting

Director of Financial Analysis

These three positions may well be of interest to you.

On the other end of the spectrum, it is also possible to be too general in your statement of objective. Some examples are:

3. *Objective.* A good job with a good company.

4. *Objective.* A good accounting position.

Vague objectives of this type will suggest to prospective employers that you have given little thought to your career objectives. Such statements of objective may also imply that you lack the ability to plan ahead or that you lack the ability to analyze your qualifications and career direction. Either way, the employer will probably not be very impressed with your objective and will likely decide not to extend an invitation for an employment interview.

Carefully study Objectives 1 and 2 above as well as the objectives presented on the sample resumes at the end of this chapter. Note the brevity, conciseness, and clarity with which these objectives are stated. Try writing your own employment objective. Remember to guard against being too specific or too general.

Although there continues to be some debate concerning the advisability of including an Objective Statement on the resume, it is important to remember that the SHRM resume survey shows that 89% of employers prefer to see one.

EDUCATION

The Education section of the employment resume should include the following facts: (1) degree awarded, (2) schools attended, (3) year graduated, (4) major field of concentration, and (5) honors. Some sample education statements have been provided below for your reference.

1. Education: Ph.D., University of Michigan, 2001
Major: Mathematics
M.S., University of Michigan, 1999
Major: Economics

   B.S., Michigan State University, 1997
Major: Economics
Magna Cum Laude

2. Education: M.S., Un. of Southern California, 2003
Major: Mechanical Engineering
Sloan Engineering Scholarship

   B.S., University of Florida, 2001
Major: Mechanical Engineering
Tau Beta Pi (Engineering Honorary)

3. Education: B.A., Bucknell University, 2002
Major: Business Administration

Generally, unless you are a recent college graduate, very little space should be allocated to the Education section of your employment resume. The general axiom to be followed in developing this section of your resume is "The further along you are in your professional career, the less important are your educational credentials and the more important are your work experience and specific accomplishments." Correspondingly, the more experienced you are, the more you should seriously consider positioning education following experience in the resume.

If you graduated from college in the last few years, you may want to highlight your educational credentials by positioning them early in the resume. If, however, you have only a bachelor's degree and most employers strongly prefer a master's degree for work in your career area or professional discipline, it is best to position education after experience.

Now try to develop the education portion of your resume using the instructions previously provided.

EXPERIENCE

The Experience section of your resume is probably its single most important component. It is this section that must convince prospective employers that you are worth investing their time in an employment interview. Therefore, you should spend the most time and devote the most attention to developing this portion of your resume. This will be time well spent and can be expected to yield appropriate rewards in the form of both more job interviews and better employment opportunities.

An important benefit to be derived from careful development of this section of your resume is that it will force you to thoroughly review your work history and accomplishments. In essence, it will serve to provide you with a thorough mental rehearsal of your background and qualifications prior to the actual job interview. This will go a long way toward increasing your overall interview effectiveness.

Careful review of the sample resumes provided at the end of this chapter and in Chapter 7 will reveal that each job listed in the Experience section has a description that includes the following:

1. Dates of employment.
2. Employer.
3. Division or location of position.
4. Job title.
5. Brief statement of major job accountabilities and scope.
6. Brief statement of major contributions and accomplishments.

A good general rule to follow in preparing this section of your employment resume is to devote the greatest amount of space to your most recent and most responsible jobs. Little space should, conversely, be devoted to positions held 20 or

30 years ago or to positions that have little bearing on your current employment objective. Most employers care very little about the jobs you held several years ago. Of great interest, however, are the positions held and contributions made to employers in recent years.

Review of the sample resumes contained at the end of this chapter and in Chapter 7 will also reveal that there are rarely any pronouns (I, you, they, he, etc.) or articles (a, the, an, etc.) used. Additionally, many sentences begin with verbs or action words which lend both brevity and a sense of "results orientation" to the resume. You will find that by starting most sentences of your resume with a verb or action word you will be forced to be brief and concise in your statements. Additionally, you will be forced to state specific results achieved and contributions made.

Starting almost every sentence with a verb or action word is probably the *greatest secret of effective resume writing!*

To assist you in getting started with this effective resume-writing technique, a list of key verbs or "action words" is provided at the end of this chapter. You are encouraged to refer to and make use of this list while developing this section of your employment resume.

Another effective technique to employ in developing the Experience section of your resume is to use quantitative descriptions when these serve to highlight your experience and contributions. Consider the following:

Wrong:	I managed a Corporate Accounting Department.
Right:	Managed Corporate Accounting Department of 50 professionals with $1.5 million budget.
Wrong:	I developed a new equipment design that saved the company a lot of money.
Right:	Developed new wrapping equipment design resulting in $2 million company savings in 2004 alone.
Wrong:	I helped to develop a new shipping system that saved a lot of shipping time.
Right:	Participated in development of new shipping system saving over 500,000 hours of labor annually ($1.5 million annual savings).

You are now ready to develop the experience section of your resume. Remember to begin your sentences with action words and to use quantitative descriptions where possible.

Start with your current or most recent job first and continue in reverse chronological order. An example is provided below for your reference.

Employment dates	From 2003 to present
Employer	National Knitting Corporation
Division/location	Corporate Offices
Job title	Engineering Manager
Job description	Manage 50-employee engineering department for this Fortune 200 manufacturer of knitting equipment (annual sales $4 billion). Direct development, design, installation, and startup of advanced technology, computer-controlled knitting machines.
Major accomplishments	(1) Developed three revolutionary knitting machines increasing company sales by 25% in last two years accounting for $50 million annual profit improvement. (2) Restructured Engineering Department with resultant labor-cost reduction of 10% and simultaneous 25% productivity increase. (3) Maintained high level of employee morale with annual employee turnover of less than 1%.

Try to list at least three to five major accomplishments for each position held.

REFERENCES

It is strongly recommended that references not be provided on the resume. The danger in providing references is that the prospective employer may elect to check these references prior to inviting you for an employment interview. The slightest bit of negative information uncovered by the employer may result in a decision against an interview. This places you at a decided disadvantage, since you will never have the opportunity to counter this negative impression.

Additionally, references are not really needed by the employer until you have been interviewed and there is interest in making an offer of employment. Why waste valuable resume space when this space could be better used to present job-relevant qualifications? Instead, have a separate list of references available in case the employer requests them. Do not volunteer this list unless the employer specifically asks for this information.

MISCELLANEOUS

Extracurricular activities and hobbies also have no place on the modern employment resume unless they are directly related to your qualifications for the position you seek. There may occasionally be some advantage to listing extracurricular activities on the resume, however, if it serves to accomplish some specific objective such as to substantiate leadership ability—president or vice-president of a related professional society or other well-known organization. Likewise, hobbies seldom add anything of real value when it comes to important job qualifications.

Technical professionals may wish to list key publications, papers, and patents that are job relevant. These could have direct bearing on their qualifications for employment and increase their marketability to prospective employers. List only those items that are truly important and meaningful, however; do not list minor or insignificant publications.

MICHAEL C. JOHNSON
822 Wilson Blvd.
Albany, NY 39406

Home: (516) 734-9215   *Email: MichJ@AOL.com*   *Cell: (722) 559-4957*

OBJECTIVE

Responsible management position in Corporate Finance or Accounting offering advancement to senior management.

EDUCATION

Degree: M.B.A., University of Wisconsin, 2001
Major: Finance

President Beta Gamma Sigma Honorary

Degree: B.A., Business Administration, Michigan State University, 1999
Major: Accounting
         Magna Cum Laude

C.P.A., May 2003

PROFESSIONAL EXPERIENCE

2003
to
Present

CORDELL ELECTRONICS, INC. (Corporate Offices)

Assistant Corporate Controller
Direct Cost Accounting, Tax Accounting and Information Services functions (36 employees) for this Fortune 500 manufacturer of cable T.V. components (annual sales $1.2 billion). Provide guidance to six Plant Controllers in cost accounting and tax practices. Major accomplishments include: implemented new equipment asset valuation program (annual tax savings $1 million), developed inventory cost accounting system (annual savings $750,000), installation/start-up of new on-line, real-time computer order entry system.

2001
to
2003

WATSON ELECTRONICS, INC. (T.V. Components Division)

Assistant Division Controller (2002 - 2003)
Reported to division Vice President of Administration with full accountability for all Accounting, Financial and Information Services functions for this 1200 employee Division (annual sales $500 million). Revamped brand manufacturing cost accounting system resulting in substantially improved managerial cost control. Developed and installed computerized brand costing system resulting in elimination of 12 positions and annual payroll savings of $480,000.

Brand Cost Analyst (2001 - 2002)
Responsible for development and maintenance of brand costing system.

LAUREN B. BRADY
622 Watson Circle
Cherry Hill, NJ 23948

Home: (609) 774-2939   *Email: LauBrad@MSN.net*   *Office: (215) 772-9485*

OBJECTIVE

Executive level position responsible for providing corporate-wide
strategic leadership to the Human Resources function.

PROFESSIONAL EXPERIENCE

2001
to
Present

ANCHOR GLASS, INC. (Corporate Offices)

Corporate Staff Human Resources Manager (2003 - Present)
Manage staff of 20 employees with responsibility for providing full range of human
resources services to Corporate Staff (900 employees) of this Fortune 200
manufacturer of glass specialties (annual sales $2.5 billion). Functions managed
include: human resource planning, staffing (internal & external), salary
administration, employee relations, organization development, safety and security.
Accomplishments include: development/implementation of employee profit-sharing
program resulting in 30% increase in employee productivity, installation of human
resources information system (clerical savings $200,000 annually) and development
of first Human Resources Policies and Procedures Manual.

Corporate Employment Manager (2001 - 2003)
Corporate-wide employment responsibility for the recruitment and employment of
exempt administrative, marketing and technical employees (annual budget $1.2
million). Managed staff of six professionals with responsibility for annual
employment volume of 500-600 new hires at all levels from college entry to
corporate vice president. Creative recruiting methods reduced annual hiring costs by
$250,000 with simultaneous reduction in average "fill time" from five to three
months. Awarded *President's Bonus* in 2002 for unique contribution to the Business.

1989
to
2001

NORTH AMERICAN MANUFACTURING, INC. (Plastics Division)

Division Human Resources Manager (1995 - 2001)
Division-wide accountability for broad range of human resources services for this
1500 employee profit center involved in the manufacture of custom plastic materials.
Directed staff of 16 with responsibilities including: salary administration, staffing,
training and development, organization design, benefits, labor relations, safety and
security. Contributions included: implementation of new job evaluation (Hay)
system, total revision of employee benefits program (25% increase in benefits with
simultaneous $50,000 annual savings), successful negotiation of three labor contracts
(no strikes, settlements averaged 10% below budgeted level), reduced engineering
manpower turnover from 20% to less than 1% per year.

Assistant Human Resources Manager (1991 - 1995)
Assisted Division Human Resources Manager in providing full range of human resources services to Division clients. Major focus was staffing (internal & external), benefits administration and salary administration.

Human Resources Assistant (1989 - 1991)
Implemented numerous special studies covering broad range of human resources topics. Managed hourly job evaluation and Division safety program.

EDUCATION

Degree: B.A., Business Administration, Union College, 1989
Major: Human Resources Management

ROGER C. REARDON
924 Willow Road
Muskegon, MI 37495
Phone: (712) 877-9412
Email: RCR924@AOL.com

OBJECTIVE

Senior operations management position at the plant, division or corporate level with full P&L responsibility.

PROFESSIONAL EXPERIENCE

2002
to
Present

KIDDIE MANUFACTURING, INC. (Muskegon Plant)

Plant Manager
Manage staff of five with full P&L responsibility for this 500 employee toy manufacturing plant (annual value of goods manufactured - $30 million). Hired in 2002 to engineer plant turnaround (2001 loss was $3.2 million). Conducted exhaustive study of operations methods and manufacturing costs, pinpointing key cost improvement opportunities. Reorganized, trained and motivated plant staff. Successfully directed ambitious profit improvement program resulting in 2003 profit of $3 million (200% improvement).

1991
to
2002

WEXLER COMPANY (Corporate Offices)

Brand Manager - Valves (1998 - 2002)
Corporate-wide profit responsibility for the full line of Tyler valves for this 5,000 employee manufacturer of specialty industrial pumps and valves (annual sales $125 million; profit $18 million). Led multi-discipline (R&D, manufacturing, sales) profit improvement task force in the development and implementation of a profit improvement plan to achieve increased annual profitability of the Valve line from $6 to $9 million in two years. Goal was achieved in one year with an additional $2 million of cost savings realized by end of second year.

Department Manager - Specialty Valves (1996 - 1998)
Managed Specialty Valve Department (four shift supervisors; 200 hourly employees) with responsibility for the profitable manufacture of some $50 million of specialty valves annually. Exceeded manufacturing cost and profit objectives for three consecutive years.

Project Engineer - Valves (1991 - 1996)
Responsible for the design, installation and start-up of a wide range of specialty valve manufacturing equipment. Major project completed was $40 million expansion of the Denver Valve Plant. Project was completed four months ahead of schedule and $1 million under budget.

1988
to
1991

MASTER VALVE, INC. (Corporate Offices)

<u>Research Engineer</u>
Developed new technology valves and related products from concept through pilot plant testing.

EDUCATION

Degree: M.B.A., Drexel University, 1988
Major: Production Management

Degree: B.S., Lehigh University, 1986
Major: Mechanical Engineering
G.P.A.   3.7/4.0

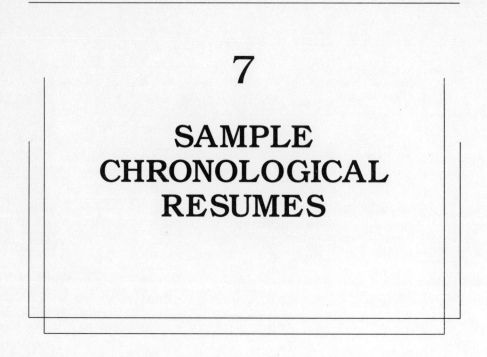

7

SAMPLE CHRONOLOGICAL RESUMES

This chapter contains 20 sample chronological resumes for your review and easy reference. You will note in reviewing these samples that there are 10 separate business disciplines or functions represented. These 10 disciplines represent a logical, functional breakdown of a typical manufacturing company and thus provide an excellent cross section of business functions. For each of these 10 functions you will find two sample resumes. The first is the resume of an experienced senior individual; the second resume represents a less experienced person.

The following Resume Locator should prove helpful in locating those sample resumes that are of greatest interest to you.

Resume Locator

Experience Level

Field or Discipline	Senior Person	Junior Person
	(Pages)	(Pages)
Accounting	72	74
Engineering	75	77
Finance	78	80
Human Resources	82	84
Information Technology	86	88
Logistics	89	91
Marketing and Sales	93	95
Operations	96	98
Procurement	99	101
Technology	102	104

BARBARA E. HENNINGS
246 Plainview Road
Fort Wayne, IN 28375

Home: (207) 822-4726   Email: BarHen@MSN.com   Office: (207) 993-2849

OBJECTIVE

Position as a corporate or business unit Controller with broad responsibility for supporting achievement of company's financial objectives.

PROFESSIONAL EXPERIENCE

2004
to
Present

TECHNOMATICS, INC. (Corporate Offices)

Assistant to Corporate Controller
Report to Corporate Vice President of Finance with full accountability for management of the Corporate Accounting and Bickford Division Accounting functions (32 employees) of this multi-division manufacturer of computer hardware (annual sales $320 million). Corporate responsibilities include: preparation of capital and operating budgets, financial statements for SEC and shareholder reporting, federal and state tax filings, external auditor coordination, consolidation and analysis of monthly financial statements, and accounting policy development. Division functional responsibilities include: general and cost accounting, accounts receivable, accounts payable and credit. Major accomplishments include: computerization of standard product cost build-up (500 hours labor savings annually), purchase/ implementation of fixed assets computer software (optimizes tax depreciation), and operational efficiencies estimated to produce annual savings of $250,000 to $300,000.

2001
to
2004

CONNER CONTAINER CORPORATION (Corporate Offices)

Manager of Corporate Accounting (2002 - 2004)
Managed staff of 14 professionals with full responsibility for the Corporate Accounting function of this $150 million manufacturer of overseas shipping containers. Reported to Chief Financial Officer with management responsibility for preparation & monitoring of budgets ($130 million), monthly and year-end financial statements, accounting system development/implementation, internal audit and payroll. Key accomplishments included: design/implementation of cost accounting system (annual savings $1.2 million), revamped department operating procedures (estimated annual savings 1,500 man hours), improved audit procedures capturing some $120,000 in unauthorized expenditures.

Senior Accountant (2001 - 2002)
Reported to Manager of Corporate Accounting with full responsibility for consolidation, review and analysis of Company's monthly and year-end financial statements.

1991
to
2001

STUBBLESTEIN & FLANDERS, INC.

Senior Accountant (1996 - 2001)
Provided wide range of consulting and auditing services to client companies for this public accounting firm. Major areas of concentration were cost accounting and taxation. Clients ranged in size from $50 to $150 million.

Accountant (1991 - 1996)
Duties similar to those of Senior Accountant. Focus was on clients with annual sales under $50 million.

1988
to
1991

MAGNUM ELECTRONICS, INC. (Winslow Plant)

Senior Cost Accountant (1989 - 1991)
Performed wide range of cost studies for this $4.5 million manufacturer of cable T.V. components.

Cost Accountant (1988 - 1989)

EDUCATION

Degree: M.B.A., University of Alabama, 1988
Major: Accounting/Finance
Bettinger Scholarship

Degree: B.A., Business Administration, Cannon College, 1986
Major: Accounting
Magna Cum Laude

C.P.A., May 1993

DAVID R. WILSON
26 Volker Village, Apt. 105
Oceanside, CA 38495

Cell: (949) 839-2849   Email: DavWil@AOL.com

OBJECTIVE

Supervisory position in general or cost accounting field with opportunity for advancement to department management based on demonstrated results.

EDUCATION

Degree: M.A., Business, Miami of Ohio, 2001
Major: Accounting
            Oceanside Businessman Fellowship

Degree: B.A., Business Administration, Ohio State University, 1999
Major: Accounting   G.P.A. 3.4/4.0
Minor: Finance   G.P.A. 3.75/4.0
            Magna Cum Laude
            Torrington Scholarship (4 years)

Activities: President, Student Government Association
             President, Accounting Honorary Society
             Captain, Varsity Football
             Captain, Varsity Track

PROFESSIONAL EXPERIENCE

2001
to
Present

STARGAZE ELECTRONICS, INC. (Oceanside Plant)

Senior Cost Accountant (2002 - Present)
Report to Cost Accounting Manager with full cost accounting responsibility for the Biostar electrical harness (annual manufacturing cost of $45 million). Provide day-to-day guidance to two Cost Accountants in the application of cost accounting standards and procedures. Responsible for researching and developing new cost standards and approaches. Major accomplishments include: development/implementation of computerized cost tracking system for early detection of negative cost trends (estimated six months savings $125,000), breakout of Rocker Assembly material costs (better material control with annual savings potential of $50,000), improved labor cost estimates for retrofits.

Cost Accountant (2001 - 2002)
Application of established cost accounting practices and procedures in the cost accounting and analysis of sophisticated electronic harnesses. Credited with $115,000 in material cost savings through unique cost tracking approach.

LINDA S. PENNINGTON
824 Stone Ridge Place
Stone Mountain, GA 94837
Phone: (205) 687-2424 (H)
(205) 557-8842 (O)

OBJECTIVE

Executive level engineering management position.

PROFESSIONAL EXPERIENCE

1990
to
Present

AIR SYSTEMS CORPORATION (Corporate Engineering)

Vice President of Engineering (2003 - Present)
Direct 250 employee engineering department in the engineering of new facilities for this Fortune 200 manufacturer of residential and commercial air conditioning and heating equipment. Successfully managed two-year, $850 million expansion program including the installation and start-up of two new residential air conditioning manufacturing plants (largest single capital program in company's history). Projects were completed three months ahead of schedule and 20% under budget. Directed wide range of engineering disciplines including Mechanical Engineering, Civil Engineering, Electrical Engineering, Systems Engineering and Chemical Engineering.

Director, Mechanical Engineering (1998 - 2003)
Provided direction to 160 employee engineering section with full responsibility for all mechanical project engineering associated with capital facilities projects (annual budget of $250 million). Major projects included installation of computer controlled Ram Shear, high speed commercial heating equipment line (project budget $245 million), complete rebuild of two obsolete Pennington residential heating equipment lines (budget of $185 million), and installation and start-up of $110 million commercial air conditioning manufacturing line. All projects were completed ahead of schedule and averaged 10% under project budget.

Manager, Systems Engineering (1992 - 1998)
Managed department of 20 electrical instrumentation and systems engineers in the application of instrumentation and control systems to manufacturing operations. Successfully managed numerous projects involving the first-time application of mini-computer and microprocessor systems to heating and air conditioning assembly lines. Average projects were in the $5-10 million range.

Senior Project Engineer, Heating (1990 - 1992)
Led project engineering teams in the design, installation, start-up and debugging of high speed, automated commercial heating system manufacturing assembly lines.

1988   **POWER ENGINEERING, INC.** (Corporate Engineering)
to
1990   Project Engineer
Design, installation and start-up of large-scale biomass boiler power generation systems.

EDUCATION

Degree: M.S., University of Colorado, 1988
Major: Mechanical Engineering
         Bartrum Scholarship

Degree: B.S., Lehigh University, 1986
Major: Electrical Engineering
         Magna Cum Laude

         President, Tau Beta Psi
         Fuller Scholarship (4 years)

KEVIN P. BAKER
1822 Prairie Trail
Austin, Texas 58694

Home: (713) 447-9583   Email: KPB18@MSN.com   Cell: (713) 757-8495

OBJECTIVE

Senior Project Engineering position in Corporate Engineering Department with responsibility for leading multi-million dollar projects involving design, installation, and start-up of new facilities and equipment.

PROFESSIONAL EXPERIENCE

1999
to
Present

PORTER METALS COMPANY, INC. (Corporate Engineering)

Senior Project Engineer (2003 - Present)
Report to Manager of Mechanical Engineering with responsibility for design, installation, start-up and debugging of aluminum and magnesium production facilities with emphasis on furnace complexes, flash calcining facilities and conveyor material handling systems. Successfully managed the mechanical design of $20 million furnace complex including coordination with Electrical Engineering Department (project on time and 5% under budget). Redesigned refractory lining in flash calciner resulting in 35% reduction in heat loss from existing units and 50% from new units. Responsible for design, installation and start-up of $12 million furnace complex. Project currently on time and under budget.

Project Engineer (1999 - 2003)
Reported to Senior Project Engineer with responsibility for design, installation, start-up and debugging of aluminum manufacturing furnace complexes and material handling equipment. Assisted in the design and start-up of $18 million furnace complex and associated material handling systems.

EDUCATION

Degree: B.S., Texas A&M University, 1999
Major: Mechanical Engineering
               Cum Laude Graduate

               Member Tau Beta Psi
               Vice President, American Society of Mechanical Engineers

AFFILIATIONS

American Society of Mechanical Engineers
Association of Aluminum Manufacturing Engineers

CARTER W. WINSLOW
187 West Lake Dive
Green Bay, WI 47589
Phone: (513) 772-6464
Email: CWWin@MSN.com

OBJECTIVE

Senior Financial Officer

PROFESSIONAL EXPERIENCE

1993
to
Present

EXCAV CORPORATION (Corporate Offices)

Vice President and Treasurer (2003 - Present)
Report to Executive Vice President, Finance and Planning for this $4 billion, Fortune 100 manufacturer of earth moving and excavation equipment. Direct staff of 48 professionals with responsibility for anticipating and providing the financial resources for short and long-term funding of all domestic and international operations. Annual financing requirements average $400 to $600 million. Functions directed include: Domestic Finance, International Finance, Money & Banking, Insurance and Pension Funding. Developed five-year funding strategy to finance $3.1 billion capital expansion plan with interest rates averaging 2% below market. Maintained top financial ratings through carefully orchestrated investor relations strategy despite substantial increase in long-term debt.

Director of Corporate Finance (1999 - 2003)
Reported to Vice President and Treasurer with responsibility for anticipating, planning and execution of effective financing for the Company on best terms and conditions available. Accountable for keeping abreast of the domestic and international capital markets to assure that financial needs were effectively accommodated. Managed departments of five Analysts with annual financing requirements averaging approximately $300 million. Developed five-year financial planning computer model permitting more accurate long-range planning of international operations' financial requirements. Secured $185 million financing for Italian affiliate at exceptionally good terms. Became major consultant to international operations in their financial planning work.

Senior Analyst, Corporate Finance (1996 - 1999)
Reported to Director of Corporate Finance. Responsible for identifying, analyzing and recommending alternative financing methods and sources for a wide range of domestic clients. Assisted top management in 5 major domestic divisions to build five-year plans. Developed and implemented user friendly computer models allowing management to forecast long range financial requirements with greater accuracy. Provided key consultation in the formulation of long-term financial strategy and analyzed and recommended a wide range of funding alternatives.

Analyst, Corporate Finance (1993 - 1996)
Reported to Senior Analyst with responsibility to assist in the identification, analysis and recommendation of a wide range of business opportunities and financing options.

EDUCATION

Degree: M.B.A., University of Chicago, 1993
Major: Finance

Degree: B.A., Western Michigan University, 1991
Major: Financial Management
Minor: Economics
             Magna Cum Laude

JANE M. KORSAN
1524 Oil Patch Drive
Houston, Texas 22375
Office: (713) 775-5757
Cell: (713) 972-3471

OBJECTIVE

Financial Management position in corporate offices of growth-oriented manufacturing company.

PROFESSIONAL EXPERIENCE

1999
to
Present

TELLSTAR DEFENSE SYSTEMS, INC. (Corporate Offices)

Senior Financial Analyst (2004 - Present)
Report to Manager of Corporate Financial Planning of this $2 billion federal contract supplier of missile guidance systems. Work with government scientists, engineers and procurement officers in developing manufacturing cost estimates for sophisticated missile guidance systems based on prototype costs. Develop program funding requirements and determine best available funding sources and options. Have developed funding estimates and recommendations for several programs in the $200 to $400 million range. Recipient of six federal commendations for outstanding service in financial planning work.

Financial Analyst (2001 - 2004)
Reported to Senior Financial Analyst and assisted in the development of funding requirements and financial strategies to support full-scale manufacture of sophisticated missile guidance systems. Researched wide range of funding options and sources recommending those with most favorable rates and terms.

Analyst (1999 - 2001)
Studied various methodologies for calculating manufacturing costs of missile guidance systems. Required conceptual scale-up from lab prototype to full-scale production model. Developed computer model which reduced time required to calculate cost estimates by 80%.

1998
to
1999

REARDON SCIENCE, INC. (Corporate Offices)

Planning Analyst
Reported to Manager of Corporate Planning. Developed computer models to support long-range financial planning process.

EDUCATION

Degree:	M.B.A., University of Texas, 1998
Major:	Financial Planning
Degree:	B.S., Georgia Tech, 1996
Major:	Management Science
	Cum Laude
	Caldwell Systems Scholarship (4 years)

DAWN M. BEATTY
106 Summit Avenue
Shillington, PA 19306

Office: (610) 252-5525   Email:DawnB106@AOL.com   Cell: (610) 377-5756

OBJECTIVE

Senior level corporate Human Resources management position.

PROFESSIONAL EXPERIENCE

1997
to
Present

LIFESRTYLE MANUFACTURING COMPANY, INC. (Corporate Offices)

Director of Human Resources (2001 - Present)
Report to Corporate Vice President, Human Resources of this $1.5 billion manufacturer of residential and commercial furniture. Direct staff of 25 professionals in providing full range of Human Resource services to the Corporate Staff Headquarters complex of 1,000 professional employees. Functional responsibilities include: Human Resource Planning, Internal Staffing, External Staffing, Organization Design, Performance Evaluation, Salary Administration and Training & Development. Major accomplishments include: design and implementation of computerized human resource information system estimated to save $500,000 per year in time and increased productivity, development of computer model which ties in human resource planning with overall business strategic and operations planning, development of a management incentive plan credited with a dramatic increase in productivity, and direction of major hiring effort requiring the employment of 90 engineers to support major capital expansion effort.

Manager Corporate Staffing (1999 - 2001)
Reported to Director of Human Resources with full responsibility for all staffing, both internal and external. Managed staff of 12 professionals and 13 support personnel, with annual budget of $2.1 million. Typical annual volume included 250 new hires and 350 internal placements. Worked closely with top management in handling search assignments at both the director and staff vice president levels. Confidentially orchestrated searches involving highly sensitive organizational changes at the corporate vice president level. Reduced average time to fill positions from six to four months. Through implementation of improved prescreening techniques, reduced the interview-to- offer ratio from six to one to a ratio of two to one. Offer-to-acceptance ratio was also improved to an 80% acceptance rate. Average cost-per-hire was reduced 45% (annual savings of $750,000).

Manager of Administrative Staffing (1997 - 1999)
Reported to Manager of Corporate Staffing with responsibility for internal and external staffing of administrative positions. Clients included Human Resources, Accounting, Finance, Law, Information Services, Logistics and Procurement. Developed and implemented internal professional level posting system which now serves as the primary source for filling most internal openings (excludes director level and above). Developed and implemented candidate assessment process credited with substantial improvement in quality of candidates selected.

1989
to
1997

HUMAN CAPITAL SOLUTIONS, INC. (Corporate Offices)

Senior Consultant (1993 - 1997)
Provided services to client companies in the design and development of employee evaluation programs for this major consulting firm in the field of Human Resources. Successfully designed and installed three major performance evaluation systems, each tailored to client company's unique requirements.

Consultant (1989 - 1993)
Performed research work in support of development of employee evaluation systems.

EDUCATION

Degree: M.B.A., Arizona State University, 1989
Major: Human Resource Management
Thesis: AThe Role of Performance Feedback in the Motivation of Professional
          Employees≅

Degree: B.A., University of Texas, 1987
Major: Human Resource Management
          Cum Laude
          Salem Scholarship (4 years)

MARTIN F. SLAUGHTER
18 Palm Drive, SW
Miami, FL 37485
Home: (715) 347-3343
Office: (715) 764-2232
Email: MarSla@MSN.com

OBJECTIVE

Overall direction of Corporate Staffing function with advancement opportunities to senior level Human Resources generalist position.

PROFESSIONAL EXPERIENCE

1998
to
Present

KOLMAR MANUFACTURING CO., INC.

Corporate Manager - Operations Employment (Corp. Offices) (2003 – Present)
Corporate-wide accountability for the employment of exempt operations and technical personnel for this 13,000 employee corporation (annual sales $1.6 billion). Direct responsibility for recruitment and employment of all operations and technical personnel (through vice president level) for corporate office complex. Additionally, provide overall staff guidance and support to decentralized employment functions of six profit centers and 14 manufacturing plants. Developed strategy and successfully directed multi-location recruiting effort to staff $1 billion capital expansion program. All critical positions filled and deadlines met. Project delivered below budget.

Manager of Employment Services (Vanstar Division) (2000 - 2003)
Responsible for all levels of salaried recruiting and employment – administrative, technical and operations – for this 2,500 employee division involved in the precision chemical coating of space vehicle parts. Position required ability to apply innovative, creative techniques to identify and recruit exceptionally hard-to-find, highly-specialized research scientists. Used combination of patent computer data base and search techniques to successfully locate and recruit two key scientists in the field of electronic scanning imaging. Developed outstanding reputation for Adoing the impossible≅.

Plant Human Resources Manager (Melville Plant) (1998 - 2000)
Responsible for providing full range of human resources services to this missile nose cone manufacturing plant of 450 employees. Areas of responsibility included: employment, employee relations, wage and salary administration, training, benefits, safety, security, medical, communications and public relations. Successfully stayed-off two attempted union drives through development and implementation of highly effective organization effectiveness program.

1994
to
1998

BAXTER FASHIONS, INC. (Fort Lauderdale Plant)

Assistant Human Resources Manager
Reported to Plant Human Resources Manager of this 800 employee clothing manufacturing facility. Responsible for assisting manager in providing full range of human resources services.

1990
to
1994

VIKING ELECTRONICS, INC.

Human Resources Assistant
Entry level human resources position for this 300 employee manufacturer of electronic equipment.

EDUCATION

Degree: B.A., University of Miami, 1990
Major: Business Administration

JOSE A. RODRIQUEZ
806 Vala Drive
Costa Mesa, CA 17283

Home: (949) 776-3546   Email: JRod@Tabor.com   Cell: (949) 883-9526

OBJECTIVE

Senior executive position in Information Technology.

PROFESSIONAL EXPERIENCE

1992
to
Present

TABOR VALVE COMPANY, INC. (Corporate Offices)

Director of IT (2002 - Present)
Report to Executive Vice President of Administration for this $2 billion, Fortune 200 manufacturer of pumps, valves and fittings. Direct 110 employee department and $8 million budget in the development, maintenance and control of corporate-wide information systems. Direct the activities of the Corporate Information Services Center and manage the corporate-wide data communications network. Provide systems development support to four divisions and 16 manufacturing facilities. Developed and implemented first five-year corporate plan for information systems development and utilization. Successfully installed $7 million system providing computerization of the sales forecasting, production scheduling and materials control functions estimated to save Company $5 million annually. Project completed three months early and 20% under budget.

Corporate Project Manager (2000 - 2002)
Managed the activities of 8 to 12 project managers in the design, installation and start-up of a wide range of management information projects. Annual budget of $5 million. All projects were completed on or before deadline with 95% of projects under budget. Major projects successfully completed include: Human Resources System, Payroll System, Order Entry System, Credit Control System, Production Scheduling System, Finished Goods Inventory Control System, Raw Materials and Vital Supplies Control Systems.

Manager of Client Planning Services (1996 - 2000)
Managed department of six professionals responsible for planning the future information systems needs of functional clients. Reviewed clients' strategic and operating plans to determine management information needs necessary for meeting plan objectives. Identified computer systems applications and developed long-range information systems plans by client area. Identified major cost savings opportunities and assisted Director of IS in establishing corporate priorities. Completed long-range plans for five functional areas including: Industrial Relations, Controllers, Finance, Manufacturing and Procurement.

Senior Programmer Analyst (1992 - 1996)
Directed the activities of Analysts and Programmers in the development of numerous systems and programs covering a wide range of client information requirements.

1990   **M&R TECHNOLOGIES, INC.** (Corporate Offices)
to
1992   Programmer Analyst
            Developed numerous programs to meet the information needs of several clients.

EDUCATION

Ph.D.,   Stanford University, 1990
Major: Computer Science

M.S.,   U.C.L.A., 1988
Major: Computer Science
          Micro Systems Corporation Scholarship (2 years)

B.S.,   Iowa State University, 1986
Major: Mathematics
          SAS Scholarship (4 years)

LILLIAN B. REED
65 Norton Road
Norristown, PA 19385
Phone: (610) 661-2239
Email: Lill65@MSN.com

OBJECTIVE

Programmer Analyst in Data Communications R&D for systems engineering and development company.

EDUCATION

M.S.,   Massachusetts Institute of Technology, 2003
Major: Computer Science
         Ransin Laboratory Fellowship (2 years)

B.S.,   Massachusetts Institute of Technology, 2001
Major: Computer Science   G.P.A. 3.85/4.0
Minor: Mathematics   G.P.A. 3.78/4.0
         Mattson Foundation Scholarship (4 years)

         President, Computer Science Society
         Vice President, Mathematics Honorary

PROFESSIONAL EXPERIENCE

2003
to
Present

DATACOM SYSTEMS, INC. (Corporate R&D)

Programmer Analyst
Provide programming support to the development of state-of-the-art data communications system for major systems engineering research firm. Responsible for the SNA/ACP/NCP functions of the Communications Controller in a PEP environment. Responsibilities include: maintaining the ACP/NCP system requirements, diagnosing software problems, and participating in network tuning, troubleshooting, testing and studies.

DERK K. JARVISON
605 North Ridge Drive
Falls Church, VA 14375
Phone: (814) 665-9399
Email: Derk605@AOL.com

OBJECTIVE

Senior level Logistics Management position with progressive company that encourages use of state-of-the-art concepts and values bottom line results.

PROFESSIONAL EXPERIENCE

2002
to
Present

TAYLOR FOODS, INC. (Corporate Offices)

Director of Logistics
Report to Senior Vice President - Operations for this $1.4 billion, Fortune 500 food processing corporation. Direct the development and implementation of both strategic and operating operation plans for the Warehousing and Transportation functions on a corporate-wide basis (eight plants, 750 employees, annual budget of $125 million). Responsible for maximum use of Logistics resources (budget, people, equipment) in assuring high level of customer service satisfaction at lowest possible cost.

Directed the development and installation of computerized order entry and distribution planning system which allows advanced planning of transportation requirements and returns $18 million in freight cost savings per year. Saved $4.7 million per year in warehouse handling costs through installation of automatic palletizers and computer controlled conveyor system. Negotiated corporate-wide rail carrier rates resulting in annual savings of $3.9 million.

1993
to
2002

BEVERTON BOTTLING COMPANY (Corporate Offices)

Logistics Manager (1999 - 2002)
Reported to Executive Vice President - Operations for this $850 million bottler of carbonated beverages. Managed the Corporate Distribution Department (250 employees, budget $85 million) with nation-wide distribution through network of company owned and leased warehouses. Responsible for development and execution of strategic and operating plans for all warehousing and transportation operations to achieve lowest possible cost consistent with customer service requirements. Consolidated all field warehousing facilities into large regional leased warehouse operations with annual savings of $10.2 million. Designed and installed computer model for determination of best shipping point and mode of transportation with resultant savings of $5 million annually.

Senior Distribution Analyst (1996 - 1999)
Reported to Distribution Manager with responsibility for conducting a wide range of studies to determine maximum use of overall Distribution resources to achieve customer service and cost objectives. Areas studied include: site selection for new distribution facilities, loading patterns for various modes and types of shipments (carriers and equipment), warehouse layout and storage patterns, warehousing operations analysis, etc. Introduced use of computer models for Distribution analysis. In three years, designed six computer models (now used in decision analysis on a daily basis), resulting in estimated annual savings of approximately $3.

Distribution Analyst (1993 - 1996)
Provided support to Senior Distribution Analyst and Distribution Manager in the analysis and study of a wide range of Distribution planning problems requiring quantitative solutions. Extensive use of statistical methods and computer techniques.

EDUCATION

M.S.,   Virginia Institute of Technology, 1993
Major: Industrial Engineering
            Weller Scholarship (2 years)

B.S.,   Virginia Institute of Technology, 1991
Major: Industrial Engineering
            Lowe Company Scholarship (4 years)

CAROLINE A. JACKSON
122 Riverview Terrace
Winslow, ME 37495

Phone: (516) 488-2927   Email: CJ122@MSN.com

OBJECTIVE

Corporate level position in Logistics Management.

PROFESSIONAL EXPERIENCE

2002
to
Present

PETCO DOG FOOD, INC. (Corporate Offices)

Manager of Warehousing
Manage Corporate Warehousing function for this $300 million manufacturer of dog food. Scope of responsibility includes 150 employees (35 salaried, 115 hourly), Corporate Distribution Center and 12 field warehouses (eight leased, four owned) and annual budget of $32 million. Accountable for development and execution of strategic and operating plans for use of all warehousing resources (capital, equipment, facilities and people) to achieve lowest storage and shipping costs consistent with customer service objectives.

Implemented palletized railcar loading resulting in $2 million annual savings. Worked with Corporate Packaging in redesign of shipping container size allowing 10% more product to be shipped per railcar (annual savings $450,000). Successfully renegotiated warehouse leases at 5% below preceding year's cost (annual savings $320,000).

1994
to
2002

HELMET METAL MANUFACTURING CO. (Portland Plant)

Distribution Center Manager (2000 - 2002)
Reported to Plant Manager with responsibility for management of plant Distribution Center for this $120 million manufacturer of metal fasteners. Directed staff of 65 employees in the daily storage and shipment of finished products.

Installed extendable powered conveyers for truck loading resulting in reduced labor costs of 10% ($300,000). Redesigned warehouse storage pattern substantially reducing product handling costs (estimated annual savings $135,000). Initiated crew training in proper product handling techniques, reducing product damage by 75% (annual savings $115,000).

Shipping Manager (1994 - 2000)
Reported to Distribution Center Manager with responsibility for managing the loading and shipment of all plant finished product. Through increased use of "gypsy carriers", was able to reduce annual shipping costs by 20% for truck shipments (savings $2.1 million)

1991
to
1994

MARSDEN TRUCKING, INC.

Dispatcher
Accepted and placed orders for truck shipments with responsibility for allocation and dispatch of all trucking equipment.

EDUCATION

Degree: B.A., Colby College, 1991
Major: Business Administration

CHARLES B. PARKER
16 Wesley Road
Eugene, OR 23118
Home: (322) 887-2938
Cell: (322) 557-9899

OBJECTIVE

Executive level position in Marketing and Sales Management.

PROFESSIONAL EXPERIENCE

2004
to
Present

OREGON CHEMICALS, INC. (Corporate Offices)

Director of Marketing
Direct marketing and sales organization of 185 employees with annual budget of $225 million for this leading manufacturer of specialty chemicals (annual sales $725 million). Functions managed include Market Research, Market Planning, New Market Development, Advertising & Promotion and Field Sales. Principle products include specialty solvents and resins. Established company as the leading marketer of solvents in the European Market through the establishment of a sophisticated marketing and dealer network which increased company's export business by 75% ($225 million) in two years. Worked with R&D in the development and test market of new low-viscosity resin product for use in the manufacture of polyurethane foams. National roll-out of this product has accounted for $150 million in new sales in first year.

1996
to
2004

HOUTON CHEMICALS, INC. (Corporate Offices)

Director of Marketing and Sales (2000 - 2004)
Reported to President with full accountability for all domestic and international marketing and sales for this specialty chemical manufacturing company (annual sales $525 million). Responsibilities included Market Research and Planning, Brand Management, Advertising and Sales. Managed sales force of 125 employees with annual budget of $130 million. In less than four years, successfully introduced eight major new products accounting for an increase in total sales of 40% ($210 million). During this same period, expanded sales force hiring and training 60 new sales representatives.

Marketing Brand Manager (1998 - 2000)
Reported to Director of Marketing and Sales with responsibility for management of company's *Canoir* brand. Worked closely with Market Research and Advertising to give this brand a new image and repositioned it in the marketplace as a low-priced, high quality product. In less than two years, *Canoir* rose from number five to number one in the marketplace and experienced a 225% increase in sales volume.

Associate Brand Manager (1996 - 1998)
Reported to Marketing Brand Manager with responsibility for coordination of all market research and test markets for the company's *Dobbins* brand. Designed and implemented test market studies that proved that customers could not distinguish the difference between *Dobbins* (second lowest priced product on the market) and two of our competitor's high-priced brands. Recommended price rise increasing revenues by 20% with no loss in volume.

1991
to
1996

CARDON CHEMICALS CORPORATION (District Sales Office)

Senior Sales Representative (1995 - 1996)
Responsible for sale of chemical specialties to the pharmaceutical industry in the states of New York, New Jersey, Pennsylvania and Delaware. Increased territory sales volume by 15% in one year.

Sales Representative (1991 - 1995)
Sold chemical specialties to the pharmaceutical industry.

EDUCATION

Degree: M.B.A., University of Washington, 1991
Major: Marketing

Degree: B.S., Oregon State University, 1989
Major: Chemistry
          President of Chemical Society

THOMAS R. SPEARS
210 Warfield Way
Huron, OH 14263

Cell: (203) 644-5658   Email: TomSP21@MSN.com   Home: (203) 652-9417

OBJECTIVE

Responsible Sales Management position with growth-oriented company in the equipment field.

PROFESSIONAL EXPERIENCE

1998
to
Present

HI-REZ GRAPHICS, INC. (Cleveland Regional Office)

District Sales Manager (2003 - Present)
Manage five employee sales force in the application sales of sophisticated computer microfilm record recording, storage and retrieval system in the states of Michigan, Ohio and Indiana. Successfully launched and marketed world's first updatable computer microfilm record keeping system to municipalities, colleges, universities, libraries, banks and insurance companies accounting for $30 million sales in first year. Creative sales strategy and strategic selling skills have accounted for over 300% sales increase in last two years, with annual sales now approaching $100 million.

Senior Sales Representative (2000 - 2003)
Worked closely with venture team in the test marketing of computer updatable microfilm record keeping system. Primary focus was on banking industry applications. Was successful in selling, installing and starting up first banking application for new system. Sale proved the viability of this application and paved the way to $330 million in third year sales.

Sales Representative (1998 - 2000)
Successfully sold wide range of microfilms and other specialty films through network of film dealerships. Selected and trained new dealers. Increased sales in the Greater Detroit market form $1.8 million to $5.2 million in two years.

EDUCATION

Degree: B.A., University of Michigan, 1998
Major: Marketing

President, Student Government
President, Delta Upsilon Fraternity
Captain, Varsity Track Team

JENNIFER T. LOGAN
1616 Ryan Circle
Marietta, GA 18274

Office: (616) 935-0978   Email: Logan1616@ MSN.com   Home: (616) 554-2374

OBJECTIVE

Senior level Operations Management position with functional responsibility for Manufacturing, Engineering, Procurement and Distribution in medium-size manufacturing organization.

PROFESSIONAL EXPERIENCE

1996
to
Present

STRATFORD TUBE, INC.

Vice President Operations (Corporate Offices) (2001 - Present)
Report to President with full P&L responsibility for two copper refineries and tube manufacturing plants for this leading producer of copper tubing (annual sales $500 million). Direct the activities of two Plant Managers, 300 salaried and 5,000 hourly employees with annual budget of $300 million. Organized and directed multi-discipline cost reduction task force which identified and implemented cost reduction opportunities resulting in 20% decrease in overall manufacturing costs in last three years (current estimated annual savings of $110 million). Directed investigation and implementation of sophisticated computerized materials management scheduling and control systems which cut raw materials inventories by 30% (annual savings $15 million).

Plant Manager (Albany Plant) (1996 - 2001)
Reported to Vice President of Manufacturing with P&L responsibility for this 2,800 employee copper refinery and tube manufacturing plan ($375 million annual production). Functions reporting included Manufacturing, Materials Management, Distribution, Maintenance & Engineering, Accounting and Human Resources. Successfully directed two-year, $125 million plant expansion program designed to double plant's annual production capacity. (All engineering done at plant level.) Project completed three months ahead of schedule and 10% below budget. In preparation for plant start-up, transferred 75% of hourly workers to new jobs in two months with no loss in plant productivity. Set plant production and safety records for four out of five years.

1986
to
1996

WOLFORD TUBE COMPANY, INC.

Manager of Engineering (Corporate Offices) (1991 - 1996)
Managed 150 employee central engineering function for this manufacturer of refrigeration tubing (annual sales $300 million). Directed engineering organization in all capital project expansion programs to include design, installation, start-up and debugging of copper tube manufacturing facilities and refineries. Successfully engineered major $250 million capital program (largest in company's history) including installation and start-up of state-of-the-art, computer controlled, integrated refinery and tube mill. Project delivered four months ahead of schedule and on budget.

Department Manager, Drawing Operations (Bradford Plant) (1989 - 1991)
Managed 100 employee tube drawing operation with annual production valued at $85 million. Increased production by 18% with simultaneous 15% reduction in manufacturing costs in two-year period.

Project Engineer (1986 - 1989)
Responsible for design, installation and start-up of major capital projects in furnace and drawing operations. Independently handled projects in the $40-50 million range.

EDUCATION

Degree: M.S., Georgia Institute of Technology, 1986
Major: Metallurgical Engineering

Degree: B.S., Virginia Institute of Technology, 1984
Major: Mechanical Engineering
              Tau Beta Psi

GEORGE T. BENNER
221 Washington Terrace
Plainfield, NJ 13448

Phone: (609) 237-9936

Email: GeoB22@AOL.com

OBJECTIVE

Manufacturing management position with medium-size company offering opportunity for advancement based upon demonstrated performance.

PROFESSIONAL EXPERIENCE

2000
to
Present

WEXLER MANUFACTURING COMPANY (Linwood Plant)

Assistant Plant Manager (2003 - Present)
Report to Plant Manager of this 1,000 employee manufacturer of silicone-based waxes and polishes ($325 million annual sales). Manage the Can Finishing and Warehousing Departments with full management responsibility for 210 employees (40 salaried, 170 hourly) and an operating budget of $130 million. Introduced automatic palletizers and palletized railcar loading, cutting warehouse operating costs by 25% (annual savings $15 million). Initiated absenteeism control program reducing absenteeism from 11% to less than 4% in one year. Reduced union grievances from 185 to 62 in two years through effective employee relations practices.

Department Manager, Formulations (2000 - 2003)
Reported to Manufacturing Manager with accountability for the formulations and mixing operations. Managed 50 employee (five salaried, 45 hourly) department with annual budget of $75 million. Organized and led hourly employee cost reduction task force implementing several programs resulting in total annual savings of 10% ($7.5 million) in one year. Increased department production by 18% in two years through employee job rotation and enrichment program. Awarded annual safety award for best departmental safety record in both 2001 and 2003.

1998
to
2000

CORDOVA WAX COMPANY (Radley Plant)

Supervisor, Formulations
Supervised 15-employee wax formulations department for this leading manufacturer of shoe polish and furniture wax (annual sales $150 million).

EDUCATION

Degree: B.S., Boston University, 1998
Major: Industrial Technology   G.P.A. 3.5/4.0
         Cum Laude

TODD E. THOMAS
3229 Colonial Place
Hartford, CT 13847
Phone: (213) 334-7495
Cell: (213) 457-9682

OBJECTIVE

Executive level position with consumer-products company offering opportunity to manage corporate Procurement function.

PROFESSIONAL EXPERIENCE

2003
to
Present

HARTFORD FOODS, INC. (Corporate Offices)

Director of Procurement
Direct staff of 15 professionals in the corporate-wide management of the procurement function for this $1.2 billion manufacturer of consumer food products. Direct the purchase of all raw materials, equipment, vital supplies and services for corporate offices and eight manufacturing plants with annual budget of $580 million. Develop, implement and control all procurement strategies and policies including centralized procurement programs on all consolidated purchases.

Implemented computerized raw materials inventory tracking and forecasting system allowing substantially reduced inventory levels (annual savings $26 million). Consolidated purchase of packaging supplies with resultant savings of $22 million. Reduced fuel costs by 20% through conversion to bio-mass boilers and long-term contracts with bio-mass fuel suppliers ($18 million annual savings)

1995
to
2003

LARSON BAKING COMPANY, INC. (Corporate Offices)

Manager of Corporate Procurement (1997 - 2003)
Directed the procurement function on a corporate-wide basis for this $850 million manufacturer of cookies, crackers and breads. Managed a staff of eight, with annual budget of $325 million and full centralized purchasing responsibility for five plants. Centralized procurement function with net headcount reduction of ten and annual savings of $300,000. Centralized purchasing and consolidated purchases of hundreds of items with first year's savings of $16.5 million.

Senior Buyer - Vital Supplies (1995 - 1997)
Managed department of two professionals and two non-exempts with responsibility for procurement of all packaging and vital supplies ($200 million budget). Developed computerized vital supplies and packing forecasting system based upon sales forecasts which permitted more efficient control of purchases and inventories (annual savings $3.2 million). Negotiated two-year contract on purchase of shipping cartons resulting in annual savings of $1.3 million. Consolidated flour and sugar purchases with estimated savings of $850,000.

1989
to
1995

BORDER FOODS, INC. (Corporate Offices)

Manager of Procurement (1992 - 1995)
Managed department of three (annual budget of $50 million) for this $150 million snack foods manufacturer. Credited with $3 million in annual savings through better inventory control and procurement practices.

Buyer (1989 - 1992)
Reported to Manager of Procurement with responsibility for purchase of all packaging materials and supplies.

EDUCATION

Degree: B.A., Syracuse University, 1989
Major: Business Administration

President of Business Club
Captain, Varsity Baseball

GORDON B. DAVIS
17 Harbor View Place, Apt. 12-A
Green Bay, WI 23568
Phone: (515) 844-8847
Email: GorDa@AOL.com

OBJECTIVE

Management position in Procurement with progressive company offering opportunity for advancement based upon achievement and bottom-line contribution.

PROFESSIONAL EXPERIENCE

2003
to
Present

GREEN BAY PAPER COMPANY, INC. (Corporate Offices)

Senior Purchasing Agent - Vital Supplies
Report to Manager of Procurement for this $350 million manufacturer of printing and converting grades of paper. Responsible for purchase of all vital supplies including: knock-down containers, poly wrap, shrink packages, etc. Annual purchase volume $18 million. Accountabilities include procurement, delivery, storage and distribution to manufacturing departments as needed. Negotiated two-year contract for knock-down containers 20% under normal purchase cost (annual savings $1.3 million). Developed and successfully installed computer system for forecasting changes in demand for vital supplies based upon changes in the sales forecast. Resultant inventory adjustments have saved estimated $575,000 annually.

2000
to
2003

FORT SMITH PAPER COMPANY (Corporate Offices)

Vital Supplies Buyer
Reported to Manager of Procurement for this $110 million converter of consumer paper products. Responsible for $4 million budget in the purchase of vital supplies in support of manufacturing operations. Managed the purchase, delivery, storage and in-plant distribution of all supplies purchased. Supplies included: knockdown cartons, poly wraps and shrink wraps. Negotiated new poly wrap contract with 10% reduction in cost (annual savings $200,000). Through use of computer forecasting, reduced vital supplies inventories by 20% with net savings of $125,000 per year.

EDUCATION

Degree: B.S., University of Wisconsin, Stevens Point, 2000
Major: Pulp & Paper Technology G.P.A. 3.8/4.0
Cum Laude
Fort Smith Paper Company Scholarship (4 years)

President, Delta Upsilon Fraternity
President, Student Government Association

SARAH B. THOMLINSON

55 Orchard Hill Road
Appleton, WI 23847
Phone: (309) 227-2999 (O)
(309) 335-5673 (H)
Email: SBT55@WPT.com

OBJECTIVE

Senior level R&D management position with responsibility for achievement of company's technology objectives.

SUMMARY

Over 20 years dynamic, innovative management and leadership in Fortune 500 companies. Demonstrated capability to achieve business goals through innovative technology. Broad range of technical expertise coupled with highly effective communications and interpersonal skills.

PROFESSIONAL EXPERIENCE

2002
to
Present

WISCONSIN TISSUE & PACKAGING, INC. (Corporate Research Center)

Vice President of Technology
Manage 500 employee Corporate Technology Center for this Fortune 100 paper and packaging manufacturer ($4.2 billion sales). Annual Technology budget of $32 million. Major accomplishments include development and successful reduction-to-practice of new, innovative magnetic fiber forming device imparting unique characteristics (softness and absorbency) to consumer tissue-based product. Process permits 30% reduction in fibers (estimated savings of $300 million annually) with enhanced product quality. Successfully developed and introduced five new products accounting for a 15% increase in total sales. Two additional major consumer products now ready for test market.

1993
to
2002

KIMBERLY NONWOVEN FIBERS, INC. (Packaging & Materials Laboratory)

Research Director, Packaging & Materials
Managed 135 professionals and technicians in the research and development of all packaging, nonwovens, plastic materials and photographic film (annual budget $12 million). Developed new technology allowing synthetic fibers to be run on a wet lay technology paper machine. Resultant web has unique strength and appears to have wide application to commercial products. Estimated five-year potential is $125 million in new sales. Developed new frozen food packaging material that prolongs thawing time by 300% at room temperature. Food processors to experience estimated 30% reduction in spoilage, providing Stratton with substantial competitive advantage.

1984
to
1993

JAMES RIVER CORPORATION (Corporate Research)

Research Manager, Synthetic Fibers (1988 - 1993)
Managed Research Department of 38 professionals in the development and application of novel synthetic fibers to packaging and consumer paper webs.

Senior Research Scientist, Polymer Research (1984 - 1988)
Pioneered and accelerated the development of proprietary polymeric materials through experimental and theoretical studies including computer modeling.

1982
to
1984

VULCAN SPACE LABORATORY

Research Specialist
Pioneered development of proprietary materials for Vulcan communications satellite heat shield. Conducted re-entry simulation tests and qualified materials for use in treating the surface of the heat shield for first satellite launch.

EDUCATION

Degree: Ph.D., University of Michigan, 1982
Major: Chemical Engineering
          Vulcan Laboratory Fellowship

Degree: M.S., Rochester Institute of Technology, 1980
Major: Materials Engineering

Degree: B.S., Rochester Institute of Technology, 1978
Major: Chemical Engineering
          Cum Laude
          Barlow Scholarship (4 years)

          President, Chemical Engineering Society

PUBLICATIONS

46 professional publications and papers (1980 - 2002)

AFFILIATIONS

American Society of Chemical Engineers
American Chemical Society
American Physical Society
Technical Association of Pulp & Paper Industry

DAVID A. FREEMAN
22 Indigo Sky Way
Split Arrow, OK 23748
Phone: (446) 757-8849
Email: DaFree22@MSN.com

OBJECTIVE

Research and Development position requiring creativity and innovation in the development of novel polymer-based products and processes.

PROFESSIONAL EXPERIENCE

2000
to
Present

WILSON POLYMER SPECIALTIES, INC. (Corporate Technology)

Senior Research Engineer, Polymers (2002 - Present)
Provided technical leadership to research team in the development of new polymer-based material for use in the manufacture of boat hulls. Developed Sampson™, a revolutionary new polymeric material having twice the strength of conventional fiberglass at half the cost and representing an annual projected market value of $300 million. Three patents awarded.

Research Engineer, Polymers (2000 - 2002)
Developed new synthetic fabric including all process steps from innovative polymerization process through fabric finishing. Transferred process from laboratory bench scale to pilot plant scale two months ahead of schedule and 30% under research budget. Awarded four patents and presented Norwood's AInventor of the Year≅ award.

1997
to
2000

GRAVERLY CHEMICAL COMPANY (Central Research)

Polymer Chemist
Developed high-temperature, resistant molding polymers and inherent fire retardant plastics. Awarded two patents for creative product development work associated with phenolic molding compounds.

EDUCATION

Degree: Ph.D., Massachusetts Institute of Technology, 1997
Major: Polymer Engineering
Thesis: ACopolymerization of Diamond Polymers≅
Hawthorne Fellowship

Degree: M.S., Rochester Institute of Technology, 1995
Major: Chemical Engineering
Ludwig Scholar

Degree: B.S., Rochester Institute of Technology, 1993
Major: Chemical Engineering
          Magna Cum Laude
          Stanton Scholarship (3 years)

          President, Polymeric Society

PATENTS

Awarded 10 U.S. patents since 1997.

AFFILIATIONS

American Society of Polymer Scientists
American Society of Chemical Engineers
National Institute for Polymer Research

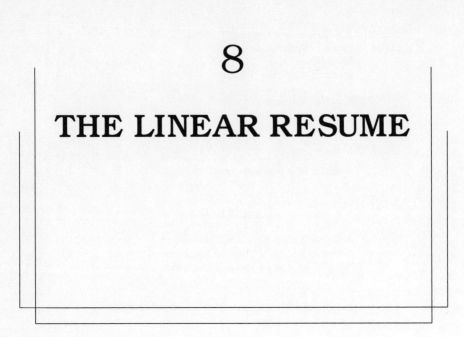

8

THE LINEAR RESUME

Throughout the later part of the 1980s, and again during the recession of the early 2000s, there has been considerable focus on corporate downsizing, with many U.S. employers stripping away at employee headcount in an effort to become more cost-effective and competitive both domestically and internationally. This trend is expected to continue through the next few years and perhaps beyond as employers increasingly feel the pressure to further cut operating costs in the face of ever stiffening competition in global markets.

Along with these employee headcount reduction programs has come the emergence of the popular linear resume format, which continues to grow rapidly in both use and popularity. This resume format has been developed and extensively promoted by many of the nation's leading outplacement consulting firms.

The linear resume format, propelled by the push from these professional outplacement consultants, has today, by far, become the most widely used and accepted resume style. This chapter, therefore, is committed to a full discussion of the linear resume; it provides complete step-by-step instructions for preparation of this highly popular and effective resume format.

TECHNICALLY A CHRONOLOGICAL FORMAT

A close study of the sample resumes at the end of this chapter, will reveal that the linear resume is a variation of the "classical" chronological resume format described in Chapter 6. What classifies it as a chronological resume is the treatment of the Experience section of the resume. You will note, as with the "classical" chronological resume samples provided in the previous chapter, the linear resume presents employers and positions held in reverse chronological order. The current (or most recent) employer and job are listed first, with each subsequent employer and job listed in reverse chronological order, ending with the candidate's first professional position held.

Although technically a chronological resume, the linear resume format has some distinct characteristics that set it apart from the "classical" chronological approach. In particular, the main feature that distinguishes it from its "classical" relative, and accounts for the name "linear," is the manner in which the Experience section of the resume is written. Comparison of the linear resume samples at the end of this chapter with the "classical" chronological resumes presented in the two previous chapters will show that the "classical" chronological resume uses a "literary" style when describing work experience. In contrast, the linear resume uses a "linear" approach when presenting much or all of this data. That is, each specific job responsibility and/or accomplishment is presented on a line-by-line (linear) basis, thus setting this data apart from the balance of the text and serving to highlight it for ease of reading.

An informal survey of several hundred linear resumes received by my company, Brandywine Consulting Group, establishes that there are typically some additional differences between the "classical" and linear chronological resume formats. Specifically, in practice, the linear resume:

1. Often lacks a "job objective" section.
2. Includes a "qualifications summary" section.

Otherwise, the two chronological formats are substantially the same.

ADVANTAGES OF THE LINEAR FORMAT

The advantages of using the linear chronological resume format over the functional resume (see Chapter 10) are several. As with the "classical" chronological resume, the key advantages of the linear chronological format are:

1. Since it is the most commonly used format, the chronological resume (including the "classical" and "linear" variations) is the format with which employers are most familiar and feel most comfortable.
2. It provides for a logical, easy-to-read flow, with point-to-point continuity from one employment position and employer to the next.
3. This same logical flow makes the linear chronological format one of the easiest resume styles to prepare.
4. This format allows the job seeker to emphasize career growth and progression (where the candidate has experienced such)—two factors viewed favorably by most employers.
5. The linear chronological format, likewise, serves to highlight continuity of employment (employer and job stability) and career continuity (growth)—both felt to be desirable factors by the majority of employers.
6. By contrast with the functional resume, this approach serves to highlight names of past employers—an advantage when these are well-known, prestigious companies.

Further, when compared to the "classical" or traditional chronological resume format discussed in the two previous chapters, the "linear" chronological resume has the following advantages:

1. The line-by-line itemization of job responsibilities and/or accomplishments greatly facilitates ease of reading (when compared to the literary approach used in the "classical" format), thus increasing the probability the resume will be read.

2. Most resume writers find it easier to delineate job responsibilities and accomplishments on a line-by-line basis as opposed to a literary format, making the linear resume easier to write.

3. The clear, separate delineation of accomplishments serves to highlight these achievements in the mind of the reader/employer.

DISADVANTAGES OF THE LINEAR FORMAT

Since it is a variation of the chronological format, the linear resume is not the "resume of choice" in all cases. As with the "classical" chronological resume, the linear chronological resume can sometimes have certain disadvantages when contrasted with the functional resume format (see Chapters 10 and 11). Such drawbacks can include the following:

1. This format can serve to highlight obvious employment handicaps (where these exist), including:
   a. Job hopping.
   b. Employment gaps.
   c. Underemployment.
   d. Lack of career progress.
   e. Little or no job-related experience.
   f. Age.

2. It focuses attention on career progression rather than specific functional skills or personal strengths.

3. It tends to highlight most recent experience when certain earlier experiences may, in fact, be more relevant to the current job objective.

4. It may serve to shortchange certain key accomplishments when these achievements occurred earlier in one's career.

Where these shortcomings are evident and could negatively affect the presentation of your qualifications, you should likely be using the functional resume format described in Chapter 10. Use of the linear chronological format, in such cases, would no be to your advantage.

In addition, when compared to the "classical" chronological format described in Chapter 6, the linear chronological format can have the following disadvantages:

1. Inclusion of the "qualifications summary" at the beginning of the resume takes up valuable space and can be viewed by some readers/employers as unnecessarily redundant because most of this information is already self-evident from the rest of the resume text.

2. Lack of an "objective" statement at the beginning of the resume may leave the reader/employer uncertain about the level and type of position acceptable to you. (This may prove a problem if you are willing to consider a lateral or even a downward career move.)

3. The line-by-line itemization of job responsibilities and/or accomplishments, although more easily read, takes up more room than the literary approach employed in the "classical" format. Thus, use of the linear approach will increase resume length.

In my judgment, exclusion of an "objective statement" by the linear resume may place you at a disadvantage, since it is known that most employers prefer to see one. Also, the additional space consumed by the line-by-line approach of the linear resume is not particularly objectionable, since the additional resume length is usually more than offset by the substantially improved ease of reading achieved by the linear format.

If space is truly a critical consideration, the resume writer could consider eliminating the "qualifications summary" since, as previously mentioned, this information is frequently self-evident and redundant to the information presented in the body of the resume. To reiterate, however, it should not be necessary in most cases to eliminate the summary section since, due to the easy readability of the linear resume format, lengthening the resume would not be found to be particularly objectionable to the reader.

Two Variations of the Linear Format

Review of the numerous linear resumes received by my company reveals that there are two basic variations of the linear resume. These are:

1. The narrative linear format.
2. The straight linear format.

Use of these format variations is unevenly divided between the two, with the narrative linear approach now clearly representing the lion's share of usage.

Sample Resume D, presented at the end of this chapter (pages 122–123), is an example of the straight linear approach; Sample Resume E (pages 124–125) exemplifies the narrative linear format. Comparison of the two will distinguish the basic differences.

You will note that in the "experience" section of the resume, the narrative linear format (see Sample Resume E) makes use of literary or narrative approach when describing the job (that is, company description, reporting relationship, job scope, and key functional accountabilities). Key accomplishments, on the other hand, are presented on a line-by-line, linear basis.

In contrast, the straight linear format (see Sample Resume D) uses *only* the linear approach to describe both the job and related key achievements. You will also note that with the straight linear approach there is no physical separation between job description factors and key achievements. The line items presented by the resume author simply flow from job description straight to achievements, with no physical demarcation between these two categories. The two are practically indistinguishable.

Although both approaches (narrative and straight linear) are certainly acceptable, I personally feel that the narrative linear approach has the distinct advantage of ease of reading. The physical separation between job description and accomplishments makes this distinction evident, and the reader does not have to wrestle with where the job and company descriptions end and key accomplishments begin. It also serves to highlight key accomplishments, which could prove advantageous during the interview process.

Additionally, the narrative format will allow you to accommodate more information in the same amount of space. For example, note how, although the sample resumes at the end of the chapter are resumes of the same person, the second resume (narrative format) permits the inclusion of the "professional affiliation" section at the end of the resume. In contrast, the first resume (straight linear format) does not allow sufficient space to accommodate this information. There is thus some loss of resume space when electing to use the straight linear format.

Although I have a preference for the narrative linear approach, it is important to emphasize that both the narrative and straight linear approaches are acceptable when writing a linear resume. Either can be used to present your credentials to a prospective employer in an effective manner. Basically, the choice is yours.

RESUME COMPONENTS

Review of the sample resumes contained at the end of this chapter and in Chapter 9 will reveal that the linear resume format is divided into the following key components:

1. Heading.
2. Summary.
3. Experience.

4. Education.

5. Military (optional).

6. Other (optional).

My study of several hundred linear resumes has shown that the "other" section of the resume is highly variable as used by different resume authors. Alternate titles for this section of the resume may include the following:

1. Professional Affiliations.

2. Patents and Publications.

3. Community Leadership.

4. Activities.

We will now start the step-by-step process of constructing a linear resume. We will examine each resume component in detail and provide practical examples so that you can tailor your own resume component accordingly. Should you follow this process, by the time we have completed this chapter, you will have prepared a highly professional looking linear resume that should serve your needs rather well.

Heading

As described in Chapter 6, the resume heading consists of four items. These are your full name, address, home telephone number, and e-mail address. Under certain circumstances, your office telephone number and/or cell number can also be provided. Some sample resume headings follow:

SAMUEL B. SWANSON
518 Barrowcroft Road
Clear Lake, WI 19847
Phone: (812) 473-9871
Email: SamSwan@AOL.com

KAREN W. WHAITLLEY
814 Yellow Duck Lane
Meadowview Farms
Portland, OR 27895

Home (716) 386-9837   Office (716) 875-2835

Your name should be typed in capital letters, with the remainder of the heading presented in lower case. Bold type should be used to highlight your name.

As discussed in detail in Chapter 6, inclusion of your office telephone number on your resume might create sensitive situations. Listing the office number can suggest that you are "at odds" with your current employer and that you are being encouraged to leave. Although this may well be untrue, use of the office phone number could nonetheless trigger unnecessary suspicion concerning your employment status on the part of prospective employers.

Summary

The intent of the Summary section of the resume is to provide the reader/employer with just enough information about your credentials to compel reading of the rest of the resume document. Generally, this is accomplished by providing a brief statement that describes the depth and breadth of your experience in your field of expertise, followed by a statement that highlights certain key strengths in relevant areas likely to interest prospective employers.

Review of the sample resumes contained at the end of this chapter and in Chapter 9 show that these "summary" sections have some similarities. You will notice that the first sentence of most summary statements cites the candidate's career or professional field and states the years of experience. The second sentence is normally used to market key job-related strengths. Finally, the third sentence (which is optional) is normally used to either further describe the breadth of the candidate's experience or, alternately, to further market some unique skill or fact that would likely be perceived as valuable to a prospective employer.

Because of today's extensive use of computers, especially keyword search, as the basis for resume scanning and candidate identification, this section of the resume needs to be carefully written to include many of the keywords employers would typically be searching for when filling the type of position you seek.

If age is a potential barrier to employment, you may want to think twice about stating the precise number of years of experience in the summary section. For example, stating that you have 40 years' experience in the electronics industry may be a dead giveaway that you are no longer a spring chicken. In such cases, you may want to be a little less specific. For example, as an alternative, you could state that you have "over 20 years" experience. In this way, the employer can't tell whether you are age 40 or age 60. Should you be concerned about how to handle age in the resume, let me suggest that you review Chapter 12, Problem Resumes, which discusses this subject in detail.

The "summary" section of the resume should be concise and to the point. It should not be a lengthy, rambling epistle. Component statements need not be written in complete sentences. Instead, they may be written as simple, descriptive phrases that are intended to be crisp, hard-hitting, and concise—much the same as the copy used in advertising. One trick to achieve this is to begin each statement with an adjective followed by a noun (or adverb followed by a verb). This will force you to be brief and to the point.

The following are a few sample summary statements for use in modeling your own summary section.

1. *Summary.* Seasoned executive with over 20 years solid career progression in Information Services field. Excellent reputation for directing development of effective systems in response to key management information needs. Known for strong interpersonal and motivational management skills.

2. *Summary.* Motivated Senior Financial Analyst with outstanding educational credentials. Five years' experience with top 10 consulting firm. Demonstrated ability to effectively manage key financial projects, from

cost estimate to final funding. Programs in the $500 to
$800 million range.

3. *Summary.* Senior electronics manufacturing executive
with 15 years' responsible line and staff experience.
Excellent record of fast-track career growth earned
through solid contributions to bottom-line results. Outstanding reputation as organizer and leader who consistently achieves committed objectives.

Experience

For the experienced person, the Experience or Work History
section is undoubtedly the single most important component
of the employment resume. It is this section on which the
employer generally focuses to determine whether or not you
have the specific experience, knowledge, and skills to effectively perform the duties of the position for which you are
being considered. It is very important, therefore, that you in-
vest the needed time and effort to do a good job of describing
these critical factors in your background summary.

The prework that you have done in Chapter 4, Preparing
to Write, should serve you very well at this point by providing the data needed to construct this section of your resume. You are encouraged to retrieve this prework and
keep it handy for easy reference as you develop this section
of the linear resume format.

Essentially, information in the Experience section of
your resume falls into three parts, as represented by the
following outline:

    I. Employer Descriptors.
       A. Dates of employment.
       B. Name of employer.
       C. Location employed.
       D. Company size, products, or services.
    II. Position Descriptors.
       A. Position title.
       B. Dates position held (from . . . to).

      C. Reporting relationship (title of boss).

      D. Position size/scope (quantitative description of position—people and budgets managed, dollars impacted, and so on).

      E. Functional responsibilities (functions performed/managed, titles of those managed).

   III. Key Accomplishments (quantitative descriptions).

      A. Results achieved.

      B. Dollars saved.

      C. Efficiencies gained.

      D. And so on.

As discussed earlier in this chapter, the linear resume follows a chronological resume format. It is for this reason, as you will note in reviewing the sample linear resumes provided, that the entire "experience section" of the resume is arranged in reverse chronological order. Thus, the "experience section" begins with your most recent (or current) employer (and position held) and then continues through previous employers (and positions held), in reverse chronology, ending with your very first employer (and position held) at the beginning of your career.

Study of the sample linear resumes provided will reveal that dates of employment are displayed on the extreme right side of the resume page. This is a deviation from older resume styles, where employment dates were positioned at the left hand margin. By positioning these dates at the right, this modern resume format saves considerable space by allowing you to move the full resume text to the left margin. Company name is presented in capital letters and is set in bold type. Location is presented in lower case letters and parentheses, and is positioned to the right of company name. Location is also set in normal rather than bold type.

Title of position held is presented on the next line. With the exception of initial capitals, this information is presented in lower case letters, and the full title is underlined. You will note the spacing between the line containing the company name and line displaying position title. This is not only aesthetically pleasing but provides for good visual separation of the material presented, greatly enhancing resume readability. Information is presented in readable "chunks" which are of a size that can be readily assimilated with a single glance.

If more than one position has been held with a single employer, each position is separated from the previous position description and key accomplishments by a line of spacing. With the exception of initial letters, position titles are always set in lower case type, and the title is fully underlined.

In the case of multiple positions with the same employer, you will also note that the dates of employment for each position are displayed in parentheses to the immediate right of position title. Placing these "position" dates just to the right of the job title, rather than at the far right margin, prevents any possible confusion with "employer" dates, which are presented at the right margin of the resume. This clear separation eliminates any possible confusion about employment stability, since there has been a clear separation between general employment dates and the dates during which the resume author held specific positions with that same employer.

In the case of the "narrative" linear format, the next line following the job title contains a brief narrative description of both the employer and position. Examination of this section will reveal that this description begins with a statement of the position's reporting relationship, followed by a description of the position's principal accountability and the employer's business (including size and products produced or professional services provided). Sometimes an additional statement is included that further outlines the position's major functional responsibilities. This is optional, but such a statement can sometimes be helpful in more fully conveying the nature and scope of the position and its accountabilities.

By contrast, as Sample Resume D illustrates, the "straight" linear format does not provide this position and employer description in a literary or narrative form. Instead, this information is presented in a line-by-line (linear) format. Typically, however, the first line of this format, as with narrative format, describes the reporting relationship and provides a brief description of the employer's business (including size, products, and/or services). The subsequent line is then normally used to describe the job's principal functional accountability along with some quantitative description of the position's principal dollar impact (that is, sales volume, operating budget, and so forth). Sometimes a third statement follows, offering a broader description of the position's functional responsibilities. This may, for example, detail positions reporting, subfunctions managed, and so on.

In the case of both the "narrative" and "straight" linear resume formats, the next section of the resume (following both the employer and position descriptions), details key accomplishments. Usually three or four major accomplishments (where appropriate) are cited for each position held. The resultant resume length will prohibit individuals with many years of experience from listing key accomplishments for all positions they have held. For such people, it is not necessary to list accomplishments in positions held earlier in their career, and a simple statement of key job accountabilities or job title alone will suffice. (Note how this has been handled on the second pages of the sample resumes at the end of this chapter.)

In reviewing these sample resumes, you will also note that each accomplishment statement is highlighted by a bullet and offset by double spacing. This makes the accomplishment stand out; it thus has a greater impact on the reader/employer and greatly enhances the resumes's readability. This is the major advantage of the linear approach to resume writing that sets it apart from other forms of the employment resume which use only the straight narrative or literary approach.

As discussed in Chapter 6, perhaps the greatest secret to brevity and conciseness in resume writing is the technique of starting each statement with an action word or verb. Review of the sample linear resumes at the end of this chapter and in Chapter 9 will show that accomplishment statements have followed this important rule. Thus, each statement is crisp, to-the-point, and conveys a sense of "results orientation" to the resume. The practice of using quantitative descriptions of results achieved is also a powerful technique that will increase the document's impact.

When selecting specific accomplishments for highlighting on your linear resume, care should be taken to list meaningful results achieved. The use of trivial results or citing only job responsibilities (as opposed to accomplishments) can backfire on you should you elect to use the linear resume format. Such choice can serve to highlight mediocrity, and will likely not serve your purpose well at all! Some careful thought about past performance can usually serve to surface at least one or two meaningful accomplishments worth highlighting. If not, however, I strongly suggest that you choose an alternate resume approach rather than employing the linear resume format.

Education

The Education section of the resume has already been described thoroughly in Chapter 6. I suggest that you review the appropriate pages of this chapter prior to constructing the Education section of the linear resume.

Military (Optional)

Review of several hundred linear resumes received by our company suggests that inclusion of a Military section (where appropriate) in the resume is entirely optional. In only a very small percentage of the cases was it shown at all. Should you elect to include it, however, the following format can be followed.

MILITARY

United States Army, 1990–1994
2nd Battalion, Armoured Division
First Lieutenant
Honorable Discharge, 6/2/94

Other (Optional)

As stated earlier in this chapter, there are many variations in titles for and contents of the Other or final section of the linear resume format. Since better than half of the linear resumes do not even bother to include this section and since there is considerable variation in content (when it is used), I will not attempt to provide details on the development of this resume segment. It must be considered optional and thus can be excluded from the resume entirely.

Should you wish to include this section in your own resume, let me suggest that you review the samples provided in Chapter 9 for ideas on how to treat this resume component.

SARAH B. CARSON
235 Rothchild Boulevard
Barron Heights, IL 18743
Phone: (312) 857-9847
Email: SarCar@MSN.com

SUMMARY

Senior executive with over 20 years experience in retail manufacturing operations, product development and marketing. Particularly strong skills in marketing and manufacturing, with ability to present well-balanced product mix, prepare and control budgets, motivate and direct people.

PROFESSIONAL EXPERIENCE

STRATHMERE FASHIONS, INC. (New York, NY) **2000 to Present**

Vice President & Division Manager, Footwear

- Report to President of this $320 million retail fashion manufacturing and marketing company.

- Full P&L for $150 million shoe marketing and merchandising operation.

- Directed marketing/merchandising for 23 operating companies, 190 store departments, 1,900 employees.

- Developed and led marketing strategy that increased sales 35% in two years.

- Profitability liquidated obsolete shoe inventory valued at $20 million ($1 million profit).

- Initiated retail sales training program that reduced customer complaints by 92%.

BEAVERTON SHOE COMPANY (Philadelphia, PA) **1993 to 2000**

Vice President, Retail Division

- Reported to Senior Vice President of this $500 million manufacturer, wholesaler and retailer of men's/women's shoes.

- Directed sales operations and merchandising/marketing for $85 million retail division.

- Initiated and coordinated northeast region co-op advertising program resulting in 20% sales increase.

- Developed successful regional marketing strategy that permitted 10% reduction in number of stores with simultaneous increase in sales of 5% ($6 million savings).

Sarah B. Carson

MAXWELL SHOE COMPANY (Hanover, PA)   **1988 to 1993**

Director of Manufacturing (1990 – 1993)

- Reported to Vice President of Operations of this $250 million quality men's shoe manufacturer.

- Full P&L for three plants, 2,200 employees, with annual operating budget of $175 million.

- Reengineered manufacturing operations, consolidating four plants into three, with no loss in production volume and annual cost savings of $25 million.

- Directed installation of SPC-based total quality program with resultant reduction in waste of more than 80%.

General Manager, Dixville Plant (1988 – 1990)

- Reported to Director of Manufacturing.

- Managed 500 employee shoe manufacturing plant with annual operating budget of $52 million.

JORDAN LEATHER & SHOE WORKS (Lancaster, PA)   **1984 to 1988**

Plant Engineer   (1987 – 1988)
Senior Project Engineer   (1985 – 1987)
Project Engineer   (1984 – 1985)

EDUCATION

Degree: M.S., Penn State University, 1984
Major: Mechanical Engineering
          Farthner Scholarship (2 years)

Degree: B.S., Bucknell University, 1982
Major: Mechanical Engineering
          Wilson Scholar (4 years)

SARAH B. CARSON
235 Rothchild Boulevard
Barron Heights, IL 18743
Phone: (312) 857-9847
Email: SaCar@MSN.com

SUMMARY

Senior executive with over 20 years experience in retail manufacturing operations, product development and marketing. Particularly strong skills in marketing and manufacturing, with ability to present well-balanced product mix, prepare and control budgets, motivate and direct people.

PROFESSIONAL EXPERIENCE

STRATHMERE FASHIONS, INC. (New York, NY)   **2000 to Present**

Vice President & Division Manager, Footwear

Report to President with full P&L responsibility for $150 million shoe marketing and merchandising operation consisting of 23 operating companies, 190 shoe departments and 1,900 employees.

- Developed and led marketing strategy that increased sales 35% in two years.
- Profitably liquidated obsolete shoe inventory valued at $20 million ($1 million profit).
- Initiated retail sales training program that reduced customer complaints by 92%.

BEAVERTON SHOE COMPANY (Philadelphia, PA)   **1993 to 2000**

Vice President, Retail Division

Reported to Senior Vice President of this $500 million manufacturer, wholesaler and retailer of men's/women's shoes. Functional responsibility for sales operations and merchandising/marketing of $85 million retail division.

- Successfully repositioned business from low end to better grade footwear resulting in 15% profit increase.
- Implemented automated inventory control system that reduced store inventories by 18% ($2 million savings).

Director of Merchandising, Retail Division (1993 – 1995)

Reported to Vice President, Retail Division with accountability for all merchandising of this $85 million retail division.

- Initiated and coordinated northeast region co-op advertising program resulting in 20% sales increase.
- Developed successful regional marketing strategy that permitted 10% reduction in number of stores with simultaneous increase in sales of 5% ($6 million savings).

MAXWELL SHOE COMPANY (Hanover, PA)   **1988 to 1993**

Director of Manufacturing (1990 – 1993)
Reported to Vice President of Operations of this $250 million quality men's shoe manufacturer. Total P&L responsibility three plant, 2,200 employee shoe manufacturing operation with annual operating budget of $175 million.

- Reengineered manufacturing operations, consolidating four plants into three, with no loss in production volume and annual cost savings of $25 million.

- Directed installation of SPC-based total quality program with resultant reduction in waste of more than 80%.

General Manager, Dixville Plant (1988 – 1990)
Reported to Director of Manufacturing. Managed 500 employee shoe manufacturing facility with annual operating budget of $52 million.

JORDAN LEATHER & SHOE WORKS (Lancaster, PA)   **1984 to 1988**

Plant Engineer   (1987 – 1988)
Senior Project Engineer   (1985 – 1987)
Project Engineer   (1984 – 1985)

EDUCATION

Degree: M.S., Penn State University, 1984
Major: Mechanical Engineering
          Farthner Scholarship (2 years)

Degree: B.S., Bucknell University, 1982
Major: Mechanical Engineering
          Wilson Scholar (4 years)

PROFESSIONAL AFFILIATION

American Manufacturer's Association:
-   President(2000 – Present)
-   Vice President   (1998 – 2000)
-   Membership Chairperson   (1996 – 1998)
-   Program Chairperson   (1994 – 1996)
-   Member   (1992 – 1994)

American Marketing Association   (1993 – Present)

American Society of Mechanical Engineers   (1983 – Present)

9

SAMPLE LINEAR RESUMES

Included in this chapter are a total of 20 sample linear resumes representing 10 different career disciplines. Although all are presented in a linear format, I have intentionally alternated between the narrative linear and the straight linear approach so that you can better make a comparison and choose which of these styles makes the most sense for you. Thus there are 10 samples of the straight linear resume and 10 samples of the narrative linear format for your reference.

If you are looking for sample resumes in a particular career discipline, perhaps the following Resume Locater will prove helpful.

Resume Locator

Experience Level

Field or Discipline	Senior Person	Junior Person
	(Pages)	(Pages)
Accounting	128	130
Engineering	131	133
Finance	134	136
Human Resources	137	139
Information Technology	141	143
Logistics	144	146
Marketing and Sales	148	150
Operations	151	153
Procurement	154	156
Technology	157	159

BARBARA E. HENNINGS
246 Plainview Road
Fort Wayne, IN 28375

Home: (207) 822-4726   Email: BarHen@MSN.com   Office: (315) 857-2345

OBJECTIVE

Corporate or business unit Controller with broad responsibility for supporting achievement of company's financial objectives.

SUMMARY

Accounting executive with over 14 years experience in increasingly responsible positions. Excellent reputation as creative, innovative and results-oriented senior manager who gets things done. Noted for applying computer systems in streamlining controllership operations. Full range of accounting experience includes: capital land operating budgets, financial statements, accounting policies and procedures, auditing, taxes, general and cost accounting, accounts receivable, accounts payable and credit.

PROFESSIONAL EXPERIENCE

TECHNOMATICS, INC. (Corporate Offices)   **2004 to Present**

Assistant to Corporate Controller

- Report to Corporate Vice President of Finance for this $320 million manufacturer of computer hardware.

- Manage Corporate Accounting and Bickford Division Accounting functions (32 employees) including consolidation of financial statements for SEC and shareholder reporting.

- Reengineered Corporate Accounting Department workflow design, revamping accounting procedures and practices (annual savings – $1.2 million).

- Directed computerization project to automate standard product cost build-up (annual labor savings – 500 hours).

- Organized, hired and trained Company's first Financial Planning Department.

- Initiated creative leaseback arrangement with foreign corporation on $52 million asset (annual savings – $1.6 million).

CONNER CONTAINER CORPORATION (Corporate Offices)   **2001 to 2004**

Manager of Corporate Accounting (2002 - 2004)

- Reported to Chief Financial Officer of this $150 million manufacturer of overseas shipping containers.

- Managed staff of 14 professionals with responsibility for budget preparation/monitoring ($130 million), monthly/ year-end closings, accounting system development/implementation.

- Computerized consolidation and analysis of monthly and year-end financial statement (annual savings – 800 man hours) and reduced closing turnaround time by 50%.

- Organized and managed task force, which provided the first breakout of individualized division P&L statements.

- Raised capital to support $35 million capital expansion program at highly favorable rates and minimal affect on Company credit rating.

Senior Accountant (2001 – 2002)

- Reported to Manager of Corporate Accounting.

- Responsible for consolidation, review and analysis of Company's monthly and year-end closing statements.

STUBBLESTEIN & FLANDERS, INC. (Richmond, VA)   **1991 to 2001**

Senior Accountant (1996 - 2001)

- Reported to Manager of Cost Accounting and Taxation of this public accounting firm.

- Provided cost and tax accounting consultation and services to clients in the $50 to $150 million range.

Accountant (1991 - 1996)

MAGNUM ELECTRONICS, INC. (Winslow Plant)   **1988 to 1991**

Senior Cost Accountant   (1989 - 1991)
Cost Accountant   (1988 - 1989)

EDUCATION

Degree: M.B.A., University of Alabama, 1988
Major: Accounting/Finance
         Bettinger Scholarship

Degree: B.A., Business Administration, Cannon College, 1986
Major: Accounting
         Magna Cum Laude

C.P.A.,   May 1993

DAVID R. WILSON
26 Volker Village, Apt. 105
Oceanside, CA 38495

Cell: (814) 972-4454

Email: DaWil@AOL.com

OBJECTIVE

Supervisory position in general or cost accounting field with opportunity to advance to department manager based on demonstrated results.

SUMMARY

Ambitious, motivated accounting professional with excellent record of growth and accomplishment. Thoroughly trained and ready for first supervisory assignment. Solid professional cost accounting foundation and excellent educational credentials.

PROFESSIONAL EXPERIENCE

STARGAZE ELECTRONICS, INC. (Oceanside Plant)   **2001 to Present**

Senior Cost Accountant (2002 - Present)

Report to Cost Accounting Manager with full cost accounting responsibility for the Biostar electrical harness (annual manufacturing cost of $45 million). Direct two Cost Accountants in the application of proper cost accounting practices and procedures. Research and develop new cost standards and approaches.

- Developed/implemented computerized cost tracking system for early detection of negative cost trends (annual savings - $250,000).

- Breakout of rocker assembly costs allowing better manufacturing control (annual savings - $350,000)

- Improved labor cost estimates for retrofits.

Cost Accountant (2001 - 2002)

Reported to Senior Cost Accountant. Applied established cost accounting standards and procedures in the cost accounting and analysis of sophisticated electrical harness.

- Implemented unique cost tracking system credited with $115,000 annual savings in material costs.

EDUCATION

Degree:	M.A., Business, Miami of Ohio, 2001
Major:	Accounting
	Oceanside Rotary Fellowship
Degree:	B.A., Business Administration, Ohio State University, 1999
Major:	Accounting G.P.A. 3.4/4.0
Minor:	Finance G.P.A. 3.75/4.0
	Magna Cum Laude
	Davidson Scholarship (4 years)
Activities:	President, Student Government Association
	President, Accounting Honorary Society
	Captain, Varsity Football and Varsity Track

LINDA S. PENNINGTON
824 Stone Ridge Place
Stone Mountain, GA 94837
Phone: (205) 687-2424 (H)
(302) 557-8842 (O)

OBJECTIVE

Executive level engineering management position.

SUMMARY

Accomplished engineering executive with over 16 years of experience in positions of increasing responsibility with Fortune 200 heating and air conditioning manufacturer. Consistently beat time deadlines and budget targets, resulting in bottom line savings in the millions.

PROFESSIONAL EXPERIENCE

AIR SYSTEMS CORPORATION (Corporate Engineering)   **1990 to Present**

Vice President of Engineering (2003 - Present)

- Report to President of this $3.7 billion, Fortune 200 manufacturer of residential and commercial air conditioning and heating systems.

- Direct 250 employee corporate engineering function in the engineering design, installation and start-up of major capital facility projects (annual budget – $320 million).

- Directed two year, $850 million expansion program with successful start-up of two complete plants (delivered three months early and $118 million under budget).

- Reengineered plant engineering functions with consolidation and centralization of most engineering work at Corporate Staff (80% headcount reduction, $120 million annual savings).

- Shifted focus from in-house to contract engineering services, reducing corporate headcount by 10% (annual savings – $8 million in wages and benefits).

Director, Mechanical Engineering (1998 - 2003)

- Reported to Vice President of Engineering with responsibility for direction of 160 employee mechanical project engineering function.

- Provided mechanical engineering support to all corporate capital projects (annual project budget – $250 million).

- Directed successful installation and start-up of new, high speed Ram Shear commercial heating equipment manufacturing line (project budget – $220 million).

- Engineered and installed $110 million commercial air conditioning line (on time and $1.2 million under budget).

<u>Manager, Systems Engineering</u> (1992 - 1998)

- Reported to Director of Systems Engineering.

- Managed department of 20 electrical, instrumentation and control engineers in the engineering of power distribution and computer control systems to support capital projects on corporate-wide basis (annual budget – $100 million).

- Successfully managed over 52 capital projects ($575 million) over six year period.

- Brought 65% of projects in under budget (total savings – $40 million).

<u>Senior Project Engineer, Heating</u> (1990 - 1992)

- Led project engineering teams in the design, installation and start-up of commercial heating manufacturing lines.

POWER ENGINEERING, INC. (Corporate Engineering) **1988 to 1990**

<u>Project Engineer</u>

- Designed, installed and started-up commercial heating equipment manufacturing lines.

EDUCATION

Degree:	M.S., University of Colorado, 1988
Major:	Mechanical Engineering
	Bartrum Scholarship
Degree:	B.S., Lehigh University, 1986
Major:	Electrical Engineering
	Magna Cum Laude
	Shearson Scholarship (4 years)
Activities:	President, Tau Beta Psi
	President, Delta Upsilon Fraternity
	Vice President, Greek Council

KEVIN P. BAKER
1822 Prairie Trail
Austin, Texas 58694

Home: (713) 447-9583   Email: KPB18@MSN.com   Cell: (713) 757-8495

OBJECTIVE

Senior Project Engineer in corporate engineering with responsibility for leading multi-million dollar projects involving design, installation, and start-up of new equipment and facilities.

SUMMARY

High-energy, results-oriented Senior Project Engineer with five years experience in design, installation and start-up of aluminum manufacturing processes and equipment. Excellent reputation for bringing projects in on time and at or below budget.

PROFESSIONAL EXPERIENCE

PORTER METALS COMPANY, INC. (Corporate Engineering)   **1999 to Present**

Senior Project Engineer (2003 - Present)
Report to Manager of Mechanical Engineering of this $1.3 billion manufacturer of aluminum. Responsible for design, installation, start-up and debugging of aluminum and magnesium production facilities.

* Successfully managed mechanical design of $20 million furnace complex, including coordination with electrical systems interfaces. (Project on time and 5% under budget.)

* Redesigned refractory lining in flash calciner resulting in 35% reduction in heat loss from existing units and 50% from new units.

* Now designing and installing $12 million furnace. (Project currently on time and under budget.)

Project Engineer (1999 - 2003)
Reported to Senior Project Engineer with responsibility for design, installation and start-up of aluminum manufacturing furnace complexes and material handling systems.

* Assisted in the design and start-up of $18 million furnace complex and associated material handling equipment.

EDUCATION

Degree: B.S., Texas A&M University, 1999
Major: Mechanical Engineering   G.P.A. 3.4/4.0
        Cum Laude Graduate

        Member Tau Beta Psi
        Vice President, American Society of Mechanical Engineers

CARTER W. WILSON
187 West Lake Drive
Green Bay, WI 47589

Phone: (513) 772-6464   Email: CWWin@MSN.com

OBJECTIVE

Senior Financial Officer

SUMMARY

Senior financial executive with 13 years experience with $4 billion, Fortune 100 manufacturer of earth moving and excavation equipment. Heavily experienced in all aspects of domestic and international financial planning. Demonstrated ability to meet major capital requirements at exceptionally favorable rates and returns.

PROFESSIONAL EXPERIENCE

EXCAV CORPORATION (Corporate Offices)   **1993 to Present**

Vice President and Treasurer (2003 - Present)

- Report to Executive Vice President, Finance and Planning for this $4 billion, Fortune 100 manufacturer of earth moving and excavation equipment.

- Direct staff of 48 professionals with responsibility for anticipating and providing the financial resources to fund all domestic and international operations ($400 to $600 million annually).

- Direct Domestic Finance, International Finance, Money & Banking, and Insurance and Pension Funding functions.

- Developed five-year funding strategy to finance $3.1 billion capital expansion plan with interest rates averaging 2% below market.

- Maintained top credit rating status, despite substantial increase in long-term debt load, through aggressive investor relations program with financial community.

- Reorganized and overhauled the Treasury function, recruiting top-flight personnel and substantially upgrading department image.

Director of Corporate Finance (1999 - 2003)

- Reported to Vice President and Treasurer with responsibility for anticipating, planning and executing financial strategy and plans to meet the Company's short and long-term capital need.

- Directed staff of five Analysts supporting annual financing requirements of $300 million.

- Managed development of five-year financial planning computer model, substantially improving forecasting and planning of capital requirements for international affiliates.

- Refinanced $185 million loan for Italian affiliate at considerably improved rates ($24 million savings).

- Created improved credibility and increased demand as a major financial consulting resource to international affiliates.

Senior Analyst, Corporate Finance (1996 - 1999)

- Reported to Director of Corporate Finance.

- Supported top management in five domestic divisions in the development of long-term (five-year) financial planning process.

- Trained management in use of PC-based financial planning models, increasing financial planning proficiency of top management and their respective staffs.

Analyst, Corporate Finance (1993 - 1996)
- Reported to Senior Analyst.

- Assisted in the identification, analysis and recommendation of a wide range of business opportunities and evaluation of alternate financing strategies.

EDUCATION

Degree: M.B.A., University of Chicago, 1993
Major: Finance
         Baxter Laboratories Scholar (2 years)

Degree: B.A., Western Michigan University, 1991
Major: Financial Management
Minor: Economics
         Magna Cum Laude

JANE M. KORSAN
1524 Oil Patch Drive
Houston, Texas 22375

Office: (713) 775-5757   Cell: (713) 972-3471

OBJECTIVE
Corporate Financial Management position in high-growth manufacturing company.

SUMMARY
Accomplished, high-energy Senior Financial Analyst with outstanding educational credentials and six years experience in financial planning with major aerospace contractor. Ability to manage financial planning programs from cost estimate through placement of funding for programs in the $200 to $400 million range.

PROFESSIONAL EXPERIENCE

TELLSTAR DEFENSE SYSTEMS, INC. (Corporate Offices)   **1999 to Present**

Senior Financial Analyst (2004 - Present)
Report to Manager of Corporate Financial Planning for this $2 billion federal contract supplier of missile guidance systems. Develop manufacturing cost estimates, based on prototype costs, and identify, evaluate and recommend program funding options and sources.

*   Developed funding estimates and recommendations for three major development programs in the $200 to $400 million range.
*   Recipient of three federal commendations for outstanding service in financial planning work.

Financial Analyst (2001 - 2004)
Reported to Senior Financial Analyst providing assistance in the development of funding requirements and financial strategies to support full-scale manufacture of sophisticated missile guidance systems.

*   Played lead role in developing funding requirements for manufacture of two electronic aiming devices (total requirements – $85 million).

Analyst (1999 - 2001)

*   Studied methodologies for calculating manufacturing costs of missile guidance systems.
*   Developed computer model, which reduced time required to calculate cost estimates by 80%.

REARDON SCIENCE, INC. (Corporate Offices)   **1996 to 1997**

Planning Analyst

EDUCATION

Degree:	M.B.A., University of Texas, 1998
Major:	Financial Planning
Degree:	B.S., Georgia Tech, 1996
Major:	Management Science
	Cum Laude
	Caldwell Systems Scholarship (4 years)

DAWN M. BEATTY
106 Summit Avenue
Shillington, PA 19306

Office: (610) 252-5525   Email: DawnB106@AOL.com   Cell: (610) 377-5657

OBJECTIVE

Senior level corporate Human Resources management.

SUMMARY

Well-seasoned senior level human resources executive with over 14 years experience in full range of human resource functions. Strong appreciation for the relationship between good human resource management and profitability. Creative leadership skills in organization development and employee productivity improvement.

PROFESSIONAL EXPERIENCE

LIFESTYLE MANUFACTURING COMPANY, INC. (Corporate Offices)   **1997 to Present**

Director of Human Resources (2001 - Present)

- Report to Corporate Vice President, Human Resources of this $1.5 billion manufacturer of residential and commercial furniture.

- Direct staff of 25 professionals in providing full range of Human Resource services to the 1,000 employee corporate staff.

- Oversee functional responsibility for Human Resource Planning, Internal/External Staffing, Organization Development and Wage & Salary Administration.

- Directed installation of human resources/payroll information system with estimated annual savings of $500,000 in labor costs.

- Developed human resource planning computer model for linking human resource planning and business planning.

- Staffed and directed major hiring effort requiring the recruitment of 97 engineers to support capital expansion program (all critical deadlines met).

Manager Corporate Staffing (1999 - 2001)

- Reported to Director of Human Resources with full responsibility for internal/external staffing.

- Managed staff of 12 professionals and 13 support personnel with annual staffing budget of $2.1 million (annual recruitment volume – 250 employees, 300 internal placements).

- Successfully orchestrated sensitive, high level replacement searches during major top level reorganization.

- Implemented improved recruiting techniques that reduced interview-to-offer ratio by ½ with an 80% improvement in the offer-to-hire ratio.

Manager of Administrative Staffing (1997 - 1999)

- Reported to Manager of Corporate Staffing with responsibility for all administrative staffing of corporate headquarters complex.

- Successfully hired 125 employees in two years to staff key positions in Accounting, Finance, Law, Information Services, Logistics, Procurement and Human Resources functions.

- Implemented psychological assessment as a selection tool in the hiring of top management personnel.

- Developed, implemented and trained key hiring management personnel in the use of "focused selection" interview techniques generally credited with substantial improvement and increased reliability of selection process.

HUMAN CAPITAL SOLUTIONS, INC. (Corporate Offices)   **1989 to 1997**

Senior Consultant (1993 - 1997)

- Reported to Senior Partner of this well-known, international human resources consulting firm.

- Designed, developed and installed new employee evaluation and feedback program at three major client locations.

- Generated $450,000 in new client consulting revenues in slightly over three years.

Consultant (1989 - 1993)
- Performed research work in support of development of new employee performance consulting product.

EDUCATION

Degree: M.B.A., Arizona State University, 1989
Major: Human Resource Management
Thesis: AThe Role of Performance Feedback in the Motivation of Professional
Employees≅

Degree: B.A., University of Texas, 1987
Major: Human Resource Management
Cum Laude
Salem Scholarship (4 years)

MARTIN F. SLAUGHTER
18 Palm Drive, SW
Miami, FL 37485

Home: (715) 347-3343   Email: MarSla@MSN.com   Office: (715) 764-2232

OBJECTIVE

Director of Corporate Staffing with advancement to senior level Human Resources generalist.

SUMMARY

Creative Employment Manger with over five years experience at the corporate and division level. Reputation for recruiting the hard-to-find. Thoroughly versed in all aspects of recruiting and employment with excellent track record of achieving results.

PROFESSIONAL EXPERIENCE

KOLMAR MANUFACTURING CO., INC.   1998 to Present

Corporate Manager, Operations Employment (Corp. Offices) (2003 – Present)
Report to Director of Corporate Employment of this $2.6 billion manufacturer of electrical products. Manage the staffing support for 25 plant facilities, employing 13,000 employees. Support the hiring of 300 to 500 professionals and managerial personnel annually at a cost of approximately $8 million.

- Successfully planned and managed the staffing of three new plant facilities employing 750 employees over seven-year period.

- Developed/implemented emergency staffing program to recruit 160 experienced engineers in 90 days to staff critical new capital program (all program goals met).

- Managed annual college recruiting program (37 campuses, 64 recruiting schedules) hiring an average of 220 professionals annually.

Employment Manager (Vanstar Division) (2000 - 2003)
Reported to Division Director of Human Resources for this 2,500-employee division involved in the precision chemical coating of space vehicle parts. Focused on recruitment of hard-to-find research scientists specializing in the development of exotic chemical coatings for space travel applications.

- Developed creative approaches to identifying rare scientists including patent and computer literature searches.

- Reduced scientific recruitment backlog from 160 to 25 positions in three years.

- Trained over 100 scientists and technical managers in the use of advanced interviewing techniques.

Plant Human Resources Manager)Melville Plant) (1998 - 2000)
Reported to Plant Manager with responsibility for providing full range of human resources services to this chemical manufacturing plant of 550 employees.

*   Successfully thwarted two union drives to maintain union-free manufacturing environment.

*   Researched and directed implementation of experimental high performance work system using cutting edge sociotechnical approach.

*   Installed new "Safety Alert" program, training all first line supervisors and reducing lost-time injuries by 63%.

BAXTER FASHIONS, INC. (Fort Lauderdale Plant)   **1994 to 1998**

Assistant Human Resources Manager
Reported to Plant Human Resources Manager of this 800 employee clothing manufacturing facility. Assisted manager in providing full range of human resources services to both salaries and hourly employees.

VIKING ELECTRONICS, INC.   **1990 to 1994**

Human Resources Assistant
Entry level human resources position for this 300 employee electronic equipment manufacturin plan. Handled wide range of projects and special studies in human resources field.

EDUCATION

Degree: B.A., University of Miami, 1990
Major: Business Administration

JOSE A. RODRIQUEZ
806 Vala Drive
Costa Mesa, CA 17283

Home: (949) 776-3546   Email: JRod@Tabor.com   Cell: (949) 883-9546

OBJECTIVE

IT Director or Chief Information Technology Officer

SUMMARY

Information Technology executive with 15+ years experience in all phases of IT work. Currently IT Director for $2 billion, Fortune 200 corporation. Strong reputation for ability to successfully lead development and implementation of modern information systems. Known for practicality, utility and cost-effectiveness. Am heavily client needs-focused.

PROFESSIONAL EXPERIENCE

TABOR VALVE COMPANY, INC. (Corporate Offices)   **1992 to Present**

Director of IT (2002 - Present)

- Report to Executive Vice President of Administration for this $2 billion, Fortune 200 manufacturer of pumps, valves and fittings.

- Direct 110-employee department and $8 million budget in the corporate-wide development, implementation, maintenance and control of information systems.

- Provide systems support to corporate headquarters, four operating divisions, 16 manufacturing plans in both the United States and Europe.

- Successfully directed completion of $12 million sales forecasting, production scheduling and materials control computer system. (Project completed three months ahead of schedule and $1 million under budget.)

- Reengineered and consolidated field IT operations with 25% headcount reduction and increased efficiency (annual savings – $6 million).

- Installed new matrix management system allowing a 10% reduction in Corporate IT headcount and greater flexibility in assignment of professional personnel (annual savings estimate – $3.2 million).

Corporate Project Manager (2000 - 2002)

- Reported to Director of IT, managing five to seven project managers in the design, implementation and start-up of wide range of IT projects ($20 million budget).

- Completed all projects on or before deadline (95% before deadline).

- Completed 87% of projects at or below budgeted target with total capital budget savings of 14% over two years.

- Major systems installed included Human Resources/Payroll, General Ledge Accounting System and Order Entry/Sales Forecasting System.

Manager of Client Planning Services (1996 - 2000)

- Reported to Corporate IT Manager.

- Managed staff of three professionals responsible for planning the future information management needs of functional clients.

- Developed long-range information management needs planning for five key corporate functions (Controllers, Finance, Operations, Procurement and Human Resources).

Senior Programmer Analyst (1992 - 1996)

- Provided daily direction to two programmer analysts in the development of numerous systems and programs.

M&R TECHNOLOGIES, INC. (Corporate Offices)   **1990 to 1992**

Programmer Analyst

- Developed over 50 programs to support five major systems areas.

EDUCATION

Degree: Ph.D., Stanford University, 1990
Major: Computer Science

Degree: M.S., U.C.L.A., 1988
Major: Computer Science
         Micro Systems Corporation Scholarship (2 years)

Degree: B.S., Iowa State University, 1986
Major: Mathematics
         SAS Scholarship (4 years)

LILLIAN B. REED
65 Norton Road
Norristown PA 19385
Phone: (610) 661-2239
Email: Lill65@MSN.com

OBJECTIVE

Programmer Analyst in data communications R&D for
systems engineering and development company

SUMMARY

Conscientious, hardworking Technology Programmer Analyst with three years experience providing programming support to Development Engineers in the development of state-of-the-art communications controller. Proficient in the use of data analyzer equipment for conducting studies and troubleshooting network problems.

PROFESSIONAL EXPERIENCE

TRANSCON SYSTEMS LABORATORIES, INC. (Corporate Offices)   **2003 to Present**

Programmer Analyst
Report to Technology Programming Manager with responsibility to provide technical programming support in the development of a state-of-the-art communications controller for major systems engineering firm.

- In-depth knowledge of SNA/ACP/NCP functions of a communications controller in a PEP environment.

- Proficiency with SDLC, various trace facilities, ALC and TSO/WYLBUR/SPF.

- Expert in the use of data analyzer equipment.

- Awarded recognition bonus in appreciation for high level of support to Development Engineering Department.

EDUCATION

Degree: M.S., Massachusetts Institute of Technology, 2003
Major: Computer Science
           Ransin Laboratory Fellowship (2 years)

Degree: B.S., Massachusetts Institute of Technology, 2001
Major: Systems Engineering   G.P.A. 3.85/4.0
Minor: Mathematics   G.P.A. 3.78/4.0
           Mattson Foundation Scholarship (4 years)

Activities: President, Computer Science Society
             Vice President, Mathematics Honorary

DERK K. JARVISON
605 North Ridge Drive
Falls Church, VA 14375
Phone: (814) 665-9399
Email: Derk605@AOL.com

OBJECTIVE

Senior level Logistics Management position in progressive company
valuing state-of-the-art practices and bottom-line results.

SUMMARY

Senior level logistics executive with demonstrated ability to direct and energize logistics functions, employing state-of-the-art concepts and realizing significant contributions to bottom-line results. Demonstrated leadership in applying reengineering, computer, and quantitative techniques to streamline operations and add substantial profits.

PROFESSIONAL EXPERIENCE

TAYLOR FOODS, INC. (Corporate Offices)   **2002 to Present**

Director of Logistics

- Report to Senior Vice President - Operations for this $1.4 billion, Fortune 500 food processing corporation.

- Direct the development/implementation of strategic and operating plans for corporate-wide Warehousing and Transportation functions (eight plants, 750 employees, $125 million annual budget).

- Directed development/installation of computerized order entry/distribution planning system allowing advance transportation planning (annual freight cost savings – $18 million).

- Directed purchase/installation of computer system controlled palletizer and conveyor system (annual warehouse handling cost savings - $4.7 million).

- Negotiated corporate-wide rail carrier rates resulting in annual savings of $3.9 million.

BEVERTON BOTTLING COMPANY (Corporate Offices)   **1993 to 2002**

Logistics Manager (1999 - 2002)

- Reported to Executive Vice President - Operations for this $850 million bottler of carbonated beverages.

- Reengineered field warehousing consolidating facilities into five leased regional hub facilities with annual space savings of $10.2 million and freight savings of 18%.
- Managed development/implementation of computer simulated shipping model to determine best shipping point and transportation mode (annual freight savings - $5 million).

Senior Distribution Analyst (1996 - 1999)

- Reported to Distribution Manager with responsibility for conducting several facilities planning and space utilization studies.
- Introduced use of MaxPlan™ computer simulation space planning software, cutting project planning time by 62%.

Distribution Analyst (1993 - 1996)

- Provided support to Senior Distribution Analyst and Distribution Manager in wide range of studies requiring use of quantitative and computer techniques.

EDUCATION

Degree: M.S., Virginia Institute of Technology, 1993
Major: Industrial Engineering
          Weller Scholarship (2 years)

Degree: B.S., Virginia Institute of Technology, 1991
Major: Industrial Engineering
          Lowe Company Scholarship (4 years)

CAROLINE A. JACKSON
122 Riverview Terrace
Winslow, ME 37495

Phone: (714) 377-2525   Email: CJ122@MSN.com

OBJECTIVE

Corporate level position in Logistics Management

SUMMARY

Ambitious, results-oriented, Logistics Manager with 12^+ years experience in all phases of warehousing and transportation. Well documented track record of translating technical knowledge and leadership into bottom-line results. Fully qualified and eager to run Logistics function for medium-sized company.

PROFESSIONAL EXPERIENCE

PETCO DOG FOOD, INC. (Corporate Offices)   **2002 to Present**

Manager of Warehousing
Report to Vice President of Operations for this $300 million manufacturer of pet food. Manage Corporate Warehousing function consisting of corporate warehouse and 12 field warehouse operations (eight leased, four owned). Direct activities of 150 employees (35 salaried, 115 hourly) with annual operating budget of $32 million.

- Implemented palletized railcar loading resulting in $2 million annual savings.
- Directed shipping container redesign allowing shipment of 10% more product per railcar (annual savings – $450,000).
- Successfully renegotiated warehouse leases at 2% below previous year's rent (annual savings – $320,000).

HELMET METAL MANUFACTURING CO. (Portland Plant)   **1994 to 2002**

Distribution Center Manager (2000 – 2002)
Reported to Plant Manager with full responsibility for Plant Distribution Center of this $120 million manufacturer of metal fasteners. Directed staff of 65 employees in the daily storage and shipment of finished products.

- Installed extendable powered conveyers for truck loading resulting in 10% reduction in labor costs (annual savings – $300,000).
- Initiated loading crew training program in improved loading techniques reducing product damage by 75%.
- Redesigned and implemented new storage pattern for warehouse (annual space savings – $135,000).

MARSDEN TRUCKING, INC.   **1991 to 1994**

<u>Dispatcher</u>
Accepted and placed orders for truck shipments with full responsibility for allocation and dispatch of 125 trailers per day.

EDUCATION

Degree: B.A., Colby College, 1991
Major: Business Administration

CHARLES B. PARKER
16 Wesley Road
Eugene, OR 23118

Home: (322) 887-2938   Cell: (322) 557-9899

OBJECTIVE

Executive level Sales & Marketing position.

SUMMARY

High energy, results-oriented sales and marketing executive with over 14 years of demonstrated achievement in all phases of sales and marketing operations. Known for bold, dynamic and creative leadership that consistently establishes employer as the market leader in most brands.

PROFESSIONAL EXPERIENCE

OREGON CHEMICALS, INC. (Corporate Offices)   **2004 to Present**

Director of Marketing

- Report to Vice President of Sales and Marketing for this $725 million manufacturer of chemical specialties.
- Direct 25 employee marketing function that includes Market Research, Market Planning, new Market Development, Advertising, Promotion and Field Sales departments.
- Developed dealer network that established Company as the leading marketer of solvents in the European Market and led to a 75% increase in exports ($225 million) in two years.
- Co-developed (with R&D) new low-viscosity resin product, which allowed national roll out in less than 18 months ($150 million new sales in first year).

HOUTON CHEMICALS, INC. (Corporate Offices)   **1996 to 2004**

Director of Marketing and Sales (2000 - 2004)

- Reported to President of this $525 million specialty chemical manufacturer with functional responsibility for market research and planning, brand management, advertising and sales.
- Directed 125-employee sales force with responsibility for all domestic and international sales volume.

- Successfully introduced eight new products, in less than four years, increasing total sales by 40% ($210 million).
- Expanded sales force, hiring and training over 60 new sales representatives.

Marketing Brand Manager (1998 - 2000)

- Reported to Director of Marketing and Sales with brand marketing responsibility for *Canoir*.
- Modified brand package and repositioned *Canoir* as low-priced, mid-quality product (through creative advertising) resulting in 225% increase in sales volume in two years. (Improved product ranking from number five to number one in market.)

Associate Brand Manager (1996 - 1998)

- Coordinated all market research and test marketing of Company's *Tetron* brand.

CARDONELL CHEMICALS CORPORATION (District Sales Office)   **1991 to 1996**

Senior Sales Representative   (1995 - 1996)
Sales Representative   (1991 - 1995)

EDUCATION

Degree:	M.B.A., University of Washington, 1991
Major:	Marketing
Degree:	B.S., Oregon State University, 1989
Major:	Chemistry
Activities:	President, American Chemical Society Chapter
	Vice President, Delta Delta Fraternity
	Captain, Varsity Rowing

THOMAS R. SPEARS
210 Warfield Way
Huron, OH 14263

Cell: (713) 559-0085   Email: TomSP21@MSN.com   Home: (203) 652-9417

OBJECTIVE

Sales management position with growth-oriented equipment manufacturer.

SUMMARY

Creative sales professional with over six years experience selling complex business systems. High producer who has consistently demonstrated ability to successfully introduce new business machine lines into intensely competitive business and institutional markets.

PROFESSIONAL EXPERIENCE

HI-REZ GRAPHICS, INC. (Cleveland Regional Office)   **1998 to Present**

District Sales Manager (2003 - Present)
Report to National Sales Manager for this $800 million manufacturer of microfilm storage, retrieval and duplicating systems. Manage five-person sales force with territorial responsibility for Michigan, Ohio and Indiana (annual sales of $90 million).

- Successfully introduced world's first updatable microfilm record keeping system into Midwest Region ($30 million in first year sales).

- Developed/implemented creative sales strategy that increased regional sales over 300% in last two years. (Sales volume now approaching $100 million.)

Senior Sales Representative (2000 - 2003)
Reported to District Sales Manager with responsibility for working closely with business venture team to introduce new microfilm record keeping system to Midwest market. Focused on developing banking industry applications.

- Sold, installed and started-up first banking system application in United States.

- Proved viability of banking industry applications, paving way to $300 million market in just over three years.

Sales Representative (1998 – 2000)
Successfully sold wide range of microfilms and other specialty films through network dealer network.

EDUCATION

Degree: B.A., University of Michigan, 1998
Major: Marketing

President, Student Government
President, Delta Upsilon Fraternity

JENNIFER T. LOGAN
1616 Ryan Circle
Marietta, GA 18274

Office: (616) 935-0978   Email: Logan1616@MSN.com   Home: (616) 554-2374

OBJECTIVE

Senior level Operations Management position having functional responsibility for Manufacturing, Engineering, Procurement and Distribution in medium-sized manufacturing company.

SUMMARY

Highly motivated Operations executive with M.S. in Metallurgical Engineering and 17+ years experience in the copper tubing industry. Strong record of engineering and manufacturing contributions. Noted for being a strong leader with solid commitment to motivating and developing subordinates.

PROFESSIONAL EXPERIENCE

STRATFORD TUBE, INC.   **1996 to Present**

Vice President – Operations (Corporate Offices) (2001 – Present)
Report to President of this leading $5 00 million manufacturer of copper tubing. Full P&L responsibility for two copper refineries and three tube manufacturing plants (5,300 employees, $ 300 million budget).

- Directed multidiscipline cost reduction taskforce which achieved 20% manufacturing cost reduction in 3 years ($60 million annual savings).

- Implemented computerized materials management control system cutting raw material inventories by 30% ($15 million annual savings).

Plant Manager (Albany Plant) (1996 – 2001)
Reported to Vice President of Manufacturing with P&L responsibility fir this 1,800-employee copper refinery and tube manufacturing facility ($120 million annual production). Functional responsibility for Manufacturing, Material Management, Engineering, Maintenance, Distribution, Human Resources and Accounting.

- Successfully directed two-year, $125 million plant expansion, doubling manufacturing capacity.

- Completed expansion 3 months early and 10% below budget.

- Transferred 75% of plant workforce to new positions with no loss in productivity.

- Set plant production and safety records for 4 out of 5 years.

WOLFORD TUBE COMPANY, INC.   **1986 to 1996**

Manager of Engineering (Corporate Offices) (1991 – 1996)
Managed 150-employee central engineering function for this $300 million manufacturer of refrigeration and specialty tubing. Directed all capital expansion programs to include design, installation, and startup of copper tube manufacturing facilities and refineries.

- Successfully engineered $250 million capital program (largest in company history) including design, installation and startup of state-of-the-art integrated refinery and tube mill.

- Delivered above project 4 months ahead of schedule and on budget.

Department Manager – Drawing Operations (Bradford Plant) (1989 – 1991)
Managed 100-employee tube drawing operation with annual production valued at $85 million.

- Increased production efficiency by 18%, with 15% reduction in manufacturing costs in two-year period.

Project Engineer (1986 – 1989)
Responsible for design, installation and startup of major capital projects in furnace and drawing operations. Independently engineered projects in the $40 to $50 million range.

EDUCATION

Degree:	M.S., Georgia Institute of Technology, 1986
Major:	Metallurgical Engineering
Degree:	B.S., Virginia Institute of Technology, 1984
Major:	Mechanical Engineering
Honors:	Tau Beta Psi

GEORGE T. BENNER
221 Washington Terrace
Plainfield, NJ 13448

Phone: (315) 772-6767   Email: GeoB22@AOL.com

OBJECTIVE

Manufacturing management position offering advancement opportunity
based on demonstrated performance and contribution to the business.

SUMMARY

Results-oriented, manufacturing manager with six years experience in wax and silicone manufacturing. Excellent record of achievement and advancement earned through demonstrated contribution to bottom-line results.

PROFESSIONAL EXPERIENCE

WEXLER MANUFACTURING COMPANY (Linwood Plant)   **2000 to Present**

Assistant Plant Manager (2003 - Present)
Report to Plant Manager of this 1,000-employee manufacturer of silicone-based waxes and polishes ($325 million annual sales). Manage the Can Finishing and Warehousing Departments (210 employees, $130 million budget).

- Introduced automated palletizers and palletized railcar loading system, cutting warehouse operating costs by 25% (annual savings $15 million).

- Installed absenteeism control program with resultant 60% reduction in days lost.

- Initiated new "open door" policy that reduced union grievances from 185 to 62 in two years.

Department Manager, Formulations (2000 - 2003)
Reported to Manufacturing Manager with accountability management of plant formulations and mixing operations. Directed department of 50 employees (five salaried, 45 hourly) with annual operating budget of $75 million.

- Implemented SPC-based "total quality" effort that identified key process variables and reduced batch rejections by 90% (annual savings – $2.1 million).

- Installed JIT materials control program that reduced on-hand raw materials inventories by 27% (annual savings – $1.3 million).

CORDOVA WAX COMPANY (Radley Plant)   **1998 to 2000**

Supervisor, Formulations

EDUCATION

Degree: B.S., Boston University, 1998
Major: Industrial Technology
         Cum Laude

TODD E. THOMAS
3229 Colonial Place
Hartford, CT 13847

Home: (213) 334-7495   Cell: (213) 457-9682

OBJECTIVE

Executive level, corporate procurement position with consumer-products company.

SUMMARY

Highly skilled negotiator with 13-year record of substantial contribution to bottom-line results. Client-focused, responsive, energetic. A motivational leader, mentor and coach, who commands the respect and commitment of subordinates. Excellent communication skills.

PROFESSIONAL EXPERIENCE

HARTFORD FOODS, INC. (Corporate Offices)   **2003 to Present**

Director of Procurement

- Report to Vice President of Operations Services for this $1.2 billion manufacturer of consumer food products.

- Direct staff of 15 professionals in the purchase of raw materials, vital supplies and services for corporate staff and eight manufacturing sites (annual budget – $580 million).

- Develop, implement and control all procurement policies and strategies including centralized buying programs on consolidated purchases of large volume/big ticket items.

- Implemented modern inventory tracking computer system allowing substantially reduced inventories ($22 million annual savings).

- Consolidated and centralized large volume, raw material purchases, with blanket order releases, permitting sizable vendor price concessions (annual savings – $15 million).

- Convinced company to convert from prime fuel to bio-mass boilers for energy generation, allowing sale of excess capacity to power company (annual savings – $12 million).

LARSON BAKING COMPANY, INC. (Corporate Offices)   **1995 to 2003**

Manager of Corporate Procurement (1997 - 2003)

- Reported to Vice President of Administration for this $850 commercial baking company.

- Managed staff of eight with full centralized purchasing responsibility for five plants (annual purchase volume – $325 million)

- Reengineered and centralized procurement function with net headcount reduction of 25% (annual savings – $1 million).
- Consolidated and centralized corporate-wide purchase of hundreds of items with first year's savings of $8 million.

Senior Buyer - Vital Supplies (1995 - 1997)

- Reported to Corporate Procurement Manager.
- Directed activities of two buyers and three support staff in the annual purchase of $200 million of vital supplies.
- Installed computer-based vital supplies/packaging forecast system permitting JIT delivery approach and substantial reduction of standing inventories (annual savings – $6 million).

BORDER FOODS, INC. (Corporate Offices)   **1989 to 1995**

Manager of Procurement (1992 - 1995)

- Managed corporate procurement function for this $150 million manufacturer of pretzels and potato chips ($50 million budget, three employees).

Buyer (1989 - 1992)

- Reported to Manager of Purchasing, providing support in the purchase of raw materials and vita supplies inventories.

EDUCATION

Degree: B.A., Syracuse University, 1989
Major: Business Administration

President of Business Club
Captain, Varsity Baseball

GORDON B. DAVIS
17 Harbor View Place, Apt. 12-A
Green Bay, WI 23568

Phone: (515) 844-8847

Email: GorDa@AOL.com

OBJECTIVE

Procurement management position offering good
growth opportunities for results-oriented achievers.

SUMMARY

Results-driven procurement professional with over five years experience in the purchase of vital supplies. Excellent track record of contribution to bottom-line through development and implementation of numerous creative cost-saving initiatives.

PROFESSIONAL EXPERIENCE

GREEN BAY PAPER COMPANY, INC. (Corporate Offices)   **2003 to Present**

Senior Purchasing Agent - Vital Supplies
Report to Manager of Procurement for this $350 million manufacturer of printing and publishing papers. Responsible for purchase of all vital supplies to support manufacturing operations – knock down cartons, poly wraps, shrink wraps, etc. ($18 million annually).

- Negotiated two-year contract for knock down carton purchase agreement with new supply source at 20% savings ($1.3 million).

- Studied historical sales forecast vs. actual purchase volume data, formulating mathematical correlation and developing computer simulation model that allows accurate purchase forecasts of within 1% of actual. (Annual savings $500,000.)

FORT SMITH PAPER COMPANY (Corporate Offices)   2000 **to 2003**

Vital Supplies Buyer
Reported to Manager of Procurement for this $110 million converter of consumer paper products. Responsible for $4 million annual purchases of vital supplies to support two manufacturing sites.

- Negotiated new poly wrap contract with 10% off previous pricing (annual cost savings of $200,000).

- Installed off-the-shelf inventory control computer software package allowing 20% reduction in vital supplies inventories (annual savings of $750,000).

EDUCATION

Degree: B.S., University of Wisconsin, 2000
Major: Pulp & Paper Technology   G.P.A. 3.8/4.0

SARAH B. THOMLINSON
55 Orchard Hill Road
Appleton, WI 23847

Office: (409) 357-2999   Email: SBT55@WPT.com   Home: (409) 357-5673

OBJECTIVE

Senior level R&D management position with responsibility
for achievement of company's technology objectives.

SUMMARY

Senior executive with 25 years of dynamic, innovative Technology leadership in Fortune 500 companies. Proven ability to deliver innovative technology that strengthens competitive market position and is the lifeline for profitable new business development. Blend of strong technical and interpersonal skills forms the basis for good management leadership and solid team participation.

PROFESSIONAL EXPERIENCE

WISCONSIN TISSUE & PACKAGING, INC. (Corporate Research Center)   **2002 to Present**

Vice President of Technology

- Report to President with responsibility for managing 500 employee corporate research center for this Fortune 100 paper and packaging manufacturer ($4.2 billion annual sales).

- Direct all basic research, product research and process development activities in support of company's strategic objectives (annual budget – $32 million).

- Directed development of innovative magnetic fiber forming device providing Company with distinct competitive advantage in the marketing of improved sanitary tissue product (200% improvement in market share).

- Introduced 22 new and/or improved products that have added over $1 billion in new business in four years.

- Developed proprietary new product expected to add $2 billion of new business over next five years (successful national rollout now underway).

KIMBERLY NONWOVEN FIBERS, INC. (Packaging & Materials Laboratory)   **1993 to 2002**

Research Director, Packaging & Materials

- Reported to Vice President of Research for this $2.9 billion manufacturer of synthetic fiber and film materials.

- Directed 135 professionals and technicians in the research and development of all packaging, non-woven, plastic packaging and photo-imaging film materials (annual budget – $12 million).

- Developed new wet lay non-woven manufacturing process expected to create high demand for Kimberly's Syntex fibers (annual sales potential – $80 million in two years).

- Developed new high technology frozen food packaging material that prolongs thaw time by 300%, reducing food processing spoilage by 30% (substantial competitive advantage).

- Directed development of TEP electronic scanning photo-imaging technology that allows pictures to be taken with electronic cameras providing clear resolution superiority over conventional photographic film.

JAMES RIVER CORPORATION (Corporate Research)   **1984 to 1993**

Research Manager, Synthetic Fibers (1988 - 1993)

- Reported to Research Director with responsibility to manage 38 professionals in the development and application of novel synthetic fibers to packaging and consumer paper webs.

Senior Research Scientist, Polymer Research (1984 - 1988)

- Pioneered and accelerated the development of proprietary polymer materials through experimental and theoretical studies using experimental design and computer modeling and simulations.

VULCAN SPACE LABORATORY   **1982 to 1984**

Research Specialist

- Developed exotic coated materials for Vulcan communications satellite heat shield. Performed re-entry simulation testing and designed predictive models using computer techniques.

EDUCATION

Degree:	Ph.D., University of Michigan, 1982
Major:	Chemical Engineering
	Vulcan Laboratory Fellowship

Degree:	M.S., Rochester Institute of Technology, 1980
Major:	Materials Engineering

Degree:	B.S., Rochester Institute of Technology, 1978
Major:	Chemical Engineering
	Cum Laude
	Barlow Scholarship (4 years)

PATENTS AND PUBLICATIONS

22 U.S. Patents (four pending)
45 professional publications and papers

DAVID A. FREEMAN
22 Indigo Sky Way
Split Arrow, OK 23748

Phone: (917) 472-3927   Email: DaFree22@MSN.com

OBJECTIVE

Research and Development position requiring creativity and innovation
in the development of novel poly-based products and processes.

SUMMARY

Highly innovative Ph.D. polymer engineer with demonstrated track record in achieving excellent product and process development results. Holder of ten U.S. patents and inventor of revolutionary, new polymeric material allowing successful entry into several new markets.

PROFESSIONAL EXPERIENCE

WILSON POLYMER SPECIALTIES, INC. (Corporate Technology)   **2002 to Present**

Senior Research Engineer, Polymers (2002 - Present)
Report to Manager of Polymer Research for this $1.2 billion chemical manufacturer. Provide technical leadership to research team in the development of novel polymer-based materials for use in boat hulls.

- Developed Sampson TM, a revolutionary new polymeric material having twice the strength of fiberglass at half the cost (projected annual sales of $1 billion).

- Awarded three key patents and generally recognized as the principal contributor to the above product development effort.

- Recipient of Norwood "Inventor of the Year" award.

Research Engineer, Polymers (2000 - 2002)
Professional accountability similar to that described above for Senior Research Engineer. Emphasis more on process rather than product development.

- Developed process for efficient manufacture of new synthetic fabric having unique finishing characteristics.

- Successfully transferred new technology from bench to full-scale production in record time.

- Awarded four patents and received special recognition bonus award for "exceptional contributions" to the commercialization effort.

GRAVERLY CHEMICAL COMPANY (Central Research)   **1997 to 2000**

<u>Polymer Chemist</u>
Developed high temperature resistant molding polymers and inherent fire retardant plastics.

EDUCATION

Degree: Ph.D., Massachusetts Institute of Technology, 1997
Major: Polymer Engineering

Degree: M.S., Rochester Institute of Technology, 1995
Major: Chemical Engineering

Degree: B.S., Rochester Institute of Technology, 1993
Major: Chemical Engineering

PATENTS

Awarded 10 U.S. patents since 1997.

AFFILIATIONS

American Society of Polymer Scientists
American Society of Chemical Engineers
National Institute for Polymer Research

10

THE FUNCTIONAL RESUME

No book on the subject of resume writing would be complete without a chapter on the functional resume. Although, as a seasoned employment professional, I must admit to not being a strong advocate of this style of resume, I will quickly add, however, that it does occasionally have its place in the employment process. As an indication of this fact, I would estimate that approximately 2 to 3 percent of all resumes received by corporations make use of the functional format. This makes the functional format the second most popular resume style (second only to the chronological format which is estimated to account for 97 to 98 percent of all resumes). The chronological resume format, as you will recall from our discussion in Chapter 8 also includes the now highly popular narrative resume, which has grown enormously in its usage.

ADVANTAGES OF FUNCTIONAL RESUME

Advocates of the functional resume are quick to point out that it makes use of an excellent marketing strategy. This resume format is designed to capture the interest of the resume reader right from the beginning. This is accomplished by positioning the candidates's most salable strengths at the beginning of the resume in the form of some brief statements that capsulize the candidate's major accomplishments and most salable professional experience.

The marketing premise upon which this resume design is based is that most employment professionals are not thorough in their reading of employment resumes. Further, advocates of this style of resume would tell you that many employment professionals in fact read only the first paragraph or two of a resume. If these initial paragraphs do not capture their interest, the reader simply discards the resume and moves on to the next.

Although there may be some employment professionals who are not particularly thorough and conscientious in their resume reading, my experience suggests that this is certainly not the case with most. In my opinion, the majority of employment professionals discover early in their professional career that thorough resume reading is a must. In having read thousands of resumes as an employment manager, I have found that the specific experience and/or skills sought by my employer were sometimes not described until the second or third page of the applicant's resume. This experience has conditioned me to read resumes with a fair degree of thoroughness. Most professional employment managers are likewise sufficiently concerned with finding well-qualified employees for their organizations that they are equally thorough in their resume-reading approach.

This is not to say that there are not those who are less diligent in their reading. To the contrary, I am sure there are some who are much less thorough. Such individuals may be superficially impressed with these opening paragraphs and may elect to invite the candidate in for an employment interview with a less than a complete screening of the candidate's qualifications. In the better companies, however, this superficial approach to resume screening will quickly attract attention and the employment professional will soon be exposed as a nonprofessional. Poor resume screening will assuredly result in unnecessary interviews, wasting the valuable time of line managers and costing the company unnecessary money in the form of candidate travel reimbursement. Such inefficiencies will not long be tolerated, and careless employment managers may well find themselves in the unemployment line.

Of course there are well-qualified candidates who without professional guidance sometimes elect to use the functional employment resume. It is up to the employment manager, therefore, to thoroughly read the *entire* resume to determine whether or not the candidate possesses the prerequisite skills and qualifications sought by his or her company.

SOME CAUTIONS

Perhaps the biggest drawback of the functional resume is that it seems to be the format most frequently chosen by individuals who wish to disguise some flaw in their credentials. In fact, as an employment professional who has read several thousand resumes, I would estimate that in seven out of every ten cases functional resumes have intentionally been chosen by the employment candidate to camouflage such problems. Awareness of this history of deception causes most employment professionals to become suspicious when this particular format is used. The tendency is thus to read these resumes as if one were on a witch hunt. Energy and focus are directed toward finding out what is wrong with the candidate instead of being directed toward whether the candidate possesses the desired qualifications.

I have discussed my feelings concerning the functional resume with several other personnel executives and have frequently found that their feelings are generally similar to my own. In general, the consensus appears to be that if an employment candidate uses the functional resume format, he or she is probably attempting to hide one or more of the following issues:

1. *Job Hopper.* The applicant has worked for an abnormally high number of employers in a relatively short period of time and would therefore be a high employment risk.

2. *Older Worker.* The applicant is older and is attempting to hide this fact.

3. *Employment Gap.* There is an undesirable or unexplained gap or break in the candidate's employment history. Since this gap is frequently unexplained, it leads the employment executive to conjure up all kinds of undesirable explanations (for example: major illness, marital problems, alcoholism). Most of these spell high risk in the minds of the employment professional.

4. *Educational Deficit.* The applicant lacks the requisite educational credentials normally required for the position for which he or she is applying.

5. *Minimal Experience.* The candidate has little if any meaningful experience related to his or her job objective.

CHOOSING WHICH RESUME FORMAT TO USE

The rule of thumb for choosing between the chronological (both classical and linear) and the functional resume is fairly simple. If you have good credentials and a solid work history, I strongly recommend that you use a form of the chronological resume. Why cast unnecessary doubt on otherwise excellent credentials?

The reciprocal of the above statement is also true. If you have some good experience and major credentials, but also have one or more of the aforementioned problems, you may well want to seriously consider use of the functional resume format.

Resume Format Test

If you are still in doubt, perhaps the following practical test may be of assistance to you in deciding whether to use the functional resume format.

Answer each of the following questions with a yes or no:

1. Have you worked for four or more employers in the last 10 years? Yes _____ No_____

2. If employed for more than 10 years, have you averaged less than three years of service per employer? Yes_____ No_____

3. Have you been employed with more than seven companies during your professional career? Yes_____ No_____

4. Are you age 50 or older? Yes_____ No_____

5. Have you been unemployed (or substantially underemployed) for a period of more than one year in the last 10 years? Yes_____ No_____

6. Have you been unemployed (three months or longer) more than once in the last five years? Yes_____ No_____

7. Do you have the necessary educational qualifications normally required by most employers for your occupation? Yes_____ No_____

8. Do you lack the experience normally required by most employers for your profession? Yes_____ No_____

If you answered yes to one or more of the first three questions, by most standards you would be considered a job hopper. Use of the chronological resume would highlight this problem early in the resume and, in many cases, would result in your being screened out. Use of the functional resume under these circumstances is to your distinct advantage.

Although illegal, the screening out of candidates because of age continues. Some inroads have been made in this area and it appears that most employers are now paying less attention to age than they are to the qualifications of the individual. Unfortunately, however, age 50 appears to be a bench mark of sorts for many employers. Rightly or wrongly, many employers assume that a candidate who is age 50 or older lacks the necessary energy and vitality to be a productive worker. This fact suggests that candidates who are in this age group should attempt, where possible, to conceal this fact. The functional resume format can be particularly effective in accomplishing this objective.

Questions 5 and 6 have to do with gaps in the employment history. Should you have such a gap or should you have been substantially underemployed for a period of time, you may wish to employ the functional resume to focus on your strengths and accomplishments and to draw attention away from this employment gap.

If you answered no to question 7, chances are that use of the chronological resume may cause you to be screened out on the basis of educational credentials. The functional resume, on the other hand, gives you the opportunity to highlight your strengths and accomplishments early in the resume and may generate interest sufficient to cause the prospective employer to disregard your educational deficiency.

If question 8 was answered yes, you will probably do better in adopting the functional resume. Here again the reader's attention will be focused on what you consider your strengths and accomplishments rather than on your lack of specific job experience.

Having satisfied yourself that you are a candidate for use of the functional resume, you should continue on with the rest of this chapter. If as a result of the above test, however, you have concluded that you are not a candidate for this type resume, I would suggest that you use either the classical chronological or narrative chronological resume formats described in Chapters 6 and 8.

FUNCTIONAL RESUME COMPONENTS

Although there are several different styles or versions of the functional resume, the most frequently used format is comprised of the following components:

1. Heading.
2. Qualification summary.
3. Major accomplishments.
4. Work history.
5. Education.

The order in which these components are presented on the resume can vary, but the sequence represented above is the most commonly used, accepted, and recommended format. The most frequent deviation from this recommended sequence, however, is the positioning of the education and work experience components. Note that the sample resume at the end of this chapter has been positioned such that education follows work experience, while other resumes in the chapter containing sample functional resumes (Chapter 11) have education positioned before work history.

The general rule for deciding whether to position education before or after work experience on the functional resume is this: Always position education after work history unless it will clearly serve to enhance your marketability to do otherwise.

In cases where the candidate has exceptionally strong educational credentials and this would be clearly recognized as the case by prospective employers, it would be in the candidate's best interest to position education prior to work history on the resume. Conversely, a candidate whose work history is extensive but whose educational credentials would be considered somewhat light by most employers' standards should definitely position education following the presentation of work history.

Additionally, it is recommended that younger candidates with good educational credentials and little work experience list education first. By contrast, older workers with considerable experience and persons who do not have strong educational credentials are generally best served by placing education after work experience.

For the older worker, placing education first in the resume can often draw attention to his or her age—something that should be avoided. This makes it easy for those employers who are in defiance of federal law, still practicing age discrimination, to weed you out. If you are successful in getting such employers to review your work experience and major accomplishments first, and thereby convince them that you have something of value to contribute to their organization, perhaps less attention will be paid to your age.

You are now ready to begin the step-by-step process of preparing the functional resume. The approach that we follow examines each resume component in some detail and provides some practical exercises that will assist you in developing each of these components. This is the same "kit" approach that was used earlier in this book in the preparation of the chronological resume. As with any kit, if you follow the step-by-step directions provided, you will conclude this chapter having prepared a logical, professional resume that will effectively portray and market your qualifications to prospective employers.

Heading

The resume heading consists of four parts: your full name, complete address, home telephone number, and e-mail address. Some sample resume headings follow:

DAVID C. JOHNSON
18 Smith Road
Richmond, Ohio 19870
Phone: (815) 852-4310
Email: DaJo@AOL.com

CAROLYN A. CRISWELL
401 East 7th Street
Knoxville, Tennessee 19760
Home: (315) 769-6588   Cell: (315) 766-4233

Your name should be typed in capital letters and in bold type so that it stands out from the rest of the heading. Your address and telephone number, on the other hand, are typed in lower case. It is advisable to exclude your office telephone number from your resume unless you are in a position to accept employment-related telephone calls at your office. Should you be on a confidential voice mail system where you are the only one who can access your messages, this is likely not a problem. Listing your office telephone number on your resume, however, sometimes raises suspicion on the part of a prospective employer that you are "on the skids" with your current employer and that your current employer is cooperating with you in your job search. It is therefore advisable to avoid listing your office telephone number on your employment resume unless by excluding it you would be making it difficult for prospective employers to reach you.

Most employment managers do not mind placing telephone calls in the evening to prospective candidates. These managers can be encouraged to do so by inclusion of a simple request to call you at home in the evenings. Such a request can easily be inserted into your cover letter. For example, you might include a statement similar to the following in the cover letter that accompanies your resume.

> *I can usually be reached at my home telephone number during the evening hours after 8:00 P.M. In the event that you find this inconvenient and wish to contact me during business hours, my husband, George, will be pleased to relay your message. George can be reached at (315) 972-8051.*

Of course, inclusion of an e-mail address in your resume heading can greatly expedite communications and eliminate the game of "phone tag" that can ensue when both parties have busy schedules and are difficult to reach.

Using the instructions provided above, try your hand at developing your own heading.

Summary

The purpose of the Summary section of the functional resume is twofold. First, it is intended to convey the breadth and scope of your experience as a professional. Second, it is intended to provide you with the opportunity to sell your key strengths. The overall intent is to hook the resume reader so that he or she will be encouraged to read further.

Let's now examine a few summary statements.

1. *Summary.* Marketing executive with over 20 years of experience in sales and marketing management. Excellent reputation as a creative, innovative manager capable of revitalizing old product lines and introducing new ones. Full range of marketing and sales experience to include: market research, market planning and analysis, advertising and promotion, sales, and sales management.

2. *Summary.* Accomplished human resources professional with over 25 years experience in all phases of human resources management. Excellent reputation as an individual who truly understands the

relationship between human resource utilization and profitability. Full range of human resources experience includes: human resource planning, internal and external staffing, organization design and development, compensation and benefits, employee and labor relations, and public affairs.

3. *Summary.* Creative design engineer with 15 years experience in innovative design of high speed electro-mechanical devices. Well known for innovative, practical, and cost-effective designs that work. A real contributor to bottom-line results.

In reviewing these summary statements, you will note certain similarities. First, the initial sentence of each summary statement gives the writer's career/professional area and indicates the number of years of experience. The second sentence is used to market particular strengths possessed by the writer. The third sentence, as in the case of the marketing executive and human resources professional, can be used to further communicate the breadth of the writer's experience. As an option to this, as shown in the designer's summary statement, the resume writer can use this third sentence to further market some unique skill or fact that would likely prove valuable to the prospective employer.

Another similarity between these summary statements is that they are fairly concise. In preparing your summary statement, you should avoid lengthy, rambling paragraphs that will only serve to dilute your message to the prospective employer. The key to this section is to be concise while stating sufficient positive information to entice the reader to continue. Additionally, your summary statement should convince the prospective employer that you have something of value to contribute to their organization.

Note that these sample summary statements are not written in complete sentences. These statements are simply descriptive phrases that are intended to convey strong meaning in as few words as possible. They are short "bullets" much the same as you would find in magazine or newspaper advertising. As with such advertising copy, each is intended to convey value and to compel the reader to respond favorably.

Review of the sample summary statements will also reveal the lack of the articles "a" and "the." Each sentence begins with an adjective followed by a noun. Following this type of format will force you to write concise, brisk statements that have considerably more marketing impact than the normal sentence.

Now try your hand at writing your own sample summary statements. Try writing this statement three times with the idea of bringing about quantum improvement with each successive writing.

Major Accomplishments

The Major Accomplishments section is intended to point out specific accomplishments that you have realized during your professional career and to highlight these accomplishments in discrete, functional areas. The functional areas under which these accomplishments are highlighted are normally major subfunctions or subactivities of your profession. Some examples of these functional areas would be as follows:

Marketing Executive

1. Market research.
2. Advertising and promotion.
3. Marketing and sales management.

Human Resources Executive

1. Human resource management.
2. Labor negotiations.
3. Employment.
4. Compensation and benefits.

Research Engineer

1. Conceptual design.
2. Prototype development.
3. Prototype testing.

4. Redesign.

5. Reduction to practice.

In preparation for this section of your resume, make a detailed listing of all of the subfunctions relating to your career specialty. Think in terms of the major components of your present and past positions—the key functional areas for which you were accountable in each of your past positions. Having done this, you are now ready to develop a listing of your major accomplishments for each of the corresponding functional areas that you have listed.

A good exercise for stimulating your memory is to list each of your past employers in reverse chronological order, including each of the respective positions you have held. Starting with the most recent employer, make a list of the most significant results that you have realized—the most significant contributions you have made to each employer. As you list each of these major accomplishments, be sure to include, wherever possible, some kind of quantitative measurement that will serve to convey to the reader the significance of this result to your past employer. Think in terms of the savings in time and money that your accomplishments provided. Additionally, think in terms of other ways you have positively affected the profitability of your employer. In this regard, actions that you have taken to increase employee productivity, sales volume, and so on should certainly be included in the category of major accomplishments.

Although the procedure described may seem laborious, it will prove to be extremely worthwhile to you as you begin the job-hunting process. In addition to providing you with an excellent basis for the construction of your functional resume, this personal analysis of major accomplishments will provide you with the information and confidence necessary to perform well during the interview phase of your employment campaign. Take time therefore to carefully develop this inventory of major accomplishments.

After you have listed your major accomplishments by functional area, you are ready to begin to rework these for inclusion in the final draft of your functional resume. Before doing this, however, review the major accomplishments section of the sample resume contained at the end of this chapter. You will note that this area of the resume is comprised of only three functional areas: market research, advertising and promotion, and marketing and sales management. It is important that your resume contain no more than three or four functional areas which you plan to highlight. Listing more than four areas will serve to dilute the impact that is intended when using the functional resume. This intent is to highlight and market your major areas of strength. Listing more than four functional areas with accompanying major accomplishments may serve to give the resume reader the impression that you are a jack of all trades but master of none. The reader will begin to question the credibility of your accomplishments rather than being impressed with a carefully chosen few.

A careful review of your list of past employers and positions held will highlight your major accomplishments and contributions. Scanning these accomplishments will show that several are similar in nature and can fit nicely under the key functions that you have chosen to feature on the resume. Picking what appear to be the most prominent three or four subfunctions, put each of these subfunctions as a heading on a separate piece of paper. Then systematically go back over your employment history, extract each major accomplishment and add it to the page containing the functional heading under which it fits. In following this procedure you will soon see the major accomplishments section of your functional resume taking shape.

Your next step is to decide in what order these key functions should be listed in the major accomplishments section of your resume. There are two schools of thought relative to the order in which these functions should be listed. The first school of thought focuses on the old adage "lead from strength." This adage suggests that you should list that function in which you have made the greatest contributions and have realized the most significant accomplishments. This approach reasons that your most marketable or salient qualifications should be listed first since they are your areas of greatest strength and therefore are those areas that will be of greatest value to any prospective employer. The second school would argue that you should position that function first that most closely parallels your job-hunting objective. For example, if you are a human resources professional and are seeking a position as director of labor relations, you would obviously wish to cite your accomplishments in the area of labor relations first. Prospective employers looking for a director of labor relations are probably less concerned about your expertise in the area of compensation and benefits.

Both of the above schools of thought have their point. This may leave you a bit confused as to which function to list first. As a general rule of thumb, I would suggest listing first that function that most closely relates to your current career objective. However, should your accomplishments in this area be less than stellar, I would suggest listing your area of strongest accomplishment first without respect to job-hunting objective. The remaining functional areas should be listed in a priority sequence based upon the significance of the accomplishments in each of these respective functions.

In this section of your resume, writing style can be extremely important if you wish to have maximum impact on the reader. I have extracted two functions from the major accomplishments section of the resume contained at the end of this chapter for your review. The first is market research:

—Investigated and analyzed European market for U.S. lumber export with resultant successful market entry.

—Worked closely with R&D in development of consumer mini pocket calculator. Careful design of test market and resultant market feedback assured successful product development and subsequent market entry ($5 million sales in 2 years).

—Developed market research computer model to forecast 10-year market projection for microwave ovens.

The second function is advertising and promotion:

—Coordinated company efforts with major New York City consumer advertising agency to develop effective campaign to revitalize failing product line (fishing reels). Campaign expenditure ($2 million) yielded annual increase in sales of $4.1 million in 1 year.

—Developed creative special value coupon and supporting advertising campaign that increased annual sales
volume for photographic film product line by 35% over
2-year period.

In reviewing these accomplishments you will note that each
statement begins with a verb or action word. By starting
most of your statements with a verb or action word, you will
be forced to be brief, concise, and to the point in your statements. Additionally, you will be forced to state specific results and accomplishments that you contributed.

To assist you in getting started with this effective resume-writing technique, a list of key verbs or action words
has been provided at the end of this chapter. You are encouraged to refer to this list and to make use of these verbs
while developing this section of your functional employment resume.

Another effective technique to employ in developing the
Major Accomplishments section of your resume is to use
quantitative descriptions, where these serve to highlight
your specific accomplishments and contributions. For example, consider the following:

Wrong: Increased sales significantly in first year.

Right: Increased sales by 50% from $100 to $150
million in first year alone.

Wrong: Developed new equipment design that saved the
company a lot of money.

Right: Developed new plastic extrusion equipment
design resulting in $1 million company savings
in 2002 alone.

Wrong: Developed and installed computerized brand
costing system resulting in substantial payroll
savings.

Right: Developed and installed computerized brand
costing system resulting in elimination of 12
positions and annual payroll savings of $385,000.

You are now ready to develop the Major Accomplishments
section of your resume. Use the format illustrated here to

carefully develop each of the functions you wish to highlight with specific accomplishments. Remember to begin
each of your statements with an action word and to use
quantitative descriptions wherever possible. Although you
will wish to highlight only three or four functional areas,
rewrite each functional area at least twice. Experiment by
attempting to upgrade your second writing of each function by being more concise and choosing words that have
greater impact.

Functional Area: _____

Accomplishments: _____

   1. _____

    _____

   2. _____

    _____

   3. _____

    _____

   4. _____

    _____

Functional area: _____

Accomplishments: _____

   1. _____

    _____

   2. _____

    _____

3. _____

_____

4. _____

_____

Work History

The Work History section of the resume should be organized in reverse chronological order. Shown first should be your most recent employer, second, your second most recent employer, and so forth back to your original employer. Shown on the left should be dates of your employment, when you began and when you left. Adjacent to these dates should be the name of the employer followed by the position or positions held. The following work history section has been extracted from the sample functional resume at the end of the chapter.

WORK HISTORY:

2003 to Present   **U.S. Paper & Wood Products**
Manager of Corporate Marketing

2001 to 2003   **Photo Films International**
National Sales Manager

1999 to 2001   **Self-Employed**
Marketing Consultant

1998 to 1999   **Microwave Ovens, Inc.**
Manager of Market Research

1997 to 1998   **Self-Employed**
Marketing Consultant

1983 to 1997   **National Computer, Inc.**
Director of Marketing   (1995–1997)
National Sales Manager   (1991–1995)
Regional Sales Manager   (1988–1991)
Salesperson   (1983–1988)

There is nothing sacred about the order of position held and employer in this section of the resume. When the candidate has been employed by major corporations and highlighting this fact could prove to the candidate's advantage from a marketing standpoint, Company Name should be listed first with job title to follow on the next line. The answer to sequence is really marketability. List first, either job title or employer, whichever you feel consistently gives you the greatest advantage from a marketability standpoint.

Listing position first followed by employer will work well as long as you have held only one position with each employer. In those cases where you have held multiple positions with a single employer, however, you will need to list employer first, followed by the positions held. (Note the National Computer, Inc. section of the above sample Work History.) You will note that National Computer, Inc. is listed first, with the positions held listed following the company name. You will also note that the dates of the positions held at National Computer are shown in brackets following each of the job titles of the positions held.

The Work History section of the resume is intended to be simple. No additional information other than company name and job title should be included in this section. Space is provided below for you to develop the Work History section of your own functional resume.

From: _____ To: _____   Employer: _____

_____

Job Title: _____

_____

From: _____ To: _____   Employer: _____

_____

Job Title: _____

_____

From: _____ To: _____ Employer: _____

_____

Job Title: _____

_____

From: _____ To: _____ Employer: _____

_____

Job Title: _____

_____

From: _____ To: _____ Employer: _____

_____

Job Title: _____

_____

From: _____ To: _____ Employer: _____

_____

Job Title: _____

_____

Education

The Education section of a functional resume should include the following items:

1. Degree awarded.
2. School attended.
3. Year of graduation.
4. Major field of concentration.
5. Grade point average (G.P.A.) (list only if good and education is recent).
6. Honoraries.

Some sample education statements have been provided below for your reference.

1. <u>Education:</u> Ph.D., Massachusetts Institute of
                  Technology, 2004
        Major: Chemical Engineering

        M.S., Rochester Institute of Technology, 2002
        Major: Chemical Engineering
        G.P.A. 3.85/4.0

        B.S., Rochester Institute of Technology, 2000
        Major: Chemical Engineering
        G.P.A. 3.75/4.0

2. <u>Education:</u> M.S., University of Pennsylvania, 2003
        Major: Statistics
        G.P.A. 3.5/4.0
        Dixon Mathematics Scholarship

        B.S., Drexel University, 2001
        Major: Mathematics
        G.P.A. 3.6/4.0
        Kettering Award (Mathematics Honorary Award)

3. <u>Education:</u> M.S., University of Michigan, 2004
        Major: Mechanical Engineering
        G.P.A. 3.4/4.0
        Sloan Engineering Scholarships

        B.S., University of Maryland, 2002
        Major: Mechanical Engineering
        G.P.A. 3.4/4.0
        Tau Beta Pi (Engineering Honorary)

4. <u>Education:</u> B.A., North Carolina State University, 2002
        Major: Business Administration

Generally, unless you are a recent college graduate, you should leave little space for the Education section of your employment resume. The general rule to be followed in developing this section of the resume is "The further along you are in your professional career, the less important are your educational credentials and the more important are your work experience and specific accomplishments." Additionally, since you have chosen the functional resume for the purpose of highlighting your experience and accomplishments, it stands to reason that the Education section of the resume will be de-emphasized.

You now can develop the Education portion of your resume using the instructions provided.

Miscellaneous

In almost all cases, extracurricular activities and hobbies should be completely excluded from the resume unless they are directly related to your qualifications for the position you seek. On occasion, however, there may be some advantage to listing a specific extracurricular activity or hobby, that is, if it further enhances your marketability to a specific employer. For example, if you are applying for a position with a sporting goods manufacturer, your athletic interests may be to your advantage. Likewise, if you are applying to a company that places a lot of stress on providing leadership in your local community, you may want to include such information as (1) President, Parent Teachers Organization, (2) Chairperson, March of Dimes Campaign, (3) President, School Board. The above are carefully chosen exceptions to the rule. In general, however, hobbies and extracurricular activities are specifically excluded from the modern resume.

In the case of technical professionals, such things as publications, papers, and patents can be important. This is particularly true for items that are directly related to the professional's employment qualifications. These may help to increase the candidate's marketability to prospective employers. List only those items that are truly important and meaningful, however, and do not list minor or insignificant publications.

GAIL A. MICHAELSON
66 Sunset Road
Provost, UT 14859

Home: (616) 355-6247   Email: GaMich@AOL.com   Cell: (616) 237-9836

SUMMARY

Marketing executive with over 20 years experience in sales and marketing management. Excellent reputation as a creative, innovative manager capable of successfully revitalizing old product lines and introducing new. Full range of marketing and sales experience to include: market research, market planning & analysis, advertising & promotion, sales, and sales management.

MAJOR ACCOMPLISHMENTS

Market Research
- Investigated and analyzed European market for U.S. lumber export with resultant successful market entry.
- Worked closely with R&D in development of consumer mini-pocket calculator. Careful design of test market and resultant market feedback assured successful product development and subsequent market entry ($5 million sales in two years).
- Developed market research computer model to forecast ten-year market projection for microwave ovens.

Advertising & Promotion
- Coordinated company efforts with major New York City consumer advertising agency to develop effective campaign to revitalize failing product line (fishing reels). Campaign expenditure ($2 million) yielded annual increase in sales of $4.1 million in one year.
- Developed creative special value coupon and supportive advertising campaign that increased annual sales volume for photographic film product line by 35% over two-year period.

Marketing & Sales Management
- Managed national sales organization of 95 employees (ten regional managers and 75 salespersons) in the sale of consumer photographic film to wholesale and retail trade.
- Directed Corporate Marketing Staff (25 employees) in the development of all marketing plans and strategies for manufacturer of consumer hardware (annual sales volume $500 million).
- Successfully organized, trained and motivated new national sales organization of 45 employees for manufacture of consumer calculators. Sales reached $20 million in four years.

WORK HISTORY

SIMPSON PAPER COMPANY   **2003 to Present**
Manager of Corporate Marketing

INTERNATIONAL PAPER COMPANY, INC.   **2001 to 2003**
National Sales Manager

SELF EMPLOYED   **1999 to 2001**
Marketing Consultant

MACRO SYSTEMS, INC.   **1998 to 1999**
Manager of Market Research

SELF EMPLOYED   **1997 to 1998**
Marketing Consultant

AMERICAN BUSINESS MACHINE, INC.   **1985 to 1997**
Director of Marketing   (1995 - 1997)
National Sales Manager   (1993 - 1995)
Regional Sales Manager   (1900 - 1993)
Salesperson   (1985 - 1900)

EDUCATION

Degree: B.A., Utah State University, 1985
Major: Business Administration

11

SAMPLE FUNCTIONAL RESUMES

This chapter contains 20 sample functional resumes for your review and reference. There are 10 separate business disciplines or functions represented. These 10 disciplines represent a logical functional breakdown of a typical manufacturing company and thus provide an excellent cross section of business functions. For each of these 10 functions, you will find two sample resumes. The first is the resume of a fairly experienced, senior individual, with the second resume representing a less experienced, junior person.

The following Resume Locator should be helpful in locating those sample resumes that are of greater interest to you.

Resume Locator

Experience Level

Field or Discipline	Senior Person	Junior Person
	(Pages)	(Pages)
Accounting	186	188
Engineering	189	191
Finance	193	195
Human Resources	196	198
Information Technology	200	202
Logistics	203	205
Marketing and Sales	206	208
Operations	209	211
Procurement	212	214
Technology	215	217

BARBARA E. HENNINGS
246 Plainview Road
Fort Wayne, IN 28375

Home: (207) 822-4726   Email: BarHen@MSN.com   Office: (207) 993-2849

SUMMARY

Accounting executive with over 21 years experience in increasingly responsible positions. Excellent reputation as creative, innovative and results-oriented senior manager who gets things done. Full rage of accounting experience includes: capital and operating budgets, financial statements, accounting policies and procedures, auditing, taxes, general and cost accounting, accounts receivable, accounts payable and credit. Noted for ability to apply computer technology in streamlining accounting operations.

MAJOR ACCOMPLISHMENTS

General Accounting
- Reviewed and revamped accounting procedures of Corporate Accounting Department with resultant annual savings of $1.2 million.
- Computerized consolidation and analysis of monthly and year-end financial statements saving 8,000 man hours annually and reducing turnaround time on closings by 50%.
- Managed a five-person task force which provided the first breakout of individual division P&L statements for a $320 million corporation.

Cost Accounting
- Developed/implemented computerized materials cost tracking system which resulted in increased raw material turnover with annual savings estimated at $500,000.
- Organized and managed cost accounting procedures task force which conducted in-depth review of cost accounting procedures and developed standard procedures manual for use by all manufacturing plants in four months.
- Developed computer model for effectively estimating material costs for new electronic circuit brands (proven accuracy of + or - 1%).

Finance
- Initiated creative lease-back arrangements with foreign corporation with resultant $500,000 annual savings.
- Raised necessary capital to support major capital expansion program ($35 million) at unusually favorable rates.
- Organized, hired and trained company's first Financial Planning Department.

WORK HISTORY

TECHNOMATICS, INC. (Corporate Offices)   **2004 to Present**
Assistant to Corporate Controller

CONNER CONTAINER CORPORATION (Corporate Offices)   **2001 to 2004**
Manager of Corporate Accounting   (2002 - 2004)
Senior Accountant   (2001 - 2002)

STUBBLESTEIN & FLANDERS, INC.   **1991 to 2001**
Senior Accountant   (1996 - 2001)
Accountant   (1991 - 1996)

MAGNUM ELECTRONICS, INC. (Winslow Plant)   **1988 to 1991**
Senior Cost Accountant   (1989 - 1991)
Cost Accountant   (1988 - 1989)

EDUCATION

Degree: M.B.A., University of Alabama, 1988
Major: Accounting/Finance
          Bettinger Scholarship

Degree: B.A., Business Administration, Cannon College, 1986
Major: Accounting
          Magna Cum Laude

CPA: May 1993

DAVID R. WILSON
26 Volker Village, Apt. 105
Oceanside, CA 38495

Cell: (949) 839-2849

Email: DavWil@AOL.com

SUMMARY

Highly-motivated accounting professional with excellent record of growth and accomplishment. Thoroughly trained and ready for first supervisory assignment. Solid professional cost accounting foundation and excellent educational credentials.

MAJOR ACCOMPLISHMENTS

Material Costs
- Developed procedure for material cost breakout of sophisticated electronic Rocker Assembly worth savings of $50,000 annually.
- Developed computerized cost accounting and analysis system for tracking material consumption during manufacture of electrical harnesses with $115,000 annual savings in reduced materials inventory.

Labor Costs
- Initiated major projects to identify labor costs for discrete manufacturing operation. Worked with Industrial Engineering to effect labor savings of $85,000 annually.
- Thoroughly experienced in all aspects of labor cost analysis.

Management
- Successfully trained and directed the daily work activity of two new Cost Accountants.

WORK HISTORY

STARGAZE ELECTRONICS, INC. (Syracuse Plant)   **2001 to Present**
Senior Cost Accountant   (2002 - Present)
Cost Accountant   (2001 - 2002)

EDUCATION

Degree: M.A., Business, Miami of Ohio, 2001
Major: Accounting
            Oceanside Businessman Fellowship

Degree: B.A., Business Administration, Ohio State University, 1999
Major: Accounting   G.P.A. 3.4/4.0
Minor: Finance   G.P.A. 3.75/4.0
            Torrington Scholarship (4 years)

Activities: President, Accounting Honorary Society
            President, Student Government Association

LINDA S. PENNINGTON
824 Stone Ridge Place
Stone Mountain, GA 94837
Phone: (205) 687-2424 (H)
(205) 557-8842 (O)

SUMMARY

Engineering executive with over 16 years of experience in positions of increasing responsibility in major facility engineering for Fortune 200 manufacturer of residential and commercial heating and air conditioning equipment. Reputation for consistently beating time deadlines and budgets on major projects resulting in bottom line savings in the millions.

MAJOR ACCOMPLISHMENTS

Engineering Management

- Managed two-year, $850 million expansion program including successful installation and start-up of two complete residential air conditioning manufacturing plants.
- Managed 120 employee Corporate Engineering Department for Fortune 200 manufacturer of heating and air conditioning equipment ($450 million annual budget).
- Directed 80 employee Mechanical Engineering Section with annual budget of $250 million.
- Managed 20 employee Instrumentation and Control Engineering Department with responsibility for installation and start-up of computer control systems.

Project Savings
- Brought largest expansion program in Company's history ($850 million) in three months early and $110 million under budget.
- Completed $245 million commercial heating manufacturing equipment installation project two months early with savings estimated at $12.5 million.
- Completed all project assignments ahead of schedule and under budget.

Technologies
- Fabrication and assembly of commercial and residential air conditioning equipment.
- Fabrication and assembly of commercial and residential heating equipment.
- Engineering application of instrumentation and control systems (including minicomputers and microprocessors) to equipment fabrication and assembly lines.
- Engineering of large scale bio-mass boiler power generation systems.

WORK HISTORY

AIR SYSTEMS CORPORATION (Corporate Engineering)   **1990 to Present**
Vice President of Engineering   (2003 - Present)
Director, Mechanical Engineering   (1998 - 2003)
Manager, Instrumentation & Control Engineering   (1992 - 1998)
Senior Project Engineer, Heating   (1990 - 1992)

POWER ENGINEERING, INC. (Corporate Engineering)   **1988 to 1990**
Project Engineer

EDUCATION

Degree:	M.S., University of Colorado, 1988
Major:	Mechanical Engineering
	Bartrum Scholarship
Degree:	B.S., Lehigh University, 1986
Major:	Mechanical Engineering
	Magna Cum Laude
	Power Engineering, Inc. Scholarship (4 years)
Activities:	President, Tau Beta Psi

KEVIN P. BAKER
1822 Prairie Trail
Austin, Texas 58694

Phone: (513) 556-7720   Email: KPB18@MSN.com   Cell: (713) 757-8495

SUMMARY

High-energy, results-oriented Senior Project Engineer with five years experience in design, installation, start-up and debugging of aluminum manufacturing processes and equipment. Excellent reputation for consistently bringing projects in on time and below budget.

MAJOR ACCOMPLISHMENTS

Facility Design
- Managed mechanical design of $20 million aluminum furnace complex. Project completed on time and 10% under budget.
- Managed mechanical design of $12 million furnace and associated material handling equipment. Project is on time and under budget.
- Designed power and free conveyor material handling equipment systems for several plant locations.

Facility Improvements
- Redesigned refractory lining in a flash calciner process to reduce heat loss by 30% in existing units and 50% in new units.
- Designed innovative material handling system which allows 50% reduction in time to convert process from one product to another.
- Installed waste heat boilers on two furnaces resulting in annual steam production valued at $400,000 annually.

Design Innovations
- Initiated use of computer assisted design to draw standard furnace designs with estimated savings of 40% in design engineering phase.
- Developed innovative furnace design projected to decrease process energy requirements by 10% annually.

WORK HISTORY

PORTER METALS COMPANY, INC. (Corporate Engineering)   **1999 to Present**
Senior Project Engineer   (2003- Present)
Project Engineer   (1999 - 2003)

EDUCATION

Degree: B.S., Texas A & M University, 1999
Major: Mechanical Engineering G.P.A. 3.4/4.0
        Cum Laude Graduate

        Member, Tau Beta Psi
        Vice President, American Society of Mechanical Engineers

AFFILIATIONS

American Society of Mechanical Engineers
Association of Aluminum Manufacturing Engineers

CARTER W. WINSLOW

187 West Lake Drive
Green Bay, WI 47589
Phone: (513) 772-6464
Email: CWWin@MSN.com

SUMMARY

Senior financial executive with 13 years experience with $4 billion, Fortune 100 manufacturer of earth moving and excavation equipment. Heavily experienced in all aspects of both domestic and international financial planning. Demonstrated capability to meet major capital requirements at exceptionally favorable rates and terms.

MAJOR ACCOMPLISHMENTS

Capital Acquisition
- Developed five-year funding strategy to finance $3.1 billion capital expansion program. Capital acquired on average of 2% below market rate. Financial rating maintained despite substantial increase in long-term debt.
- Successfully manage annual capital requirements of $400 to $600 million at very favorable rates and terms.
- Secured $185 million loan for Italian affiliate at exceptionally favorable rate and term.

Financial Planning
- Developed financial strategy to support $3.1 billion, five-year expansion program.
- Provide leadership in the development of planning strategy to support annual capital requirements of $400 to $600 million.
- Developed and implemented computer model to assist five domestic divisions in forecasting and planning financial requirements as part of five-year plan.

Investor Relations
- Cultivated many key financial contacts in a wide range of financial institutions in both the domestic and international markets.
- Excellent rapport with key outside analysts with resultant maintenance of top financial ratings despite substantially increased long-term debt.

WORK HISTORY

EXCAV CORPORATION (Corporate Offices)   **1993 to Present**
Vice President and Treasurer   (2003 - Present)
Director of Corporate Finance   (1999 - 2003)
Senior Analyst, Corporate Finance   (1996 - 1999)
Analyst, Corporate Finance   (1993 - 1996)

EDUCATION

Degree: M.B.A., University of Chicago, 1993
Major: Finance

Degree: B.A., Western Michigan University, 1991
Major: Financial Management
Minor: Economics
          Magna Cum Laude

JANE M. KORSAN
1524 Oil Patch Drive
Houston, Texas 22375
Office: (713) 775-5757
Cell: (713) 972-3471

SUMMARY

Accomplished, energetic Senior Financial Analyst with outstanding educational credentials and six years experience in financial planning with major aerospace contractor. Ability to manage financial planning projects from cost estimate to placement of funding for programs in the $200 to $400 million range.

MAJOR ACCOMPLISHMENTS

Capital Planning
- Developed manufacturing cost estimates and funding requirements for sophisticated missile guidance systems ($200 to $400 million range).
- Developed computer model to automate process for performing manufacturing cost estimates reducing manual effort by 80%.
- Developed several computer models to support long-range financial planning process.

Capital Acquisition
- Provided capital funding for $1.5 billion of expansion programs over five-year period.
- Received six government commendations for outstanding work in financial planning.

WORK HISTORY

TELLSTAR DEFENSE SYSTEMS, INC. (Corporate Offices)   **1999 to Present**
Senior Financial Analyst   (2004 - Present)
Financial Analyst   (2001 - 2004)
Analyst   (1999 - 2001)

REARDON SCIENCE, INC. (Corporate Offices)   **1998 to 1999**
Planning Analyst

EDUCATION

Degree: M.B.A., University of Texas, 1998
Major: Financial Planning

Degree: B.S., Georgia Tech., 1996
Major: Management Science
           Laude
           Caldwell Systems Scholarship (4 years)

DAWN M. BEATTY
106 Summit Avenue
Shillington, PA 19306

Office: (314) 872-4467   Email: DawnB106@AOL.com   Cell: (610) 377-5756

SUMMARY

Senior level human resources executive with over 14 years experience in full range of human resources functions. Strong appreciation for the relationship between good human resource management and profitability. Enjoy excellent reputation for innovative programs designed to maximize human productivity and overall organization effectiveness.

MAJOR ACCOMPLISHMENTS

Human Resource Planning
- Designed and installed company's first human resource information system resulting in estimated annual savings of $500,000 in time and productivity.
- Designed and implemented human resources computer model providing first-time link between human resources planning and business planning.

Employee Productivity
- Developed and implemented bold new management incentive system credited with significant morale improvement and substantially increased management productivity.
- Designed and installed professional exempt employee internal posting system recognized as a key factor in improving the overall morale and productivity of professional employees.

Employee Staffing
- Successfully directed major hiring campaign resulting in the employment of 90 engineers in five months to meet stringent deadline in support of major capital expansion programs.
- Saved $750,000 per year in recruiting costs through the implementation of effective prescreening and recruiting techniques.
- Implemented unique candidate assessment process credited with substantial improvement in the quality of employee assessment and selection.

Management
- Managed Corporate Human Resources Department of 52 employees with annual budget of $3.2 million.
- Managed Corporate Staffing Department of eight employees and annual budget of $2.1 million.

WORK HISTORY

LIFESTYLE MANUFACTURING CO., INC. (Corporate Offices)   **1997 to Present**
Director of Human Resources   (2001 - Present)
Manager Corporate Staffing   (1999 - 2001)
Manager of Administrative Staffing   (1997 - 1998)

HUMAN CAPITAL SOLUTIONS, INC. (Corporate Offices)   **1989 to 1997**
Senior Consultant   (1993 - 1997)
Consultant   (1989 - 1993)

EDUCATION

Degree: M.B.A., Arizona State University, 1989
Major: Human Resource Management
Thesis: AThe Role of Performance Feedback in the Motivation of
          Professional Employees≅

Degree: B.A., University of Texas, 1987
Major: Human Resource Management
          Cum Laude
          Salem Scholarship (4 years)

MARTIN F. SLAUGHTER
18 Palm Drive, SW
Miami, FL 37485
Home: (715) 347-3343
Office: (715) 764-2232
Email: MarSla@MSN.com

SUMMARY

Creative employment manager with over five years experience at the corporate and division levels. Reputation for recruiting the hard-to-find. Thoroughly versed in all aspects of recruiting and employment with excellent track record for achieving results.

MAJOR ACCOMPLISHMENTS

College Recruiting
- Developed and successfully directed first corporate-wide college recruiting effort covering six divisions and 14 manufacturing plants.
- Prepared and distributed the ACollege Recruiters Guide≅ - a complete Ahow to≅ guide for the new recruiter.
- Conducted corporate-wide recruiter training program designed to improve the interviewing and selection skills of campus recruiters.
- Developed company's first integrated college relations program including all divisions. Highly effective programs begun at 18 colleges and universities in first year alone.

Technical Recruiting
- Developed novel, creative approaches to locating hard-to-find technical scientists and engineers making use of computerized patent database.
- Used direct mail for first time in the recruitment of technical personnel. Bought computer printed mailing lists and initiated letter campaign that resulted in 30 engineering hires in two months at a total cost of $3,000.

Recruiting Costs
- Reduced the average cost per hire from $4,000 to $2,000 in three years – a 50% decrease!
- Reduced candidate travel expense by 35% through more extensive use of telephone prescreening.
- Reduced the offer-to-hire ratio to an acceptance rate of 80%.

WORK HISTORY

KOLMAR MANUFACTURING CO., INC. (Corporate Offices)   **1998 to Present**
Corporate Employment Manager - Operations Employment   (2003 - Present)
Manager of Employment Services   (2000 - 2003)
Plant Human Resources Manager   (1998 - 2000)

BAXTER FASHIONS, INC. (Westerly Plant)   **1994 to 1998**
Assistant Personnel Manager

VIKING ELECTRONICS, INC.   **1990 to 1994**
Human Resources Assistant

EDUCATION

Degree: B.A., University of Miami, 1990
Major: Business Administration

JOSE A. RODRIQUEZ
806 Vala Drive
Costa Mesa, CA 17283

Home: (949) 776-3546   Email: JRod@Tabor.com   Cell: (949) 883-9526

SUMMARY

Information services executive with over 15 years experience in all phases of IS work. Currently Director of IS for $2 billion, Fortune 200 corporation. Strong strategic and leadership skills in planning and implementing information systems that contribute to company profitability.

MAJOR ACCOMPLISHMENTS

Planning
- Developed and implemented first five-year corporate information systems strategic plan for Fortune 200 manufacturer.
- Developed long-range information requirements plans for five key business functions including: Manufacturing, Human Resources, Controllers, Finance and Procurement.

Project Implementation
- Successfully directed development and start-up of $7 million system for control of the sales forecasting, production scheduling and materials management functions with estimated annual savings of $6 million. Project completed three months early and 20% under budget.
- Delivered numerous systems ahead of schedule and under budget including the following major projects: Human Resource Information System, Payroll System, Production Scheduling System, Finished Goods Inventory Control System and Raw Materials & Vital Supplies Control System.

Management
- Directed 60 employee ($8 million budget) Corporate IS function for Fortune 200 corporation.
- Managed eight to 12 project managers and an annual budget of $5 million in corporate-wide implementation of information systems projects.
- Managed six professionals in development of long range information systems plans for functional clients.

WORK HISTORY

TABOR VALVE COMPANY, INC. (Corporate Offices)   **1992 to Present**
Director of Information Management Services   (2002 - Present)
Corporate Project Manager   (2000 - 2002)
Manager of Client Planning Services   (1996 - 2000)
Senior Programmer Analyst   (1992 - 1996)

M&R TECHNOLOGIES, INC. (Corporate Offices)   **1990 to 1992**
Programmer Analyst

EDUCATION

Degree: Ph.D., Stanford University, 1990
Major: Computer Science

Degree: M.S., U.C.L.A., 1988
Major: Computer Science
         Micro Systems Scholarship (2 years)

Degree: B.S., Iowa State University, 1986
Major: Mathematics
         SAS Scholarship (4 years)

LILLIAN B. REED
65 Norton Road
Norristown, PA 19385
Phone: (610) 661-2239
Email: Lill65@MSN.com

SUMMARY

Research and development programmer analyst with three years experience in providing programming support to development engineers in the development of state-of-the-art communications controller. Proficient in the use of data analyzer type equipment for studies and troubleshooting network problems.

TECHNICAL HIGHLIGHTS

- In-depth knowledge of the SNA/ACP/NCP functions of a communications controller in a PEP environment.

- Proficiency in SNA/ACP/NCP internals.

- Proficiency with SDLC, various trace facilities, ALC and TSO/WYLBUR/SPF.

- Expert in use of data analyzer equipment

WORK HISTORY

DATACOM SYSTEMS, INC. (Corporate R&D)   **2003 to Present**
Programmer Analyst

EDUCATION

Degree:	M.S., Massachusetts Institute of Technology, 2003
Major:	Computer Science
	Ransin Laboratory Fellowship (2 years)

Degree:	B.S., Massachusetts Institute of Technology, 2001	
Major:	Computer Science	G.P.A. 3.85/4.0
Minor:	Mathematics	G.P.A. 3.78/4.0
	Mattson Foundation Scholarship (4 years)	

Activities:	President, Computer Science Society
	Vice President, Mathematics Honorary

DERK K. JARVISON
605 North Ridge Drive
Falls Church, VA 14375
Phone: (814) 665-9399
Email: Derk605@AOL.com

SUMMARY

Senior level logistics executive with demonstrated ability to effectively organize and lead logistics function that employs state-of-the-art concepts and realizes significant contribution to bottom line results. Leadership in the application of computer and quantitative techniques that streamline operations and add substantial profits.

MAJOR ACCOMPLISHMENTS

Management
- Director of Logistics for Fortune 500, $1.4 billion corporation. Manage eight warehouses, 750 employees and annual budget of $125 million.
- Managed Corporate Distribution function for $850 million beverage bottler – 250 employees, budget $85 million.
- Functions managed include both Warehousing and Transportation.

Cost Savings
- $18 million per year through computerization of order entry and distribution planning system.
- $10.2 million per year through regional consolidation of leased warehouse facilities.
- $5 million per year through development of computer model for use in determining best carrier and routing.
- $4.7 million per year through installation of automatic palletizers and computer controlled conveyor system.
- $3.9 million per year through corporate-wide negotiation of rail carrier rates.

Information Systems Applications
- Designed corporate order entry and distribution planning system.
- Installed computer controlled conveyor system and automatic palletizers.
- Implemented use of computer model for determination of best shipping point for best delivery and cost by order received.

WORK HISTORY

TAYLOR FOODS, INC. (Corporate Offices)　　　　　　　　　**2002 to Present**
Director of Logistics

BEVERTON BOTTLING COMPANY (Corporate Offices)　　　**1993 to 2002**
Distribution Manager　　　　(1999 - 2002)
Senior Distribution Analyst　(1996 - 1999)
Distribution Analyst　　　　(1993 – 1996)

EDUCATION

Degree:　M.S., Virginia Institute of Technology, 1993
Major:　 Industrial Engineering
　　　　 Weller Scholarship (2 years)

Degree:　B.S., Virginia Institute of Technology, 1991
Major:　 Industrial Engineering
　　　　 Lowe Company Scholarship (4 years)

CAROLINE A. JACKSON
122 Riverview Terrace
Winslow, ME 37495

Phone: (516) 488-2927   Email: CJ122@MSN.com

SUMMARY

Ambitious, results-oriented logistics manager with over 12 years experience in all phases of warehousing and transportation. Demonstrated track record of translating technical knowledge and leadership into bottom line results. Fully qualified and eager to run logistics function of medium-sized company.

MAJOR ACCOMPLISHMENTS

Management
- Managed Corporate Warehousing function for $300 million manufacturer of dog food (150 employees, 12 warehouses, $32 million budget).
- Managed Corporate Distribution Center for $120 million manufacturer of metal fasteners (65 employees, $12 million trucking company, 85 trucks).

Cost Savings
- $2.1 million per year in shipping costs for truck shipments through greater use of "gypsy" carriers.
- $450,000 per year through packaging redesign allowing 10% more product to be shipped per railcar.
- $320,000 through renegotiation of warehouse leases.
- $300,000 per year through installation of extendable power conveyors for truck loading.
- $135,000 per year through redesign of warehouse storage pattern.
- $115,000 per year in reduced product damage through product handling training for warehouse crews.

WORK HISTORY

PETCO DOG FOOD, INC. (Corporate Offices)   **2002 to Present**
Manager of Warehousing

HELMET METAL MANUFACTURING CO. (Portland Plant)   **1994 to 2002**
Distribution Center Manager   (2000 - 2002)
Shipping Manager   (1994 - 2000)

MARSDEN TRUCKING, INC.   **1991 to 1994**
Dispatcher

EDUCATION

Degree: B.A., Colby College, 1991
Major: Business Administration

CHARLES B. PARKER
16 Wesley Road
Eugene, OR 23118
Home: (322) 887-2938
Cell: (322) 557-9899

SUMMARY

High-energy, results-oriented sales and marketing executive with over 14 years of demonstrated achievement in all phases of marketing and sales. Excellent track record of bottom line results. Noted for innovative ideas that dramatically increase sales volume and establish brand leadership in the marketplace.

MAJOR ACCOMPLISHMENTS

Marketing
- Established unique network of dealerships which catapulted company to number one in European sales in specialty resins. Export sales increased 75% to $225 million in two years.
- Led national roll-out of new low-viscosity resin product accounting for $150 million new sales in first year.
- Introduced eight major new products accounting for increase in total sales of 40% ($210 million) in less than four years.
- Realized a 225% increase in sales volume of old product in two years through repositioning of product in market and creative advertising program.
- Conducted market research resulting in successful recommendation to increase price of major product by 20% with no loss in sales volume.

Management
- Directed 115 employee marketing and sales organization for major chemical specialties manufacturer (annual sales $725 million).
- Managed 95 employee marketing and sales function for $525 million manufacturer of chemical specialties.
- Managed five-employee brand management function.

Sales
- Increased sales by 15% in one year while selling chemical specialties to pharmaceutical industry in four-state area.
- Received national sales award for greatest sales volume increase for years 1993, 1995 and 1996.

WORK HISTORY

OREGON CHEMICALS, INC. (Corporate Offices)   **2004 to Present**
Director of Marketing

HOUTON CHEMICALS, INC. (Corporate Offices)   **1996 to 2004**
Director of Marketing and Sales   (2000 - 2004)
Marketing Brand Manager   (1998 - 2000)
Associate Brand Manager   (1996 - 1998)

CARDON CHEMICALS CORPORATION (District Sales Office)   **1991 to 1996**
Senior Sales Representative   (1995 - 1996)
Sales Representative   (1991 - 1995)

EDUCATION

Degree: M.B.A., University of Washington, 1991
Major: Marketing

Degree: B.S., Oregon State University, 1989
Major: Chemistry

President of Chemical Society

THOMAS R. SPEARS
210 Warfield Way
Huron, OH 14263

Cell: (203) 644-5658   Email: TomSP21@MSN.com   Home: (203) 652-9417

SUMMARY

Creative sales professional with over six years of experience in selling complex business systems requiring exceptional application sales skills. Demonstrated ability to successfully introduce new business machine product lines involving complex business and institutional applications.

MAJOR ACCOMPLISHMENTS

New Product Introduction
- Successfully launched and marketed world's first updatable microfilm record keeping and retrieval system with sales now approaching $100 million.
- Sold and developed first banking industry application for new microfilm storage system. Annual sales now $300 million.

Equipment Sales
- Increased sales of new microfilm systems by 300% in last two years.
- Developed and trained dealership network increasing sales of microfilm and other specialty photo-imaging films from $1.8 million to $5.2 million in two years. – a 189% increase!

Marketing
- Worked as part of venture team in the test marketing of new updatable microfilm record keeping system. Work resulted in highly successful marketing strategy.

WORK HISTORY

HI-REZ GRAPHICS, INC. (Detroit Regional Office)   **1998 to Present**
District Sales Manager   (2003 - Present)
Senior Sales Representative   (2000 - 2003)
Sales Representative   (1998 - 2000)

EDUCATION

Degree: B.A.,   University of Michigan, 1998
Major: Marketing

Activities: President, Student Government
             President, Delta Upsilon Fraternity
             Captain, Varsity Track Team

JENNIFER T. LOGAN
1616 Ryan Circle
Marietta, GA 18274

Office: (616) 935-0978   Email: Logan1616@MSN.com   Home: (616) 554-2374

SUMMARY

Senior operations executive with 19 years experience in responsible operations management and engineering positions. Excellent record of fast-track growth based upon solid contribution to bottom line results. Outstanding reputation as organizer and leader who never fails to achieve goals and objectives.

MAJOR ACCOMPLISHMENTS

Manufacturing
- Directed successful $125 million, two-year capital expansion program doubling plant manufacturing capacity. (Completed three months ahead of schedule and 10% under budget.)
- Directed cost reduction task force resulting in overall reduction of manufacturing costs by 20% ($110 million) in three years.
- Cut raw material inventories by 30% ($15 million) through implementation of computerized production scheduling and inventory control system.
- Moved 75% of hourly employees to new jobs in less than two months with no loss in plant output.

Engineering
- Managed company's largest capital expansion program ($250 million, two years) with start-up four months ahead of schedule and project under budget.
- Engineered numerous projects in the $40-$50 million range with all projects completed ahead of schedule and within budget.

Management
- Directed all manufacturing activity for 5,300 employee manufacturer of copper tubing (sales $500 million).
- Managed $2,700 employee copper refinery and tube manufacturing facility ($375 million budget).
- Managed 150 employee Central Engineering Department for major manufacturer of refrigeration tubing.

WORK HISTORY

STRATFORD TUBE, INC. (Corporate Offices)   **1996 to Present**
Vice President of Operations   (2001 - Present)
Plant Manager (Norfolk Plant)   (1996 - 2001)

WOLFORD TUBE COMPANY, INC. (Corporate Offices)   **1986 to 1996**
Manager of Engineering   (1991 - 1996)
Department Manager, Drawing Operations (Bradford Plant)   (1989 - 1991)
Project Engineer   (1986 - 1989)

EDUCATION

Degree: M.S., Georgia Institute of Technology, 1986
Major: Mechanical Engineering

Degree: B.S., Virginia Institute of Technology, 1984
Major: Mechanical Engineering
          Tau Beta Psi

GEORGE T. BENNER
221 Washington Terrace
Plainfield, NJ 13448

Phone: (609) 237-9936

Email: GeoB22@AOL.com

SUMMARY

Results-oriented manufacturing manager with six years experience in wax and silicone manufacturing. Excellent record of achievement and advancement earned through demonstrated contribution to bottom-line results.

MAJOR ACCOMPLISHMENTS

Manufacturing
- Introduced automatic product palletizing and palletized railcar loading, cutting warehouse operating costs by 25% ($15 million annual savings).
- Organized and coached hourly employee cost reduction task force accounting for implementation of several cost savings projects with $7.5 million savings in one year.
- Increased department productivity by 18% in two years through employee job rotation and enrichment program.

Management
- Managed 210 employee, two-department manufacturing operation in the manufacture of silicone-based waxes and polishes (annual budget $130 million).
- Managed wax Formulations Department of 50 employees and annual budget of $75 million.

Employee Relations
- Initiated absenteeism control program reducing absenteeism from 11% to less than 4% in one year.
- Reduced union grievances from 185 to 62 in two years through effective employee relations practices.
- Awarded best department safety award in both 1998 and 1999.

WORK HISTORY

WEXLER MANUFACTURING COMPANY (Linwood Plant)   **2000 to Present**
Assistant to Plant Manager   (2003 - Present)
Department Manager, Formulations   (2000 - 2003)

CORDOVA WAX COMPANY (Radley Plant)   **1998 to 2000**
Supervisor, Formulations

EDUCATION

Degree: B.S., Boston University, 1998
Major: Industrial Technology G.P.A. 3.5/4.0
         Cum Laude

TODD E. THOMAS
3229 Colonial Place
Hartford, CT 133847
Phone: (213) 334-7495
Cell: (213) 457-9682

SUMMARY

Procurement executive with over 13 years demonstrated effectiveness in contributing substantially to bottom-line results. Knowledgeable in all facets of modern procurement management including computer applications. Fully qualified to direct procurement function of major corporation.

MAJOR ACCOMPLISHMENTS

Management
- Direct procurement function for $1.2 billion manufacturer of consumer food products (eight plants). Direct staff of 15 professionals and $580 million budget.
- Managed corporate procurement function of $850 million baking company with professional staff of eight and annual budget of $325 million.
- Managed department of four with annual budget of $200 million in the purchase of all vital supplies.
- Managed department of three and annual budget of $50 million with corporate-wide procurement responsibility for $150 million manufacturer of pretzels and potato chips.

Cost Savings
- Saved $36 million per year through computerization of raw materials tracking and forecasting.
- Saved $22 million through corporate-wide consolidation of all packing supply purchases.
- Realized $18 million annual savings through conversion to biomass fuels with long-term purchase contract.
- Centralized procurement function realizing $16.5 million annual savings through corporate-wide consolidation of all purchasing.
- Saved $3.2 million per year through installation of computer systems for vital supplies and packaging materials forecasting and inventory control.
- Negotiated two-year shipping carton purchase contract worth savings of $1.3 million annually.

WORK HISTORY

HARTFORD FOODS, INC. (Corporate Offices)   **2003 to Present**
Director of Procurement

LARSON BAKING COMPANY, INC. (Corporate Offices)   **1995 to 2003**
Manager of Procurement   (1997 - 2003)
Senior Buyer - Vital Supplies   (1995 - 1997)

BORDER FOODS, INC. (Corporate Offices)   **1989 to 1995**
Manager of Purchasing   (1992 – 1995)
Buyer   (1989 - 1992)

EDUCATION

Degree: B.A., Syracuse University, 1989
Major: Business Administration

Activities: President of Business Club
Captain, Varsity Baseball

GORDON B. DAVIS
17 Harbor View Place, Apt. 12-A
Green Bay, WI 23568
Phone: (515) 844-8847
Email: GorDa@AOL.com

SUMMARY

Results-driven procurement professional with over four years of experience in procurement of vital supplies. Excellent track record of contribution to bottom-line results through finding and implementing major cost savings opportunities.

MAJOR ACCOMPLISHMENTS

Cost Savings
- Saved $1.3 million through negotiation of two-year contract to purchase knockdowns at 20% below current price.
- Realized annual savings of $575 through inventory reductions resulting from tighter control through computer forecasting.
- Saved $200,000 annually through renegotiation of poly wrap contract at 10% reduction in purchase price.
- Saved $125,000 annually through use of computer forecasting of vital supply requirements and subsequent inventory reductions.

Information Systems
- Developed and implemented computer system for accurate long-range forecasting of vital supply requirements permitting reduced supply inventories.
- Computerized vital supplies delivery schedule with all deliveries made to manufacturing on time and with no shortages.

WORK HISTORY

GREEN BAY PAPER COMPANY, INC. (Corporate Offices)   **2003 to Present**
Senior Purchasing Agent - Vital Supplies

FORT SMITH PAPER COMPANY (Corporate Offices)   **2000 to 2003**
Vital Supplies Buyer

EDUCATION

Degree: B.A., University of Wisconsin, Stevens Point, 2000
Major: Pulp & Paper Technology   G.P.A. 3.8/4.0
         Cum Laude
         Fort Smith Paper Company Scholarship (4 years)

         President, Delta Upsilon Fraternity

SARAH B. THOMLINSON
55 Orchard Hill Road
Appleton, WI 23847
Phone: (409) 357-2999 (O)
(409) 357-5673 (H)
Email: SBT55@WPT.com

SUMMARY

Over 20 years of dynamic, innovative technology management leadership in Fortune 500 companies. Demonstrated capability in achieving business goals through innovative technology. Broad range of technical expertise coupled with highly effective communications skills.

MAJOR ACCOMPLISHMENTS

Managerial Leadership
- Managed 500-employee corporate research center for Fortune 100 paper company ($32 million annual research budget).
- Directed packaging & materials laboratory of 135 professionals for leading fiber corporation ($12 million budget).
- Managed 38 professional employee synthetic fiber research department ($1.2 million budget).

Technical Leadership
- Realized $300 million in annual savings through invention of unique forming device permitting 30% reduction in product raw material fiber.
- Allowed entry into $125 million new market through development of unique paper-like synthetic material.
- Increased sales by 15% in two years through development and introduction of five major new consumer products.
- Pioneered development of revolutionary new freezer wrap prolonging room temperature thaw time by 300% and reducing frozen food spoilage by 30%.

Innovation
- Invented unique and highly successful magnetic forming device for high-speed sheet formation of non-woven materials.
- Pioneered new innovative process permitting the forming of a synthetic fiber web on high speed wet lay technology paper machine.
- Developed thermal mechanical pulping process allowing 5% reduction in TMP energy requirements.

WORK HISTORY

WISCONSIN TISSUE & PACKAGING, INC. (Corporate Research Center)   **2002 to Present**
Vice President of Technology

KIMBERLY NONWOVEN FIBERS, INC. (Packaging & Materials Laboratory)   **1993 to 2002**
Research Director, Packaging & Materials

JAMES RIVER CORPORATION (Corporate Research)   **1984 to 1993**
Research Manager, Synthetic Fibers   (1988 - 1993)
Senior Research Scientist, Polymer Research   (1984 - 1988)

VULCAN SPACE LABORATORY   **1982 to 1984**
Research Specialist

EDUCATION

Degree: Ph.D., University of Michigan, 1982
Major: Chemical Engineering
          Vulcan Laboratory Fellowship

Degree: M.S., Rochester Institute of Technology, 1980
Major: Materials Engineering

Degree: B.S., Rochester Institute of Technology, 1978
Major: Chemical Engineering
          Magna Cum Laude
          Barlow Scholarship (4 years)

          President, Chemical Engineering Society

PUBLICATIONS

45 professional publications and papers (1980 - 2002)

AFFILIATIONS

American Society of Chemical Engineers
American Chemical Society
American Physical Society
Technical Association of Pulp & Paper Industry
American Management Association

DAVID A. FREEMAN
22 Indigo Sky Way
Split Arrow, OK 23748
Phone: (446) 757-8849
Email: DaFree22@MSN.com

SUMMARY

Highly innovative Ph.D. polymer engineer with demonstrated track record in achieving excellent product and process development results. Hold ten U.S. Patents and am credited with development of major new polymeric materials allowing successful entry into several new markets.

MAJOR ACCOMPLISHMENTS

Creativity, Innovation
- Invented fiberglass substitute with twice the strength and half the cost, allowing successful entry to $300 million new market.
- Pioneered new synthetic wool-like fiber from product development stage through successful pilot plant testing.
- Recipient of Norwood Chemical "Inventor of the Year" award.
- Holder of ten U.S. Patents.

Bottom Line Contributions
- Developed polymer material for manufacture of boat hulls with estimated annual market potential of $300 million.
- Developed synthetic wool substitute allowing successful entry into market valued at $150 million annually.
- Invented five new polymer-based products, four of which have led to new market entry and one of which is now in test market (estimated annual sales of $350 million to date).

WORK HISTORY

WILSON POLYMER SPECIALTIES, INC. (Corporate Technology)   **2000 to Present**
Senior Research Engineer, Polymers   (2002 - Present)
Research Engineer, Polymers   (2000 - 2002)

GRAVERLY CHEMICAL COMPANY (Central Research)   **1997 to 2000**
Polymer Chemist

EDUCATION

Degree: Ph.D., Massachusetts Institute of Technology, 1997
Major: Polymer Engineering
Thesis: "Copolymerization of Diamond Polymers"
          Hawthorne Fellowship

Degree:	M.S., Rochester Institute of Technology, 1995
Major:	Chemical Engineering
	Ludwig Scholarship

Degree:	B.S., Rochester Institute of Technology, 1993
Major:	Chemical Engineering
	Magna Laude
	Stanton Scholarship (3 years)

President, Polymeric Society

PATENTS

Awarded ten U.S. Patents since 1997

AFFILIATIONS

Society of Polymer Scientists
American Society of Chemical Engineers
National Institute for Polymer Research

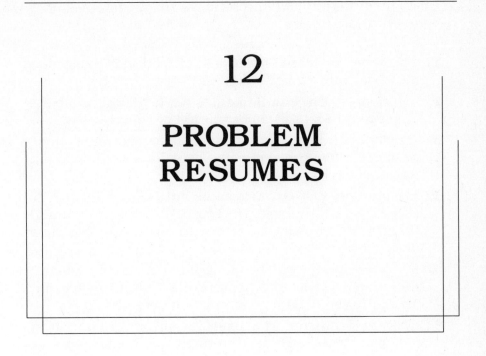

12

PROBLEM RESUMES

Chances are fairly high that, if you have elected to read this particular chapter, you anticipate having some difficulty with your resume that could prove detrimental to your employment candidacy. Knowing how to treat this problem in the employment resume is imperative if you are to be successful in competing with the thousands of other resumes that find their way into the employment manager's mail folder. Failure to handle this problem in an appropriate manner could result in the screening out of your resume, with little or no consideration given to your qualifications for employment.

Since there are probably tens, if not hundreds, of reasons why a resume may be a "problem resume," it is not my intent to attempt to deal with the unusual or rare problem. Thorough coverage of such a broad topic would require a book in itself. Instead, this chapter will focus on the seven most common reasons for classifying a resume as a problem. These seven reasons are believed to account for approximately

80 percent (or better) of all problem resumes. The seven most common resume problems can be classified as follows:

1. *Age.* The applicant is over age 40 and may experience age discrimination.

2. *Job Hopper.* The candidate has worked for a number of employers in a fairly short period of time.

3. *Employment Gap.* The applicant has had one or more periods of lengthy unemployment (or substantial underemployment).

4. *Educational Deficit.* The applicant lacks a formal degree or generally lacks the requisite educational qualifications necessary to attain his or her employment objective.

5. *Experience Deficit.* The candidate has insufficient experience or lacks the appropriate type of experience normally required for the position sought.

6. *Chronic Handicap.* The applicant suffers from a physical or mental handicap that might be thought by some employers to impede performance.

7. *Changing Careers.* The candidate wishes to enter a new field in which he or she has little or no experience.

We examine each of these problems in some detail, and I share some practical and effective ways to deal with these problems in the employment resume. Here again, as in other chapters of this book, this advice is based on firsthand observation as a former Fortune 200 human resources executive who has played a very active role in his company's employment process. Hopefully my practical experience will help you over what otherwise might prove a difficult obstacle to your development of an effective employment resume.

AGE

When is age an obstacle to employment? This question is becoming more and more difficult to answer for two basic reasons. First, there is the matter of demographics. Second, there is the factor of civil rights legislation. Let's take a moment or two to consider the effect of these two items on the employment process and therefore the employment resume.

Most of you are familiar from reading about the previous financial plight of Social Security, U.S. census data, and other similar articles and reports dealing with the changing age demographics in the United States, that the age mix of the population is moving from younger to older. As this population ages, older persons are becoming an increasingly larger percentage of the total, with younger individuals becoming a proportionately smaller percentage of the population. Along with this shift in demographics there is a corresponding change of attitude toward age in the employment process. With fewer younger workers and an increasing number of older workers now constituting the labor market, employers have been forced to give stronger consideration to older workers than in the past. Thus age is becoming less and less of an employment barrier with the passage of time. Depending on circumstances, however, age may still be a very real barrier to employment—all things being equal.

An important civil rights law, the Age Discrimination in Employment Act of 1967, made it illegal for employers to discriminate against individuals on the basis of age when making employment decisions. This law, coupled with highly publicized age discrimination lawsuits, has served to direct the focus of the employment professional's attention away from age as the basis for screening out employment candidates. It has forced employment managers to refrain from using age alone to screen out employment candidates who are otherwise qualified for a given employment opening. Thus the average age of candidates employed by enlightened companies has gradually risen over the years. However, this does not mean that such discrimination has been eliminated. It simply means that blatant cases have all but disappeared, and employment managers have become more sophisticated and creative in practicing this form of discrimination.

Both the changing demographics and the age discrimination legislation have served to make companies more flexible in hiring older workers. The question of age, however, still remains a relative factor. When faced with otherwise equal qualifications, many employers would still prefer to hire the younger worker. Since the law forbids this, however, the employment professional may scrutinize the qualifications of the older candidate more thoroughly in an effort to eliminate this candidate on the basis of some job-related qualification.

For many employment managers, the question of age is a relative one—usually relative to the level of the position sought. Thus an individual who is 45 or 50 years of age may not be thought of as too old for a position as vice president. It would take 25 to 30 years to accumulate sufficient experience to qualify for such a position. Likewise, candidates who are 35 to 45 years of age may be acceptable candidates for a director-level position for similar reasons. By contrast, however, a 25-year-old person may well be preferable to a 45-year-old individual for a position as a project engineer, a position that may require only three or four years of experience. Many firms might question the motivation and drive of a 45-year-old engineer who had only attained the level of project engineer after 24 years of experience.

You can see from this discussion that age still plays a role in the employment process. Therefore, if you are an older worker and have not reached a reasonable level or position for your peer group, you should attempt to disguise your age on the employment resume. Should you still have some questions on whether age represents an obstacle to your employment, let me suggest the following guidelines:

1. Age 30—Junior-level professional position.
2. Age 35—Senior-level professional position.
3. Age 35—Lower-level managerial position.
4. Age 40—Mid-level managerial position.
5. Age 45—Director-level position.
6. Age 50—Vice president-level position.

These are not hard and fast rules but merely guidelines based on my discussions with numerous human resources and employment professionals. The supply-to-demand ratio for a given field (computer programming, for example) may dictate that age cannot be a factor when considering the qualifications of such a scarce resource in a high-demand market. Likewise, firms with compensation packages (wages and benefits) that are considered substandard for their industry may be considerably more flexible on the age issue. Nonetheless, you would be well advised to keep the above guidelines in mind when considering whether to reflect age on your resume.

To disguise your age on the employment resume, simply apply the following basic rules:

1. Do not list your age or birthdate on your resume.
2. Do not list the year you graduated in the Education section of the resume.
3. Do not list all of the positions that you have held or all the employers for whom you have worked since the beginning of your career. Simply list your most recent positions and employers, going back in time only as far as is necessary to convince the prospective employer that you have sufficient experience to handle the position for which you are applying.
4. When listing patents, professional publications, and so forth on your resume, omit issue and publication dates.
5. Carefully review your resume for any dates that may give a prospective employer a clue regarding your age and remove the date (or item) from your resume.

You shouldn't feel guilty in applying these rules for disguising your age since it is illegal for employers to discriminate against you on the basis of age. Additionally, you could well be better qualified than your younger counterparts but never have the opportunity to establish this through a personal interview if you provide prospective employers with the chance to screen you out on the basis of your age.

There is no written law or rule that says the employment resume *must* include *all* employers or past positions held. The purpose of the resume is simply to provide the prospective employer with a synopsis of your employment credentials. It does not purport to reflect all qualifications. On the other hand, the employment application form normally requires that the applicant list all past employers and positions. Should you have a potential age problem, therefore, it is recommended that you skillfully avoid completion of a formal application form until after you have had the benefit of an employment interview. By all means avoid indication (or giving clues) of your age on the resume when doing so could cause you to be screened out. If you are otherwise qualified for the position in question, you deserve the benefit of a personal employment interview. Don't deny yourself this opportunity!

JOB HOPPER

As with the subject of age, it is difficult to establish set rules or guidelines for the job hopper. Simply put, the job hopper is one who is considered to have held too many jobs with too many employers in too short a period of time. As with age, the frequency of changing employers can vary considerably between industries. What may constitute an acceptable level of job hopping in one industry may well be totally unacceptable in another.

For example, engineers who work for a contract firm or "job shop" are subject to frequent layoffs throughout their careers compared to professionals in many other fields. As large contracts wind down these firms simply don't have a need for as many engineers, and if no new contracts are on the horizon, they are forced to lay off many of their professional workforce. These firms are economy dependent. When the economy is healthy and expanding, many companies are engaged in vigorous capital-expansion programs requiring the services of engineering contract firms in the engineering and construction of new facilities. During such periods the contract firms undergo substantial hiring programs and expand their professional ranks. Conversely, when things get tough and the economy is contracting, most companies forego expansion plans and the demand for contract engineering support drops off. The result of this decreased demand is the layoff of engineers.

For the most part, experienced employment professionals are very much aware of those industries in which high employee turnover is a normal fact of life. When reviewing the resumes of professionals working in such industries, therefore, the employment manager will not be alarmed to see a large number of employers in a fairly short period of time. The knowledgeable employment professional is fully aware that this unusually high job turnover probably has little to do with the candidate's ability or performance and is simply a reflection of the normal turnover pattern within that particular industry. Thus a contract engineer who has averaged a new employer every two or three years does not raise any unusual concern.

Where the pattern of job turnover is considered high for a particular industry, however, the employment professional becomes most reluctant to give serious consideration to the employment applicant. High job turnover conjures up a wide range of negative assumptions in the mind of employment managers. The single word used to categorize individuals with high job turnover is "unstable." The causative factors underlying this pattern of instability could be poor performance, incompetence, incompatibility with management or fellow workers, absenteeism, alcoholism, marital problems, and so on. The list of possibilities is almost endless.

Bear in mind that the resume review process is essentially a negative screening process. The employment manager's objective is to screen out those candidates who are either unqualified on the basis of technical skills and experience or who are considered undesirable on the basis of some other factor that suggests that the candidate is a high risk. If the applicant's past has been one of high job turnover, why would this pattern be any different in the future? Why should the employment manager risk hiring this individual when other candidates are available who have demonstrated a history of low job turnover and great stability in the past? The answer to these questions is simple: They won't!

Consider for a moment the risks associated with hiring an individual who has had a poor history of job stability. The financial implications of a poor employment decision are fairly dramatic. First, there is the employment agency fee. Assuming an annual salary of $70,000 and a fee of 30 percent, the agency fee amounts to $21,000. Second, there is the matter of reimbursement of moving expenses. Most companies with a fairly comprehensive moving-expense reimbursement policy estimate moving expenses at approximately 1½ times annual salary (for a homeowner with a family). In our example, therefore, moving expenses are estimated at approximately $105,000. Thus direct replacement costs (agency fee and moving expenses) alone total $126,000. This does not even begin to take into consideration such indirect replacement costs as dual training costs (the cost of having trained the departed employee plus the cost of training the replacement) and the loss of productivity while both the past and present incumbents were in training.

Considering the substantial costs associated with making a poor employment decision, it can be readily understood why employment managers are reluctant to give much consideration to job hoppers. This is especially true when other candidates with more favorable employment histories are available. Additionally, the costs associated with bringing a candidate in for interviews can also mount up in a hurry. First, there is plane fare (say $800 round trip). Next, there is the cost of meals and lodging (estimate one day at $175). Third, there are the salaries of those managers and professionals who participate in the interview process (estimate four at one hour each at $50 per hour). Thus the typical costs associated with interviewing just one employment candidate can quickly add up to hundreds of dollars for the employer. The employment manager is responsible for keeping these expenses to a minimum by inviting in for interviews only those candidates who have a reasonable probability of being made an employment offer.

Being classified as a job hopper will place you at a decided disadvantage when compared to others of equal qualifications but whose employment history is considerably more stable. This is not to say that you are not a good candidate or that you don't have good reasons for having changed employers with some frequency. This may well be true. I am in no way passing judgment on your qualifications and abilities. What I am doing is attempting to be realistic with you—

sharing with you the truth of how your resume will be perceived by the typical employment professional as he or she reviews your overall qualifications relative to other candidates with whom you may be competing. If you believe that you might be classified as a job hopper, there are some steps that you can take to at least minimize the overall effect of your employment history. The following recommendations should prove helpful.

Use of the functional resume format (see Chapter 9) can be fairly effective in reducing the potentially negative impact of a high frequency of past job turnover. The organization of this format is to list major areas of experience and accomplishment on the resume first, followed by a listing of past employment history (dates, employers, and positions held). If you have made substantial contributions to past employers, citing these early in the resume may create sufficiently positive impact on the reader to overcome concerns regarding your past employment record. This is especially true when the employer has had a particular problem where it is felt that your major contributions of the past are directly related to these areas of need. In such a case the employer may well feel that the value of solving this particular problem far outweighs the risk of turnover. In any event, use of the functional resume format is strongly recommended where there has been a history of high job turnover but where significant past contributions and accomplishments can be cited.

Although this technique is *not* recommended for those who have had a solid record of employment stability, it is one that can prove helpful to the individual whose resume must reflect a poor employment history from a turnover standpoint. Where appropriate, consider offering an explanation for leaving past employers. This should be shown in the Work History section of the functional resume format as follows:

2003 to 2004   Manager of Contract Sales
                Smith Collison Corporation
                Reason for Leaving: Change in marketing
                strategy—company went to cash sales
                only—position eliminated.

2002 to 2003   Controller
Johnson and Parker
Reason for Leaving: Replaced by owner's
son.

2001 to 2002   Corporate Vice President,
Manufacturing
Hollingsworth Company
Reason for Leaving: Company purchased by
Karlson Reed Corporation—all top
management replaced by Karlson Reed
personnel.

If using the chronological resume format, a reason for leaving should be positioned following description of position and accomplishments. It should not follow either name of employer or title of position held. To do so could distract the reader from giving full attention to the description of the position held and accomplishments. This is not the case with the functional format, however, where major accomplishments have already been described at the beginning of the resume.

In the general parlance of most employment professionals, certain reasons for having left past employers are considered to fall into the "acceptable" category. Perhaps the following categories may serve to give you some ideas as to the parameters of acceptability from the employment manager's standpoint.

1. *Job Elimination.* Elimination of position, department, or function (especially if your previous duties have not been absorbed by others).

2. *Acquisition.* Acquisition of your employer by another company (especially where the new parent company has replaced the management of the acquired company with its own personnel).

3. *Nepotism.* Where the candidate has been replaced by a relative of the owner (especially where there has been a past pattern of this type of practice within the company).

4. *Contraction.* Where there has been significant contraction of the company with reduction in future advancement opportunity.

5. *Deemphasis of Function.* Where there has been significant deemphasis on the candidate's functional specialty (for example: Research and Development budget reduced by 50%).

6. *Lack of Advancement Opportunity.* Where it can be demonstrated there has been little or no opportunity for professional growth. (Care should be exercised in using this as a reason since it is frequently used by individuals to disguise other forms of discontent with past employers.)

7. *Health.* Where the candidate is allergic to certain chemicals or other items used in the manufacturing process, or when a family member has a health problem requiring relocation to a different climate. (Care should be used in citing health reasons if the effect is to create the impression that you are not a healthy individual or could be prone to excessive absenteeism.)

On the other hand, the following reasons for separation from past employers are considered unacceptable by most employment professionals:

1. *Poor Performance.* Where the candidate has been discharged from a past employer on the basis of poor performance.

2. *Incompatibility.* Where the candidate has either been discharged or has left a past employer voluntarily for reasons of incompatibility with management or fellow workers.

3. *Absenteeism.* Where the individual has been discharged by a past employer for absenteeism or chronic lateness.

4. *Dishonesty.* Where the candidate has been discharged by a past employer for lying, cheating, or stealing.

5. *Quit.* Where the individual has quit without providing the past employer with reasonable advance notification (normally at least two weeks).

If your past employment history could potentially classify you as a job hopper, you can readily see why it may be important to state your reasons for leaving past employers, especially where such reasons would be considered acceptable. If no reason is cited, the employment manager is left to assume the worst, that is, poor performance, incompatibility, dishonesty, and so on. It is strongly recommended, therefore, that you list the reasons for leaving past employers on your employment resume.

If your reasons for departure from past employers are deemed acceptable in most cases, and you elect to show these on your resume, it is not necessary to list reason for departure in the case of all past employers. In those cases where your reason for leaving would be considered unacceptable, simply do not show a reason or, where appropriate, indicate "personal—will discuss during interview." When in doubt as to whether a specific reason for leaving a past employer is acceptable, the general rule to be followed is "Don't show a reason." Why show information that could provide the basis for the reader to screen you out?

EMPLOYMENT GAP

Another topic of major concern to the novice resume writer can be how to handle employment gaps, that is, periods of unemployment or substantial underemployment. By the term "underemployment" I mean being employed for a period of time in a position that is substantially below your obvious experience level or professional capability. Either of these events can sometimes cast a shadow of doubt on what otherwise may be excellent credentials. The obvious question that is raised in the mind of the employment manager when encountering such employment gaps is: "How could a person with otherwise good credentials possibly be unemployed or underemployed? Something is wrong. What is it?" As with the case of the job hopper, periods of unexplained unemployment or underemployment represent a high risk to the employment professional and must be dealt with effectively if you are going to be successful in landing an employment interview.

One rule to follow when dealing with periods of unemployment or underemployment of less than one year is "Simply don't show it." Thus, if you were unemployed for the period from January 21, 2004 until August 1, 2004, your resume would show the following:

WORK EXPERIENCE

2004 to Present	Senior Project Engineer	
	Deltoid Corporation	
1980 to 2004	Project Engineer	
	Syntaf Corporation	

There is no written rule that says the employment resume must list all periods of employment and unemployment. To the contrary, the resume is intended to be a brief sketch or synopsis of one's employment credentials. Why then list information that is not relevant to one's professional qualifications and which may have an adverse effect on one's employment candidacy? In my opinion, to list this information is utter foolishness.

This is not to say that I believe in dishonesty. To the contrary, I believe that there is a time and place to disclose this information to the prospective employer. For example, if at the time of the employment interview you are asked to complete a formal employment application that requires that you account for all time spent, by all means don't try to hide this period of unemployment. Additionally, at an appropriate time in the interview process (preferably after you have had an opportunity to interest the prospective employer in your qualifications), you should volunteer this information to the interviewer (I suggest the employment or human resources manager) along with an appropriate explanation. In fact, if you don't share this information with the company and should they accidentally discover this information during a subsequent background investigation or reference check, such action might result in the decision not to make you an employment offer. At best it would cause feelings of distrust and uneasiness about your integrity. Therefore, should you elect not to show this information on the resume itself, be sure to voluntarily disclose it at an appropriate point in the interview process.

If the period of unemployment or underemployment extends to a year or longer, there are two suggested ways of dealing with this problem period on the resume. Assume that the period in question is December 12, 1994 until January 3, 1996. Here are the two ways:

Example 1:

2003 to Present	Senior Project Engineer Delray Corporation
2001 to 2003	Personal (will discuss during interview)
1999 to 2001	Project Engineer Johnson & Lipford Corporation

Example 2:

2003 to Present	Senior Project Engineer Delray Corporation
1999 to 2001	Project Engineer Johnson & Lipford Corporation

In Example 1 there is no attempt to hide an unexplained time gap on the resume. The designation as "personal," although raising some questions in the mind of the employment professional, leaves a somewhat neutral feeling. There is simply not sufficient information provided for the employment manager to make a decision one way or another. Chances are if you were unemployed or underemployed, you will at least have an opportunity to discuss this with the employment manager and offer a reasonable explanation. Otherwise, had you shown this information on the resume, you might well have been screened out without the opportunity to explain the circumstances.

Example 2 simply omits this information from the resume entirely, including dates. Here again the argument that could be used to defend this intentional omission is that the resume is intended to summarize the highlights of one's employment credentials only. It is not intended to provide complete information as in the case of the formal employment application form, which requires that complete information be furnished.

EDUCATIONAL DEFICIT

For purposes of this discussion, the term "educational deficit" means lacking the requisite educational qualifications normally required by employers in filling the type of professional position that you are seeking. There are still many employers who get hung up when the applicant does not have a college degree, does not have the appropriate degree level (B.S., M.S., Ph.D.), or does not have a degree in the appropriate field. This is one of those employment facts of life that must be dealt with, however, if you expect to have the opportunity to interview and discuss your qualifications in person.

The first step in dealing with this particular resume problem is to determine the magnitude of your problem. If most employers require a B.S. degree in Mechanical Engineering and you have no degree at all, your educational deficit represents a fairly major stumbling block. If, on the other hand, most employers prefer a B.S. degree in Mechanical Engineering and your degree is a B.S. in Electro/Mechanical Engineering, you do not have a major problem. In fact, in the latter example, you probably have no problem at all.

Another type of educational deficit problem is having an unusual degree with which most employers are unfamiliar. An example of this would be a B.S. degree in Pulp and Paper Technology. The term "technology" suggests that it is a science degree, but where is the emphasis? Is it heavily chemistry oriented, biology oriented, or more oriented toward engineering? Another example is a B.S. degree in Engineering Technology. Here again several questions are raised in the mind of the resume reader. Is this a heavy applications-oriented degree light on engineering theory? Which of the traditional engineering educations does this degree most resemble—chemical engineering, mechanical engineering, electrical engineering, or civil engineering?

Each of these educational deficits is slightly different and requires, therefore, a slightly different solution. Let's examine these situations one at a time and arrive at some possible answers.

The first basic premise to keep in mind is that most employment professionals are primarily interested in whether the individual can perform the position in question. Stated differently, does the candidate have the necessary understanding of the technical principles necessary to solve the more complex problems he or she will be called upon to address? Is there reasonable evidence, based upon past experience and accomplishments, that the candidate has the technical qualifications to perform the job at a reasonably high level and make important contributions to the business? Questions of this type are paramount in the mind of the employment manager when attempting to gauge the technical competence of an individual employment applicant. Believe it or not, in most cases educational qualifications are secondary to experience and accomplishment. This is especially true in markets where certain skills are in great demand and the supply of qualified candidates is limited. Unfortunately, it is less true where there are many candidates but few openings. In the latter case, the probabilities are high that proper educational credentials will play a much greater role and will become a primary factor in the resume screening process.

Not having a degree, having the wrong degree, or not having the right level of degree in most cases is far from fatal to your employment candidacy assuming you have the right experience and can cite demonstrated accomplishments. If you can impress the prospective employer sufficiently with your actual experience and accomplishments in the field in question, the fact that you have an educational deficit may be overlooked or at least substantially discounted as a factor in determining whether you should be invited in for an interview.

The key to dealing with this type of educational deficit is to cite your experience and accomplishments near the beginning of the resume with your educational credentials shown later. Both the chronological resume format (see Chapters 6 and 8) and the functional resume format (see Chapter 10) provide for such positioning of your educational credentials. If your resume is to be successful in overcoming this educational handicap, however, the experience and accomplishments sections of your resume must be well developed. You are counting on these portions of your resume to convince a prospective employer that you are well worth interviewing even though you do not possess the educational credentials required. Chapters 6, 8, and 10 will provide you with a great deal of help in developing the experience and accomplishments sections of your resume and should help to maximize your resume's effectiveness.

Possession of an unusual degree, with which many prospective employers will be unfamiliar, requires a slightly different tactic. In this case, educational credentials should also be positioned later in the resume (following description of experience and accomplishments); however, some reasonable description of the degree will also be needed to provide the resume reader with a better understanding of the degree. Where possible, and without stretching the truth, some correlation should be cited with more commonly known degrees and academic disciplines. For example, if a B.S. degree in Pulp and Paper Technology has a strong chemical engineering concentration, it might be shown on the resume as:

B.S. Pulp and Paper Technology (heavy emphasis in Chemical Engineering)

or

B.S. Pulp and Paper Technology (approximates B.S. ChE)

Handling the degree description in this fashion helps the resume reader to associate the degree with a more traditional and commonly understood academic curriculum, usually making the reader feel more comfortable.

In extreme cases of educational deficit, you may not want to list education on the resume at all. For example, let's assume that following high school you took some trade school courses in mechanical drafting. Let's assume further that you are bright and have read several engineering textbooks on your own. Further, you have 25 years of experience, starting as a draftsman and advancing into the professional engineering ranks. Your current job title is Senior Project Engineer, and you are handling relatively sophisticated engineering projects related to the design, installation, and start-up of multimillion-dollar steel-rolling equipment. Even though you are heavily experienced and exceptionally well qualified, showing that you lack a formal degree in mechanical engineering could prove to place you in a disadvantaged position and cause you to be screened out automatically with no opportunity to demonstrate your capability through a personal interview. In such cases I strongly recommend that you exclude the education section of the resume entirely.

Here again, I am not proposing that you be dishonest or devious in your approach. On the contrary, you should volunteer the fact that you do not have a formal degree during the course of the employment interviews when people will have the opportunity to explore your technical knowledge and competence and to satisfy themselves that you have what it takes to perform the job. At least you will have the benefit of these discussions rather than being arbitrarily screened out on the basis of having no degree.

EXPERIENCE DEFICIT

In this discussion, the term "experience deficit" means that the individual lacks either sufficient experience or the appropriate type of experience normally required by employers in filling the position that the candidate is seeking. By sufficient experience I mean the required number of years of experience. We will explore both of these experience deficits in some detail, and I will provide you with some helpful advice in effectively dealing with them.

The experience deficit is perhaps one of the most difficult resume problems to handle. Most employers put considerably more weight on experience than any other factors when judging a candidate's qualifications for employment. The professional employment community has long subscribed to the belief that the best single predictor of future success is past experience coupled with past success. Thus it is felt that there is considerably less risk involved in hiring someone who has actually performed the work in question than in hiring someone who has never performed this type of work before.

The problem with this thinking is that it does not take into consideration the individual's desire to do the work or the level of motivation required to do the work at an exceptionally high level of quality and/or volume. In other words this philosophy ignores the potential for individual productivity. It ignores the fact that some individuals, who have minimal or no experience but have sufficient technical knowledge and training, may well have the motivation and desire to far outproduce their experienced counterparts! Although most employment professionals are willing to concede this possibility, they are still faced with the dilemma of somehow distinguishing such individuals from the large population of applicants. Second, there is the problem of convincing the line manager to whom the potential employee would be reporting that he or she should consider interviewing someone who clearly does not have the experience called for in the candidate specification. These are two very difficult hurdles to overcome and, if there are sufficient experienced candidates from which to choose, most employment professionals will not even try. In such cases, it is simply not an efficient use of their time.

The truth of the matter is that the employment resume itself can do little to overcome this particular problem. Attempting to establish personal contact through a mutual acquaintance with the individual having the opening is the best-known method for overcoming this barrier. Second, the cover letter that accompanies the employment resume provides some limited opportunity to convince the prospective employer that you are "short on experience but long on motivation and desire." From the resume standpoint, however, there are some things that you can do to at least improve your chances. Here are some basic ideas.

In this case the functional resume format (see Chapter 10) is clearly your best bet. The following minor modifications to this format, however, are in order:

1. Eliminate the Summary section at the beginning of the resume. If you do not have appropriate experience, there is no point drawing attention to this fact at the beginning of the resume.

2. In the place of the summary statement, substitute an objective statement setting forth your job-hunting objective. Care should be taken that this objective is not too narrowly stated. This could serve to screen you

out from other related opportunities that could be of
interest to you. See Chapter 6 for specific instructions
on how to prepare an effective objective statement.

3. Instead of the heading Major Accomplishments, use
the heading Key Qualifications. (Instructions for
preparing this section of the resume follow.)

Some thoughtful analysis at this point can make a considerable difference in the effectiveness of your resume.
Therefore, make a careful list of the probable qualifications
that an employer will be looking for in a good candidate.
Since it is already a foregone conclusion that your experience is inadequate, you should focus your analysis on other
factors. In order to get started, try answering the following
questions:

1. *Technical Knowledge:*

What specific technical knowledge is required to perform
this job? Describe in the space provided below:

_____

_____

_____

_____

Are you proficient in any of these areas of required knowledge? If so, which areas? List below:

_____

_____

_____

_____

_____

How did you obtain this proficiency (education, hobbies, other)? Describe below:

_____

_____

_____

_____

_____

2. *Technical Skills:*

What specific technical skills are required to perform this type job successfully? (for example: mathematical, statistical, analytical, instrumental analysis, oral communications, written communications.) Which are the most critical skills? List below:

_____

_____

_____

_____

_____

Are you proficient in any of these critical technical skills? If so, which ones? List below:

_____

_____

_____

_____

How did you acquire these skills? What have you done to attain this level of proficiency? Describe below:

_____

_____

_____

_____

_____

_____

Now that you have completed this exercise, go back and review your answers. Try to place yourself in the role of an employment manager. Which of these areas of knowledge and/or skill are the most impressive and convincing? Which might tempt you to give serious consideration to the candidate even though he or she lacks the specific experience required?

Returning to the functional resume format (see Chapter 10), substitute these key technical knowledge and skills as headings in place of the functional headings normally used on the functional resume format. A typical key qualifications section might read as follows:

Key Qualifications:

Instrumental Techniques—Proficient in a wide range of instrumental techniques including gas chromatography, ultrasonic scanning, electron microscopy. Over 60 credit hours in Physical Chemistry and Physics dealing with the use of instruments and instrumental techniques.

Biological Science—Thoroughly schooled in the field of Biological Science with over 30 credit hours in Zoology. Worked as laboratory assistant to Dr. Charles Von Zeit, world renowned in the area of DNA genetic research.

Written Communications—Excellent written communications ability. Have written several technical articles for *Biological Science Magazine* summarizing Dr. Von Zeit's experimental findings in the field of genetic research. Served as editor of college newspaper.

With this style of organization the reader's attention is drawn away from the fact that you lack specific work experience and is instead focused on those areas of job-related knowledge and skills critical to the successful performance of the position in question. This should be sufficient to carry you through to the interview stage.

CHRONIC HANDICAP

For purposes of this discussion, the term "chronic handicap" means a physical impairment that interferes with the performance of a normal life function: that is, seeing, hearing, walking, using arms or hands, exercising muscular control, and so on. This terminology also applies to diseases or medical disorders of life-threatening proportion (cancer, heart disease, M.S., etc.) as well as those that are temporarily disabling (asthma, migraine headache, chronic allergy, etc.).

The subject of chronic handicap is a difficult one to deal with from a resume perspective since these handicaps are individually unique and manifest themselves in symptoms dependent upon the individual case in question. Due to this variance in severity it is difficult to generalize about any one particular type of physical handicap. I therefore attempt to deal with the question of severity rather than to simply lump similar conditions into a single category.

Federal law prohibits employers from discriminating against the employment of individuals on the basis of physical handicap. Even when such a handicap may impair the individual's ability to perform the job at normal productivity, employers are prohibited from using the handicap as an excuse not to hire. In such cases, under the law, the employer is required to provide "reasonable accommodation" to allow the handicapped individual to perform the job. The term "reasonable accommodation" is interpreted to include minor modification and adaptation of the work environment to allow the handicapped person to function in a normal manner. Thus adaptations such as special desks, chairs, ramps, and modified rest room facilities are today commonplace.

From a resume standpoint, the biggest issue confronting the handicapped person is whether to disclose the fact that he or she is physically handicapped in the resume. This is not an easy question to answer.

There is little doubt in my mind that discrimination on the basis of physical handicap is still practiced today. People who are severely handicapped can readily attest to this statement if they have tried time and time again to find meaningful employment. I am convinced, however, that such discrimination is rooted in productivity issues rather than in disdain or discomfort with the handicap itself. There is genuine concern on the part of the employer, or more specifically the hiring manager, that the individual may not be able to perform the job and that as a result department productivity will fall. Since the department manager's performance evaluation and salary increases are based on the overall productivity of the department, it is important that the most productive workers available are hired. Thus, the issue is principally one of productivity. Managers would much prefer to hire a highly motivated and productive handicapped person than hire a nonhandicapped individual who is poorly motivated and nonproductive.

In my opinion, a good deal of discrimination based on physical handicaps stems from general ignorance of the disease and/or condition. The idea of cancer or heart attack, for example, conjures thoughts of fatality in the mind of the employer. It also brings to mind the thought of lost productivity and long periods of absence from work. Although there may be reasonably high probabilities for both of these in the most chronic of cases, there are substantially increasing numbers of individuals with these diseases who can expect to live a fairly normal existence thanks to numerous advances in medical technology. From the employment standpoint, however, unless specific information is provided concerning future prognosis, employers will tend to think the worst, and many will avoid the issue entirely by moving on to the next resume.

I have a recommendation regarding how to handle your physical handicap from a resume standpoint. The answer is a fairly simple one. It is principally related to your level of comfort with handling your handicap in an interview situation. If you feel fairly comfortable with your handicap and are not easily embarrassed by someone else's (namely, the interviewer's) surprise or feelings of awkwardness, *by all means do not list your physical handicap on your resume!* If, however, you are severely handicapped and feel compelled to advise the employer of this in advance, then do so, *but not in the resume!* Instead, make use of the cover letter to accomplish this objective. Be sure, however, to offer a fairly detailed and accurate description of your physical limitations and how these relate to your ability to perform the job. If you must disclose your handicap to employers, then don't leave them guessing concerning your ability to perform the job. If you do, they'll assume the worst.

If you elect to make use of the cover letter to disclose your physical handicap, make sure that you don't overdo it. Remember, the employer is really interested in your qualifications for the job. It is important, therefore, that you start the letter by very convincingly summarizing your qualifications for the position so that you create interest on the part of the reader in your employment candidacy. Introduce the subject of your handicap along with a frank description of your limitations and some convincing evidence of how this condition will not prohibit your performance of the job for which you have applied.

CHANGING CAREERS

Changing careers or fields is one of the more difficult problem areas from the standpoint of resume preparation. The degree of difficulty, however, is related to how far along the individual is in their current career and their overall qualifications for the new field of endeavor. For those who are early in the occupational life cycle, say a year or two, changing fields can be a fairly simple matter (assuming reasonable qualifications). Conversely, for someone who has invested several years in a particular occupational endeavor and who then elects to make a switch, the barriers can be substantial.

Here again it is difficult to generalize since there are several variables that affect one's ability to make an occupational change. Perhaps the single greatest factor is the law of supply and demand. When an individual elects to move into a new field that is categorized by high demand and a limited number of qualified applicants (computer programming, for example), the transition can be fairly easy, provided he or she has the appropriate technical qualifications. By contrast, transition to a field of little demand and an oversupply of qualified candidates (eg., forestry) can be extremely difficult unless the applicant has some unique credentials or has personal contacts in the field.

In addition to supply and demand, the relative qualifications of the individual wishing to make a career change are extremely important to success probability. By "relative" I mean the individual's credentials as compared to the employment qualifications of the other candidates with whom he or she must compete. Obviously, for individuals with strong qualifications the transition can be fairly smooth one. In such cases, however, the individual does not have a resume problem to address.

The obvious drawback to changing careers from a resume standpoint is lack of specific experience in the new field. Although educationally you may be well qualified, the fact is that you will probably be competing with individuals who have equivalent educational credentials and also have the added advantage of direct experience in the field. In such a case you are obviously at a competitive disadvantage.

There is an added dimension to making a career switch that you must also take into consideration. The fact that you elected to pursue a different career path initially may cause some understandable concern on the part of prospective employers. They are going to wonder why you have elected to make this change. Unless properly addressed, there may be a lot of negative concern surrounding your decision. Some of these feelings center on the following notions:

1. *Judgment.* There will be concerns about your judgment. The decision to change directions implies that you did not think through your initial decision properly. Will this be indicative of the judgment you exercise on the job?

2. *Patience.* Employers may question why you didn't stick it out. Some may deduce from your decision to make a change that you are a person who is unable to exercise patience, constraint, or self-control—that you may have a tendency to abandon things when the going gets tough.

3. *Maturity.* Some employers may interpret your actions as a sign of immaturity. They may be concerned that you are somewhat impulsive and don't think things through before acting.

These feelings must be addressed in a positive manner if you expect your resume to be effective in leading to the interview stage of the employment process. Some logical, rational explanation of your decision must be offered.

As with a chronic handicap, the most logical place to present your reason for making a job change is the cover letter that accompanies your employment resume. A brief, logical explanation of your rationale for making this change should be provided at the beginning of the letter. Be sure not to dwell on all the negative reasons that caused you to make this transition. Pick only one or two and then quickly change the focus of the letter to the positive reasons that have attracted you to the new field as well as your qualifications for entry. The following is a brief example:

Having watched the rapid decline of the steel industry and realizing the long-range implications from a career standpoint, I have elected to pursue opportunities elsewhere.

I have observed, with great interest, the rapid expansion and growth of the pharmaceutical industry in recent years. Your company, Stanford Pharmaceutical, in particular, has made great strides in the development and introduction of several new drugs used in the treatment of malignant melanomas. I find this area of research interesting and

*exciting since I was a research assistant to Dr. James R.
Dwight, a renowned cancer researcher, while a graduate student at the University of Pennsylvania.*

As you can see in this example, the explanation offered to
the prospective employer for making a career change is
brief, to-the-point, and very plausible. You will also note
how quickly the transition is made to the new area of career
interest and the tie-in with the applicant's qualifications for
the new job objective. You are encouraged to be equally brief
and to-the-point—don't waste time before quickly moving
the reader's attention to your job objective and employment
qualifications.

In most cases, the single biggest problem in making a career change is the lack of specific experience in the new
field or occupational specialty. This was referred to earlier
in this chapter as "experience deficit." Although as the say-
ing goes, "there is no substitute for experience," there are
some steps that you can take to address this problem and to
improve the overall effectiveness of your resume. Rather
than repeat these recommendations here, however, I suggest
you refer to the section entitled Experience Deficit earlier in
this chapter.

13

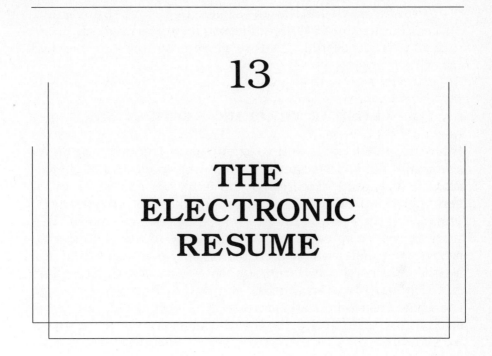

THE ELECTRONIC RESUME

Reengineering of work processes, and the resultant rush by businesses to electronically automate much of their repetitive, nonvalue-adding work, has not escaped the employment functions of most corporations. Many human resources functions, hard hit by corporate downsizing, have adapted computer automation as an answer to the growing demand on their functions to do more work with reduced staffs and fewer resources.

Recent research shows that better than 95% of all larger employers today make use of software systems in the identification and selection of people for positions in their firms. These systems are known as resume management and applicant tracking systems.

Clearly there has been rapid growth in the use of computers as a replacement for people in the reading, storage, and retrieval of employment resumes. This fact alone provides compelling reason for the job seeker to become knowledge-able of the guidelines for producing resumes that can be efficiently read, stored, and retrieved by modern resume tracking technology.

HOW RESUME TRACKING SYSTEMS WORK

When received by an employment department using a resume management system, the resume may either be electronically posted directly to the employer's website or, if sent by "snail mail," read through an electronic scanner. The electronic resume image created by the scanner is then transferred to a computer using OCR (optical character recognition) software, which converts the resume text into a universal computer language known as ASCII. Stored as ASCII text, this allows other computers that are tied into the same resume database system to electronically access, search, retrieve, and print out the resume text of qualified candidates.

The process used by employers to identify the resumes of qualified candidates in the computerized resume tracking system is known as *keyword search.* By inputting a combination of keywords (e.g., project engineer, paper machines, towel, tissue, design, installation, start-up, forming devices, transpiration dryers, mechanical engineering, B.S.M.E.), the computer searches out those resumes having the prescribed combination of keywords contained in them. These keywords are most often the same words as contained in the candidate specification being used by the employer to conduct the employment search.

When using the system to conduct a search, the employer can either expand or contract this list of keywords to yield a different size population of qualified candidates. For example, if the number of resumes initially identified is too voluminous, by expanding the list of keywords to include additional "qualifiers," the number of resumes matching the keyword criteria can be reduced to a more manageable number. Conversely, by decreasing the list of keywords being used to conduct the resume search, the employer can expand the number of qualified candidates identified by the system.

THE IMPORTANCE OF KEYWORDS

Having your resume contain the right keywords is absolutely critical to the computer's identification and selection of your resume for the type of job you are seeking. To assure success, prepare your resume by being sure that those keywords, most likely used by employers to identify candidates for this type of work, are incorporated into your resume document right from the start.

Most resume tracking systems, when conducting a keyword search of resumes stored in their database, tend to "key in" primarily on nouns. Thus, it is important, when constructing your resume, to be sure that the resume document is well stocked with specific, concrete nouns that describe the areas in which you have experience and expertise.

THINKING LIKE THE EMPLOYER

To be sure that your resume fully captures the keywords that are required for your resume to be selected as part of a computerized keyword search, it is important for you to think like the employer. Pretend you are the employer, and that you are conducting a keyword search of a resume database to fill the target position you are seeking. What keywords would you input into the computer to identify candidates having the basic qualifications for this position?

Here are some guideline questions that might prove helpful in determining what keywords should be included:

1. What is the industry(ies) you have targeted for purposes of your job search? (Examples: steel, chemical processing, pharmaceutical, paper.)

2. By what alternate names is this industry known (if any)? (Example: The paper industry is sometimes referred to as the "pulp and paper industry" or the "forest products industry.")

3. What is the business function in which you would be working (e.g., accounting, finance, manufacturing, human resources)?

4. What synonyms might be used by employers as alternative titles for these business functions? For example:

(a) Human resources could also be called "personnel" or "employee relations."

(b) Manufacturing is also known as "operations."

(c) Distribution might also be called "logistics."

(d) Purchasing is often referred to as "procurement."

(e) Product development and "process development" are often used interchangeably.

5. What are the major areas of accountability (or subfunctions) for which you would be accountable in your target position (and for which employers may be looking in their keyword search)?

For example:

(a) Human resources can include subfunctions or principal accountability areas such as internal staffing, external staffing (or employment), training, development, management development, organization design, compensation, benefits, labor relations, safety, security, employee wellness.

(b) Subfunctions of finance might be international finance, domestic finance, money and banking, financial planning, financial analysis, investor relations.

(c) Subfunctions of technology might encompass areas such as basic research, product development, process development, analytical testing, technology transfer.

(d) Accounting subfunctions could include auditing, cost accounting, taxes, payroll, accounts payable, accounts receivable.

6. What specific skill or knowledge areas are normally required by a successful candidate to perform this type of job? Examples might be:

(a) Statistical process control.

(b) Design of experiments.

(c) Behavioral interviewing techniques.

(d) Reengineering.

(e) Total quality.

(f) Wet lay technology.

(g) Transpiration drying equipment.

(h) Computer modeling.

(i) Knowledge of WordPerfect.

7. For a management position, what words best describe the organizational environment and management style sought? (Assume an employer is seeking someone who has managed in a participative, team environment.) Examples are:

(a) keywords describing organizational environment:

(1) Participative management.

(2) Team environment.

(3) High-performance work team.

(4) Sociotechnical systems.

(b) keywords describing management style:

(1) Coach.

(2) Teacher.

(3) Facilitator.

(4) Enabler of others.

Thus, if you were an employer seeking a mechanical project engineer with five or more years experience in the design, installation, and start-up of a tissue paper machine utilizing transpiration drying technology, keywords would likely include: B.S.M.E., mechanical, project engineer, design, installation, start-up, tissue, paper machine, transpiration drying.

Each of these keywords is critical to your selection by the resume tracking system. If any keywords are missing from your resume, but are all contained in the resume of a competitor job applicant, you are likely to be passed over in favor of the other candidate, despite the fact that you may well be the better qualified person.

The computer is totally impersonal and impartial, making no exceptions when doing a keyword search. A keyword is either there or it is not. If the keyword is present, your resume will be selected. If the keyword is missing, the computer will simply pass your resume by in search of resumes containing the keyword it has been programmed to select.

The lesson for the job seeker is simple. Make sure you carefully think through the list of keywords most likely to be chosen by employers using wordsearch to find someone with your qualifications, and make sure that these keywords are in your resume!

KEYWORDS SUMMARY

One approach to capturing these important keywords in the resume is the growing use of the "keywords summary." Such a summary might be positioned at the beginning of the resume, perhaps immediately following the statement of the job search objective. Although this is the preferred location, it could also be positioned later in the resume immediately following work experience or education. Titles for use with this section vary, but might include: Qualifications Summary, Key Skills, Functional Expertise, Technical Skills. The specific heading probably matters less than the keywords contained in the summary itself. It is, after all, these keywords that the computer will be seeking.

Using the project engineering position previously described as our example, the following might be incorporated into the resume in the form of a keyword summary.

Technical Expertise

Have technical expertise in the following areas:

- Paper machines.
- Transpiration dryers.
- Yankee dryers.
- Control systems.
- Wet lay technology.
- Tissue machines.
- After dryers.
- Beloit machines.
- Twin wire formers.
- Wet end formation.
- Sheet formation.
- Black Clawson machines.

Another example of how such a keyword summary might be incorporated into a resume is illustrated next. This resume section, for example, might routinely be placed in an administrative assistant's resume, where it is commonly known that such positions frequently require extensive computer software skills.

Computer Software Proficiency

- MS Office 2000.
- MS Excel 2000.
- HTML Tools.
- Windows Me.
- MS PowerPoint 2000.
- MS Word 2000.
- PageMaker 7.5.
- Adobe Photoshop 6.5.

When considering the possible creation of a keyword summary on the resume, a good rule to follow is first to utilize the conventional resume formats as described earlier in this book to write your resume. Then, once written, carefully scan the resume to determine whether or not you were able to incorporate all of your keywords naturally as part of this conventional resume design. In most cases, if the resume has been well written, you will find that you have been able to do so.

When this is not the case, however, think of an appropriate resume section heading that might be used to incorporate those keywords missed in the original resume design. Perhaps a good catch-all might be "Additional Skill Areas," for example:

Additional Skill Areas

Additional areas of expertise include the following:

- Design of experiments.
- MRP 2.
- Reengineering.
- Statistical process control.
- SAP R/3.
- Total Quality Management.
- Just-in-time Management.
- ISO 9002.
- Dry forming technology.

OTHER TIPS

Using relatively sophisticated word search software, most modern resume tracking systems today have the ability to extract key qualifications and skills from many different resume styles. Because of their common usage, however, both the chronological (narrative and linear forms) and functional resumes, as described earlier in this book, are formats that lend themselves particularly well to these electronic resume systems. The developers of these systems have paid particular attention to creating systems that would be particularly adept at handling these style resumes due to their wide usage.

Beyond the standard formatting of chronological and functional style resumes, however, there are some additional tips that you will want to heed in assuring that your resume will serve you well in the world of computer-based resume management, including:

- Use standard 8½" × 11" white or off-white paper (avoid other darker or off-colors).
- Use common typefaces such as Times, Arial, Courier, Helvetica, Palatino (avoid out-of-the-ordinary fonts).
- Provide original copy using high-quality printing that is crisp and neat (preferably a laser printed original—high quality photocopy, although not preferred, is acceptable).
- Use 12 point font size, although 10 and 14 point are normally acceptable.
- Minimize use of bold highlighting and underlining; avoid unusual effects such as shadows, reverse typeset (i.e., white type on dark background), and so on.
- Keep it simple—sticking to text only and avoiding use of graphics, tables, charts, and the like.
- Follow standard resume formats employing common resume section headings (as already described in detail earlier in this book).
- Describe your qualifications and skills in specific, concrete terms (avoiding vague or broad-sweeping statements).

- Use standard terminology when describing your field, specialty, type of work performed, and skills.
- Scan your resume carefully to be sure you have made effective use of keywords that will most likely be used to identify candidates for the type of position you are seeking.

Once you are satisfied that you have prepared a resume that will serve you well in the new electronic age, you may want to further explore the many new job search options now available to you using electronic means. Knowing how to get your resume out onto the Internet, for example, will expose your qualifications to the thousands of employers now using on-line systems to identify employment candidates.

14

PHYSICAL APPEARANCE OF THE RESUME

The physical appearance of the resume is an extremely important factor, since the resume almost always represents the first contact with a prospective employer. It is imperative, therefore, that it create a favorable impression.

A well-organized, concise, neat resume will go a long way toward achieving that important favorable first impression: The candidate is neat, well-organized, and concise. Conversely, a resume with ragged margins, misspelled words, and coffee stains will leave a very different impression.

Review the sample resumes included in Chapters 7, 9, and 11. Note the neatness, organization, concise layout, and overall readability. Copy is well-spaced, margins are even, and key areas are thoughtfully highlighted with capital letters and effective underlining.

Once the final draft of your resume has been completed and is ready for typing, if you are not skilled at word processing, seek out a professional typist and have the job done right. Remember, you will be counting solely on your resume to create a sufficiently favorable impression to lead to an employment interview. It is well worth the extra money to achieve this important objective.

If you do not know a professional typist, check the Yellow Pages of your telephone directory. Such services are normally listed under the headings of "Word Processing Services," "Secretarial Services," or "Typing Services." Do some competitive shopping by phone; you will find that fees can vary substantially. You may also wish to use the same typing service for typing cover letters later in your job-hunting campaign. Take care to select a good one with reasonable fees.

Be sure that resume typing is done on a top-quality word processor (using a laser or other comparable quality printer). Select neat, clean, conventional type and have the resume typed on a high-quality, white bond paper. Your professional typist can usually advise you on the best style of type to use and the proper grade and color of paper for reproduction purposes.

Before trotting off to the printer or your local copy service, be sure to carefully proofread your resume. Make sure that the original is neat, well-spaced, uncluttered, and easy to read. Check carefully for proper punctuation and spelling. If you do not have a high level of confidence in your own punctuation and spelling skills, it may be a good idea to have a friend who is proficient in these skills give your resume the once-over prior to going to print.

Printing should be done by a professional using quality photo-offset printing equipment. In many quarters, high-quality Xerox copies or copies printed on a high-quality laser printer will be just as acceptable. Printing should be done on quality bond paper that is off-white or white in color.

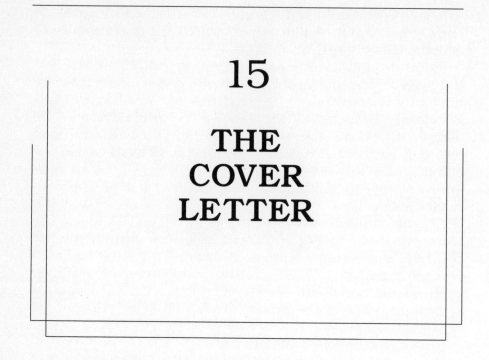

15

THE
COVER
LETTER

Quite a bit has been written on the subject of cover letters and their importance to the employment process. Much has been said about the supposed power and mystique of these letters as they relate to an effective job-hunting campaign. Some claim that the cover letter is more important than the resume itself. Proponents of this viewpoint argue that the resume alone is nothing more than a sterile document and that the cover letter is the instrument that compels the reader to act. It is sometimes argued that without the cover letter many resumes would, in fact, go unread. I do not support this contention.

The *truth* of the matter is that most employment professionals pay little initial attention to the cover letter. In the course of a year, the professional employment manager may frequently read in excess of 20,000 resumes along with accompanying cover letters. Considerable experience in reading these letters has led most employment professionals to conclude that most cover letters add little meaningful, new information. Most are of the "broadcast" variety and are redundant to the actual resume. Faced with thousands of applications, therefore, valuable time would be lost if the employment manager were to read each and every cover letter thoroughly. From the employment manager's standpoint, it is much more important to proceed with the reading of the resume, since this is the document that details the specifics of the candidate's background and qualifications, and as such, is used for comparing these qualifications with the candidate specification of the position that the employment manager is attempting to fill.

When first glancing at a cover letter the employment manager is usually looking to see whether the letter is a mass mailed "broadcast" form letter, or whether it contains something of a more personal and specific nature. Care is taken to ferret out those letters that indicate a firsthand association with the company, that is, friends of employees and executives, shareholders, local community leaders, and so forth. Each of the aforementioned categories usually requires a more personalized response. Care is thus taken to read such cover letters with greater diligence so that an inappropriate form response is not sent. Letters of a less personal type such as general broadcast letters, however, receive very little attention from the employment professional.

Admittedly there are some cases when a cover letter has been particularly cleverly written and may heighten the interest of the reader. Such letters are extremely rare, however, and the reader's interest is normally increased only because of the relationship between the candidate's qualifications and the position that the employer is attempting to fill. Additionally, when the resume has been sent to someone other than the employment manager (e.g., the director of marketing, research and development manager, personnel director, or some other executive), the cover letter may serve to increase interest in the applicant's employment candidacy.

In general, the cover letter serves as a business letter used for transmitting one's resume to a prospective employer. The purpose of the cover letter is to create sufficient interest on the part of the reader to warrant further reading of the employment resume. If written particularly well, it can also convey a sense of value to the employer. This is particularly true if the writer emphasizes his or her ability to contribute something of importance or value to the prospective employer.

TYPES OF COVER LETTERS

There are essentially four types of cover letters used for transmittal of the employment resume. They are as follows:

1. Broadcast letters—to employers.
2. Broadcast letters—to executive search firms.
3. Employment advertising responses.
4. Personal referral letters.

Although there are some similarities between these various types of cover letters, there are also some differences. You should be aware of these differences and should tailor your cover letter appropriately. Please take a few minutes to review the sample cover letters contained in Chapter 16 of this book. You will note that there are five sample letters for each of the four cover-letter categories. We now examine each of these different letters in greater detail and provide you with the necessary instructions for the development of interesting and effective cover letters.

The Broadcast Letter—To Employers

The broadcast letter is the transmittal letter used by the job applicant to mass mail his or her resume to a number of prospective employers. Although the technique of mass mailing one's resume is frequently used by many if not most job seekers, it is also known for not being a particularly effective technique. Experts generally agree that a favorable response of 2 to 5 percent is considered an excellent response rate. I have personally been involved in several outplacement programs and have observed the results of mass-mailing campaigns on a firsthand basis. This 2 to 5 percent return rate is borne out by my own experience.

Thus in a broadcast campaign, where the individual mails his or her resume to 500 companies, he or she can expect to elicit favorable response from only 10 to 25 employers. After the initial phone screen by the employer, however, these numbers may be quickly reduced to three or four actual employment interviews. This would appear to be a tremendous amount of effort for a minimal result. However, if such a campaign results in an interview for the "perfect" position, this effort will have paid off handsomely.

Design of an effective cover letter for a broadcast campaign need not be a cumbersome task. Essentially, the letter is comprised of the following components:

1. Return address.
2. Employer's address.
3. Salutation.
4. Introductory paragraph.
5. Statement of purpose.
6. Brief summary of qualifications.
7. Reason for making change (optional).
8. Salary requirements (optional).
9. Geographical preferences/restrictions (optional).
10. Request for response.

Wherever possible, it is preferable to mail letters of this type to a specific individual within the corporation. This individual should be at a reasonably high level in the corporation and should be within the discipline or business function most closely related to the position for which you are applying. Thus if you are an Engineering professional, you should mail your letter to the manager or director of Engineering. Similarly, if you are a human resources professional seeking a managerial position, you should be writing to the director of human resources. An individual who is already at the director level, however, should be writing to the company president or chief operating officer.

Notice that I have not recommended that you send your resume to the human resources department or to the attention of the employment manager. The reason for this is simple.

Since I have been a corporate human resources executive, I most certainly am not suggesting that you circumvent the human resources function, but the human resources manager or the employment manager may have knowledge of only those positions that are *currently* open. He or she may not be aware of the positions that the director, chief operating officer, or other line manager is thinking about filling. A good resume, appropriately timed, may actually trigger the line manager to advise the human resources manager of the opening and, at the same time, deliver your resume along with a request that you be scheduled for an employment interview. Even if the line manager does not take the time to read your resume, chances are it will be forwarded to the employment department for a response. In any event, directing your resume to the top functional officer in your discipline gives your campaign an added dimension and increases the likelihood of a favorable response.

If your employment search is intentionally limited to a specific industry, one key source for executive names is the trade directory for that industry. Although some industries do not have directories, many, in fact, do. If your industry does have a trade association, a simple phone call in many cases is all that is necessary to obtain a trade directory. Additionally, if you are currently employed, chances are that your research or marketing libraries will already have a copy of the trade directory that you can use. Also, if your funds are limited, and you do not wish to pay the cost of such directories, you could try your local or county library.

In addition to industry trade directories, professional associations frequently publish membership rosters. These rosters contain the names, addresses, and titles of various members. Such membership rosters can be extremely helpful in obtaining the names and titles that you need, adding a personal dimension to your cover letter.

Another approach that can be used to develop a mailing list to include specific names, titles, and addresses is personal contact. Make a thorough list of every professional acquaintance who you know or have met. Call them and ask for the names, titles, and addresses of the appropriate functional manager from their own company. In addition, ask them for contacts at additional companies as well. Although from the same industry, these contacts need not be from the same professional specialty. They, in turn, can be used as contacts to find out the names, titles, and addresses of the appropriate individuals within their own companies. Although this is a time-consuming task, it is far better than simply mailing your resume to a title or to the human resources department. Additionally, it is possible that these contacts will be aware of specific openings and provide you with some direct leads!

You will note in reviewing the five sample broadcast letters to employers in Chapter 16 that although the exact same format is used in showing return address, employer's address, and salutation, the introductory paragraphs are all different. There is no standard or uniform way to introduce the subject of the letter to the reader. This fact stresses the individuality of letter writing. All are quite effective introductory paragraphs, however, and any one would serve its purpose effectively.

One fairly uniform component of each of these five sample letters is a brief summary of qualifications. The emphasis is on the word "brief." You don't want to bore the reader or insult his or her intelligence by repeating a lot of the information already contained in the resume. Whenever possible, try to provide some additional information beyond that reflected in the employment resume. Additionally, whenever possible, cite some specific results or accomplishments you feel will be of particular interest to the prospective employer.

Early in the letter, it is important to make the prospective employer aware that you are seeking employment. In most cases it is appropriate to list a generic job title (corporate credit manager, research scientist, director of engineering, and so on) to communicate effectively the level and type of position you seek. This is particularly true if you are absolutely firm on the type and level of position that is acceptable. Otherwise, be fairly general about your objective or state no job objective at all. Remember, if too narrow a position objective is stated, however, it could have the effect of screening you out from job opportunities in which you might be very interested.

In some cases, you will want to include an explanation of your reason for making a job change. This is particularly true in cases of massive layoffs, shutdown of facilities, severely limited future advancement opportunity, and so forth. If you elect to include this information, be sure your explanation is reasonable, plausible, and understandable. Where this information is fairly positive in nature, it can help remove some of the suspicion in the mind of the reader and satisfy his or her curiosity.

If, on the other hand, your reason for leaving your current employer could be construed to be negative, do not volunteer this information in either the cover letter or the resume itself. Thus, if you were or are being terminated involuntarily for reasons of poor performance, absenteeism, negligence, misconduct, or anything similar, do not provide this information. There is no rule that requires you to voluntarily furnish this information in the cover letter or on the resume. It is best left off both. Inclusion is sure to result in your being eliminated from further consideration.

The issue of salary requirements is also a subject of great debate when it comes to cover letters and resumes. Some argue that it should be included, others that it should be excluded. Those that favor exclusion argue that to state either current salary or salary requirements in the cover letter could serve to automatically screen you out from career opportunities in which you would have been quite interested.

I personally feel that this type of argument is a lot of nonsense! Employers are usually dealing with a salary range and frequently have some flexibility in what they are able to pay. If they see somebody who looks particularly good and whose salary requirements are a little high, there is usually some way of addressing this issue. In some cases, it may mean upgrading the current job, and in others it may mean an increase for the person to whom the position is reporting. Either way, there is normally some way around this problem if the interest is strong enough. If on the other hand your salary requirements are totally out of range for the prospective employer, why not know in advance? A lot of valuable time can be saved by you and the prospective employer if this information is known at the onset!

I would argue in favor of the inclusion of salary requirements in the cover letter. This is provided you are firm on what you are willing to accept as fair compensation for your skills and ability. Certain situations, however, may warrant an exception to this general rule. Essentially, this is related to two factors: (1) how high you are now paid and (2) how desperate you are for employment. If you are working for the highest-paying employer in your industry and you know that your salary is already usually high, you may want to moderate your salary requirements or simply not state them in the cover letter. Also, if you have been unemployed for several months and future prospects look glum, you may likewise wish to exclude salary requirements from the cover letter.

With the preceding exceptions in mind, I generally recommend inclusion of salary requirements in the cover letter. It is recommended, however, that appropriate wording be used to allow for some flexibility. As with statement of job objective, too narrow a statement of salary requirement could also have the effect of screening you out from what otherwise would have been a very interesting opportunity. Note how salary requirements are worded in the sample cover letters in Chapter 16.

A statement of geographical preference or restriction is another optional requirement of the cover letter. Here again, care should be taken not to automatically screen yourself from an excellent opportunity by statement of a restriction. For example, if the employer is located in upper New York State, but most division and plant locations are in the South, a geographical restriction to the Northeast may screen you from consideration for a home-office opportunity. The employer may realize that future advancement would require relocation to an area in the South and automatically eliminate you from further consideration.

The rule of thumb to be followed when deciding whether or not to include a statement of geographic restriction in the cover letter is "don't include it unless it is an absolute requirement." You can always decide at a future point whether the opportunity is truly worth the exception. Stating a geographical preference is not nearly so final. It will not automatically screen you from further consideration.

The final component of the letter is the request for response. Let the employer know that you expect to hear something regarding your employment candidacy. Request that you be advised of the outcome of your employment inquiry. Obligating the employer to respond to your application may force him or her to be a little more thorough in reviewing your credentials.

The Broadcast Letter—To Executive Search Firms

Before reading this section, it is suggested that you carefully review the five sample broadcast letters to executive search firms in Chapter 16. This will give you a better understanding and appreciation for the recommendations and ideas contained in this section of the chapter. It will also serve to familiarize you with those letters that most appropriately fit your particular circumstances.

This particular type of letter is very similar to the broadcast letter to employers. In addition to executive search firms, this letter will suffice for use with employment agencies as well. Components of this type of letter are:

1. Return address.
2. Search firm or employment agency address.
3. Salutation.
4. Introductory paragraph or statement.
5. Statement of job objective.
6. Brief summary of qualifications.
7. Reason for making change (optional).
8. Salary requirements (optional).
9. Geographical preferences/restrictions (optional).
10. Statement of willingness to provide additional information.
11. Contact instructions for reaching you.
12. Thank you.

When contrasted with the letters to employers, there are only a few minor differences. First, there should be an acknowledgment that the firm is an executive search firm and that you realize that they do search work for client companies. Don't make the mistake of asking them to help you to find a job. This would imply that you are somewhat naive in business-related matters and would reflect poorly on your general awareness and employment candidacy. This is not the case, however, with the employment agency. Employment agencies work both sides of the fence. They act as agents on behalf of the employment candidate by helping him or her to find employment. Likewise, they may also represent client companies by helping them to locate and recruit candidates to fill their personnel requirements. For purposes of the cover letter, however, I would use the same approach with the employment agencies. Some will feel complimented that you do not make this distinction and are aware that they represent client companies as well.

Most of the comments and qualifications made earlier in this chapter regarding letters to employers apply to letters to executive search firms as well. This is particularly true in the areas of statement of job objective, summary of qualifications, salary requirements, geographical preferences/restrictions, and reason for making the change. I won't repeat the same information.

When writing to the search firm or employment agency, it is important to volunteer to provide additional information should they require it. Additionally, you may wish to include contact instructions in the cover letter to make it easy and convenient to reach you. Don't forget to thank them for their consideration of your credentials and tell them that you look forward to the possibility of hearing from them.

Rest assured, if you have appropriate qualifications to fill one of their current client searches, you will be hearing from the search firm quickly. Chances are, if they do not have a compatible current search and you have reasonably good credentials, they will file your resume and cover letter for future reference. Many now use computers and may scan your information into their computer resume data base as well.

Cover Letter—Response to Advertisement

Review of the sample cover letters headed "response to advertisement" in Chapter 16 of this book will reveal the presence of the letter components below. These components are in addition to the normal return address, employer's address, and salutation.

1. Reference to advertisement.
2. Expression of interest in position.
3. Comparison of position requirements with own qualifications.
4. Statement of additional reasons for serious consideration (optional).
5. Statement of salary requirements (optional).
6. Statement of geographical preference (optional).
7. Contact information.
8. Request for response or interview.
9. Thank you for consideration.

Careful review of the sample letters will reveal that not all of these components are included in each of the letters. With the exception of additional reasons for serious consideration, other components designated as optional can be included or excluded dependent upon whether each adds or detracts from your overall employment candidacy. Again, these components have been thoroughly discussed earlier in this chapter, but I will spend some time exploring the more standard letter components in some detail.

In each of the five sample letters, the introductory paragraph makes specific mention of the position advertisement. Included in this reference are the name of the publication in which the ad appeared, the date of publication, and the position title. It is important that all three of these components be included so that the employer can readily identify the position for which you are applying. It is possible that the employer may be running more than one recruitment ad (sometimes 30 or 40 if a large company) at a time, and, without this specific reference, there may be some confusion concerning your interests.

Also, in all five letters there is a specific statement of interest in the position being advertised. In addition to merely stating your interest in this position, it is important to convey some sense of enthusiasm. This adds a note of positive energy, which does not go unnoticed and suggests to the reader that he or she might have a special need to read your cover letter and resume with a little greater care. Your interest and enthusiasm suggest that you feel that you have some fairly good credentials for the position in question. This serves to heighten interest in your candidacy.

Another commonality between these sample cover letters, and by far the most important, is the comparison of position requirements with your own qualifications. You will note the line-by-line comparison of qualifications with the candidate specification as set forth in the ad. This approach is extremely powerful! It has the effect of leading the reader to one simple conclusion—you *are* qualified (if not well qualified) for the position.

In reviewing the sample letters in Chapter 16, it should be absolutely clear to you that your cover letter must go far beyond simply stating that you are qualified. You must offer direct proof of this fact by offering the reader a point-by-point comparison of your qualifications and the job requirements. To maximize the effectiveness of this technique requires more than a cursory stab at providing a general description of your qualifications. Instead, it will require a much more systematic and analytical approach on your part. The following section will help you to more effectively employ this technique.

The first step in organizing your comparison is to do a careful analysis of the advertisement itself. In doing so, here are the questions that you need to ask. (I suggest that in order to make this exercise more meaningful, you perform an analysis on an actual employment advertisement, especially if you can find one that is close to your career objective.)

1. What are the educational requirements (degree level and major) of the position? Describe below:

_____

_____

2. What is your educational background (degree level and major)? Describe below:

_____

_____

_____

3. Beyond the formal educational degree, is any special skill training required or preferred? If so, describe below:

_____

_____

_____

4. Have you had this special skill training? If so, describe the skill and nature of training you received.

_____

_____

_____

5. What technical or scientific knowledge does the job require (for example: polymer chemistry, Hay job evaluation, contract negotiation, Occupational Safety & Health Act, and so on)? List below:

_____

_____

_____

_____

6. In which of these areas are you knowledgeable? What is your level of knowledge or proficiency? What have you done that demonstrates this level of proficiency?

_____

_____

_____

_____

_____

7. If a managerial position, what is the scope of experience required (for example: functional areas managed, number of people and levels, budgets, and so on)? Describe:

_____

_____

_____

_____

_____

_____

8. Which of the above managerial experience requirements do you meet? Describe below:

_____

_____

_____

_____

_____

9. How many years of experience are sought and at what level? (By "level" I mean professional versus managerial level.) Describe:

_____

_____

_____

10. How many years of experience do you have at these levels? Show below:

_____

_____

_____

Having completed this analysis, you are in excellent shape to make a direct comparison between your own qualifications and the qualifications required by the position. Review of the five sample form letters in Chapter 16, however, will reveal that there are two ways in which this comparison can be made. Which one should you use for greatest effect?

The first approach is a point-by-point delineation of qualifications preceded by a statement of your belief that you are well-qualified for the position. In this approach, there is no specific mention of the qualifications required in the ad, only a general reference to these "specs." The second is a more literary approach, in which each key qualification stated in the ad is mentioned followed by a brief description of the candidate's qualifications as related to this requirement. For ease of discussion, I will refer to the first approach as the "linear" approach and the second approach as the "literary" approach.

In general, of the two approaches, I recommend using the linear approach. This is particularly true when the candidate has most or all of the qualifications called for in the ad. This line-by-line description of qualifications is easily read. Also, the reader may find this a little less offensive since it does not repeat what is contained in the advertisement. Although such cases are few, there are instances where the reader might be offended by this repetition of ad content. It may imply to some that you feel they are incapable of recalling the qualifications of the position as stated in the ad.

Where only some of the qualifications are met, however, do *not* use the linear approach. This approach tends to make it easy for the reader to check off those qualifications that you have. The drawback, however, is that it also tends to highlight those qualifications that you are missing. In a nutshell, it makes it too easy for the reader to make this direct comparison. In this case, I recommend use of the literary approach.

There is one more additional point to be made if you are going to get the most out of this comparison approach. This has to do with the focus of the ad. Most ads are slanted to emphasize the need for particular strength in a given area. Reread the ad to see if you can discover the slant or focus. What is it?

Here are a few clues to help you identify the slant or focus of the ad. Look for the following keywords or phrases:

Must be.

Must have.

Required.

Must be capable of.

Ability to _____ is highly desirable.

Must have strength in.

Must be thoroughly knowledgeable of/versed in.

Additionally, look for thoughts or qualifications that are repeated more than once in the ad. The statement may not be identical, but the thought or theme might be repeated in a slightly different way. Such repetition usually signals that the author of the ad wanted to make sure that the point was well covered. It will usually tell you that the writer was preoccupied with this particular need as a key requirement.

Where you are able to discover this slant or focus in the ad, be sure to take full advantage of it. If you have strong qualifications in this area, include in your cover letter a brief, separate paragraph that highlights your qualifications in this key area of need. Such a paragraph can often prove to be the clincher that gets you an interview.

The balance of the components of the cover letter that is a response to an advertisement are pretty straightforward. They have been well addressed earlier in this chapter, so I will not repeat them here. Let's now move on to the final type of cover letter, the personal referral.

Cover Letter—To Personal Referral

As suggested earlier, I would recommend that you take a few minutes to review the five sample cover letters of this type shown toward the end of Chapter 16. This will enable you to better understand the recommendations and thoughts represented in this section.

Review of these sample, personal-referral cover letters reveals that they can be divided into two categories: direct and indirect. The direct letter is one in which the applicant makes the addressee aware that he or she knows of a specific opening in their company. This type of letter is represented by the sample letters addressed to B. David Carter and J. Perrington Russel (see Chapter 16). By contrast, the indirect letter (sometimes called the networking letter) professes no specific knowledge of an opening and simply solicits the assistance of the addressee in helping the applicant in his or her job search. The indirect approach is typified by the sample letters addressed to Mr. Marcus, Mr. Davis, and Ms. Harrison.

Careful analysis of these letters reveals the following common components. Although not *all* of these components appear in every sample letter, *most* are used in each letter.

1. Personal opening.
   (a) Name of person making referral.
   (b) Relationship to applicant.
   (c) Something of a personal nature.
2. How referral came about.
3. Reason for job change.

4. Direct reference to existing opening (where known opening exists).

5. Indirect approach (where no known opening exists).

6. Reference to enclosed resume.

7. Action to initiate personal meeting.

8. Thank you.

If carefully written, the personal referral or networking cover letter can be a very effective tool. If a good job is done in establishing a sense of close personal relationship with the individual making the referral, a strong sense of personal obligation is created, and the addressee feels compelled to respond.

After all, friends don't let friends down. When there is a need, they respond and offer to help. This is a somewhat sacred relationship, however, and one should not abuse it.

The personal tie-in is usually established in the first paragraph of the letter. Note the first paragraphs of the sample letters. They include the name of the person making the referral, the relationship of the referror to the applicant, and usually some special story or other experience of a personal nature.

Although not always included in the first paragraph, the writer usually tells the addressee how the referral came about. Care should be taken in how one goes about describing the events that led up to the referral. If made to sound too casual, it may give the addressee the idea that the referral was made on a courtesy or polite obligation basis, as opposed to a strong, meaningful referral. This lessens the sense of obligation on the part of the addressee. Be careful, on the other hand, not to overdo it. It will surely turn the addressee off if you take advantage of the relationship and claim a stronger referral than the referror intended.

Unlike other kinds of cover letters, the personal referral letter almost always offers an explanation as to why the writer/applicant wishes to make a job change. In a more personal relationship, such as that represented in the personal-referral cover letter, there is a stronger sense of needing to share this information with the addressee. There is an almost unwritten obligation to do so. If the reason could be construed to be fairly negative (poor performance, misconduct, etc.), however, I would question the wisdom of volunteering this information prematurely. Once again, I would recommend excluding this information from the cover letter. It is better to discuss it during the personal interview. If you value your friendship, however, you had better think long and hard about not sharing this information with the addressee during your personal meeting. At least you will have the opportunity to explain any extenuating circumstances that led to this decision. If you have a reasonable explanation, chances are he or she will give you the benefit of the doubt.

In the sample letters addressed to Mr. Carter and Mr. Russel (see Chapter 16), there is a direct reference to a specific opening. In fact, in the Carter letter the applicant indicates that the referror, John Bristol, has given him permission to use him as a reference. This type of direct approach is quite acceptable. This is one of the special things about friendship—you can sometimes go a little further than you might with a complete stranger. You must be careful, however, to walk a fairly narrow line but not cross over and give the impression that you are acting in poor taste or are abusing this special relationship. The sample letters provided in Chapter 16 are in good taste and professional in their approach. By tailoring your personal referral letters with these as your guide, you should be right on target.

You will note that those personal referral letters using the indirect style use a much more subtle approach than the direct letters. In these cases the applicant does not know whether the addressee is aware of an appropriate opening with his or her company. In such cases the applicant should avoid putting the addressee on the spot. Instead, as shown in the sample letters, the applicant takes a more casual approach indicating that he or she realizes that "it is unlikely" that an appropriate opening exists, and then goes on to solicit the addressee's counsel and assistance in helping to make contacts with others who may be aware of appropriate job opportunities.

Review of the sample letters in Chapter 16 will also reveal that in every case the applicant has initiated action to arrange a personal meeting with the addressee. This is a very important part of the process. This action creates a greater sense of obligation on the part of the addressee to help in some way. Chances are, therefore, that he or she will make a greater effort to develop a more meaningful list of contacts, check openings of the current employer, and so on. Thus taking action to initiate such meetings is important to the overall effectiveness of the referral process. In those cases where geography makes such meetings impractical, indicating that you will be phoning to discuss the matter can be almost as productive as the personal meeting.

Manners are always an important part of any friendship. Although it may sound trite, don't forget a "thank you" near the close of the letter. Little things like this are important. It at least acknowledges your appreciation for any effort that the addressee may make on your behalf.

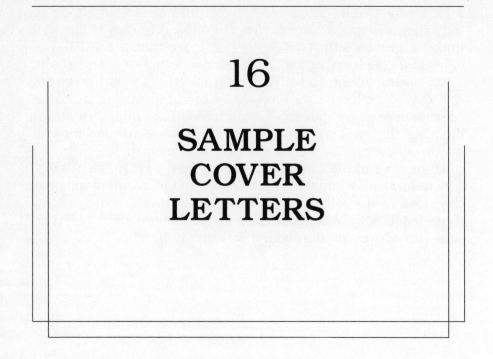

16

SAMPLE
COVER
LETTERS

This chapter contains 20 sample cover letters. They represent a variety of approaches and styles, and you should be able to find samples that will help you with most of your letter-writing requirements. They, of course, follow the basic letter-writing principles and guidelines as outlined in Chapter 15. As with Chapter 15, these sample cover letters are organized into four basic categories. For each category there are five sample letters. Each uses a slightly different approach from the others. I have also attempted to provide a fairly good cross section of career disciplines and fields. You should find these helpful as guidelines in designing your own cover letters. The samples are of professional quality and should enable you to write effective and professional quality cover letters of your own.

2222 Strenton Drive
Sharon Hills
Utica, NY 82289
August 3, 2000

Dr. Richard P. Stevenson
Director Research & Development
Kriston Laboratories, Inc.
1435 Claymont Way
Wawa, OR 57338

Dear Dr. Stevenson:

As you are undoubtedly aware, Keystone Chemical Corporation has made a decision to close its entire Research Center in Utica, New York effective October 15th of this year. I am thus seeking a responsible position in R&D management requiring a Ph.D. with 18 years of experience and proven skills in polymer and specialty chemical research.

I have extensive experience and knowledge in the following chemical specialties:

- Organic & Polymer Specialty Chemicals
  - Water Treatment Chemicals
  - Oil Field and Mining Chemicals
  - Consumer Products Based on Water Soluble Polymers

- Polymers, Rubbers and Plastics
  - New Polymers and Plastics – Synthetic Approach
  - New Polymers and Plastics – Physio-Chemical Approach

- Adhesives, Coatings, Polymer Alloys and Composites

As you can see from the enclosed resume, my reputation as a creative, innovative scientist has led to 35 registered patents and 14 new product introductions. Perhaps I can make a similar contribution to your company?

I have no geographical restrictions and, in fact, would enjoy living on the West Coast. My current salary is $75K per year.

Should you have an appropriate opening in your Research Center, I would welcome the opportunity to meet with you personally. I can be reached at (312) 472-5535 during the day and at (312) 472-0088 during evenings and weekends.

Thank you for your consideration, and I look forward to hearing from you.

Sincerely,

Carolyn R. Steinman

Carolyn R. Steinman

Enclosure

125 Deerborne Street
Heeley, VT 43506
March 18, 2001

Ms. Sarah D. Bowlings
Senior Vice President
Human Resources
Hawthorne Publishing Company
8000 Monroe Avenue
Chicago, IL 37787

Dear Ms. Bowlings:

I am an attorney with broad corporate experience in industrial relations and labor law.

My background includes substantial experience in collective bargaining, arbitration, equal employment opportunity, NLRB proceedings, contract administration and preventive employee relations programs.

I am seeking a corporate position with emphasis on employee relations law. I am open to relocation. Salary requirements are in the mid $70K range.

I will be happy to provide additional information. Thank you for your consideration.

Sincerely,

Rodney G. Smith

Enclosure

822 Fern Avenue
Forest Glen, IN 23994
October 4, 2000

Mr. J. Walter Pringe
President & Chief Operating Officer
Walburn Manufacturing, Inc.
18 Collings Way
Trenton, NJ 08330

Dear Mr. Pringe:

As President & Chief Operating Officer of a leading firm in the small appliance manufacturing field, I am sure that you are aware of the importance and value of a top-flight Chief Financial Officer. If you are in the market for such an individual, you may want to give serious consideration to my credentials.

With 14 years of progressively senior financial management experience in manufacturing, I have logged a very satisfying record of achievement in such areas as cash flow improvement, profit enhancement and application of sophisticated IS techniques. In my current position as Controller and Chief Financial Officer for a $10 million autonomous division of a major company in the healthcare industry, I have established an excellent reputation for cost control. Under my leadership, cost reduction task forces have been successful in improving net earnings by 15% through application of creative cost reduction control techniques.

Since my current company is family owned, it has become quite apparent to me that meaningful future advancement is not a realistic probability. I have, therefore, decided to seek employment elsewhere.

My current compensation is $95,000 per year plus bonus. My requirements are in the $90K range plus comprehensive benefits package.

Should you be in the market for a top-flight Financial Officer who can add profits to your bottom line, I would appreciate hearing from you.

Sincerely,

Sandra A. Dawson

Sandra A. Dawson

Enclosure

725 Peachtree Lane
Rochester, NY 27132
July 2, 2000

Mr. David Ramstead
Vice President Operations
Smith Burgstrom Company
2732 Birmingham Way Road
Fort Smith, AK 13950

Dear Mr. Ramstead:

Because of the outstanding reputation of your company as a leader in the field of small electrical devices, I am interested in exploring the possibility of employment with your firm in a senior operations management capacity.

An M.S. degreed Electrical Engineer with over 20 years experience in the electrical and electronics industries, I have held a variety of positions of increasing responsibility. Most recently, I have been Plant Manager of Davidson Electronics' plant in Rochester, New York, where I have enjoyed a reputation for efficiency and profitability. During the last three years, this plant has consistently set new production and profitability records with 1999 showing an increase in net profits of nearly 25%!

Unfortunately, although Davidson has been good to me, there appears to be little opportunity for advancement in the foreseeable future. As you may be aware, Davidson has only three manufacturing facilities with the Rochester Plan being the largest. At this point in time, Davidson management is not aware of my decision to seek other employment.

I have no geographical preferences or restrictions. Salary requirements are in the high $80K range and are negotiable as appropriate with the specific opportunity.

Should you have a suitable opportunity and wish to discuss my qualifications in greater detail, I can be reached on a confidential basis at my office during normal business hours. My office number is (315) 472-5252.

I look forward to hearing from you.

Sincerely,

Donald P. Carlton

Enclosure

2004 Jansen Street, NW
Atlanta, GA 33405
February 22, 2001

Ms. Carolyn A. Tarkin
Vice President Technology
Orlando Pharmaceutical Corporation
1825 Bisque Avenue, SW
Orlando, FL 88795

Dear Ms. Tarkin:

During my 20-year career in research and development, I have successfully managed numerous product development programs in the pharmaceutical and healthcare industries. As a leader in the pharmaceutical field, I felt that perhaps Orlando Pharmaceutical might have an interest in my background and accomplishments.

In addition to the qualifications set forth on the enclosed resume, I feel that it is important for you to know that I have a reputation for being extremely creative in the area of new product development. I also possess the ability to effectively translate market need into practical laboratory solutions. This has accounted for an excellent reputation with marketing management for developing products, which consistently meet marketing objectives.

While the work at Sampson Chemical is both challenging and rewarding, recent downsizings in the economy have forced severe reduction of the Company's R&D budget. This has seriously hampered my ability (and the ability of other R&D scientists) to respond to business requirements. For this reason, I am seeking a position in a growth-oriented organization where I may more fully utilize my talents and energy.

Salary requirements are in the $70-80K range with some flexibility dependent upon cost of living, future opportunity and other similar factors. Although I have no absolute geographical restrictions, I do have a preference for the Southeast.

Thank you for your consideration. I look forward to hearing from you.

Sincerely,

Linda R. Barlett

Enclosure

825 Needham Road
Bellville, OH 13970
July 27, 2000

Mr. R. James Drillpenny
Burstrom & Bailings
Executive Search Division
795 Fifth Avenue, Suite 2075
New York, NY 01320

Dear Mr. Drillpenny:

Enclosed please find my resume for your review and consideration against either current or future search assignments in the field of human resources.

I am seeking a responsible and challenging corporate or division level position as a human resources generalist. Consideration would also be given to a senior level position in the field of organization effectiveness with either a manufacturing company or consultant. As you can see from my resume, I am well qualified for either of these areas.

My decision to leave Faulings Manufacturing, Inc. is a confidential one and is predicated by lack of company and personal growth. In five short years, Faulings has sold two divisions and four manufacturing plants. Shutdown of a fifth plant is scheduled for year-end. Future business strategy calls for further consolidation and the outlook for future personal growth, therefore, does not look particularly encouraging.

My current salary is in the mid $70K range with salary review scheduled for next month. Salary requirements will vary depending upon nature of position, defined advancement opportunity, location, cost of living, etc. Although I admittedly have a preference for the East Coast, I would be willing to discuss the possibility of other locations.

Since Faulings Manufacturing, Inc. is unaware of my decision to seek other employment, I would appreciate your treating this inquiry with appropriate sensitivity. In this regard, I would prefer, if at all possible, to keep contact to my home during evenings or weekends. Should this prove inconvenient, however, my wife, Peggy, will be pleased to relay messages to me during working hours, if necessary.

Thank you for your consideration, and I look forward to the prospect of discussing appropriate career opportunities with you or a member of your staff.

Sincerely,

Jonathan P. Peters

Jonathan P. Peters

Enclosure

45 Puritan Road
Plymouth Meeting, PA 19377
September 21, 2000

Mr. Craig Holston
President
Holston Executive Search, Inc.
22 Wollington Avenue
Charton Circle, PA 18537

Dear Mr. Holston:

I am an experienced Controller and CPA seeking an opportunity for further career advancement in accounting/financial management. Some of my accomplishments are outlined in the enclosed resume.

My ability to creatively deal with rapid growth and to manage and develop people, in addition to my technical qualifications, should allow me to make a significant contribution to the right company.

My compensation, with performance bonuses, has averaged in the high $90K range for the past three years.

I will be happy to provide additional information if my experience and qualifications match the requirements of any of your current search assignments.

Sincerely,

Mary C. Walters

Mary C. Walters

Enclosure

33 Bakers Row
Cedar Hill, WA 98873
May 26, 1999

Ms. Michele Brown
Executive Search, Ltd.
1835 Washburn Avenue
Chicago, IL 60634

Dear Ms. Brown:

In the course of your search activities, you may have a requirement for an accomplished Manager of Operations.

My career has covered responsible positions with major companies in their industry: General Electric, U.S. Steel, I.B.M. and International Paper Company. I have substantial experience in the manufacture of electronics, steel, business machines and paper. Review of my resume will demonstrate a record of increasing responsibility and personal growth.

The enclosed resume briefly outlines my manufacturing accomplishments over the past 14 years. There are no geographical restrictions and salary requirements are in the $85-95K range.

If it appears that my qualifications meet your current needs in the manufacturing or related fields, I would be happy to further discuss my background with you in greater depth.

Thank you for your consideration.

Sincerely,

Samuel G. Kingstone

Enclosure

3807 Green Tree Terrace
Smithsonville, OH 45878
August 24, 2000

The Brenton Company
Executive Search Division
215 East Market Street
Detroit, MI 87705

Dear Search Consultant:

I am writing to you in hopes that you are currently providing service to client firms seeking uniquely talented sales and marketing management professionals. With a consistent track record of success within the plastics and specialty chemical industries, I believe that I could contribute immediately to a variety of business development situations.

I have enclosed my resume to provide you with the details of my background and skills. I would be most anxious to discuss my career goals with you – even if on a purely exploratory basis.

If you have any immediate questions, do not hesitate to call. Should you have employment opportunities, which you feel may be of interest to me, I would appreciate hearing from you.

Thank you for your consideration.

Sincerely,

Cynthia A. Ruthers

Cynthia A. Ruthers

Enclosure

35 Pierce Street
Grasson, TX 77534
April 5, 2001

Ms. Judith Beerson
Senior Account Executive
Baxter, Wilcox & Sloan Executive Search
325 Ollander Circle
Cleveland, OH 43762

Dear Ms. Beerson:

If any of your client searches require a seasoned International Sales Manager, I would appreciate your consideration of the enclosed data.

While my international experience with technical products has permitted me to sell successfully in a variety of markets, I feel that I have the most to offer a company that wants to build a solid, international distributor network. This would be true of either a company new to the export market or an established firm that would like to improve their oversees market position.

By nature, the enclosed resume is only a brief summary of my qualifications. I would be pleased to expand on it personally at your convenience and should you have an appropriate opportunity with one of your clients. My current compensation at Pearson Plastics is $85,000 per year.

I hope to hear from you soon.

Sincerely,

Barbara A. Johnson

Enclosure

1832 Briarwood Circle
Radley, VA 23031
November 12, 1999

Mr. Joseph B. Cartigen
Technical Employment Manager
Hartwell Engineering, Inc.
78 Riverside Place, Suite 108
Norfolk, VA 24772

Dear Mr. Cartigen:

Your ad in the Sunday edition of *The Baltimore Sun* for a Senior Project Engineer caught my attention and interest! It appears that my professional qualifications and career interests are very much in line with your requirements. Consider the following:

Your ad calls for a B.S. in Mechanical Engineering with five plus years project experience in the design, installation, start-up and debugging of modern high-speed tissue paper machines. Project responsibility, including supervision of three to five professionals, with focus on forming devices is highly desirable.

I have eight years experience with Brunson Paper Company as Project Engineer in the area of paper machine project engineering. I have handled projects up to $25 million with supervision of five to eight contract engineers and designers. Project responsibility has included preliminary design, installation, start-up and debugging. I have just completed successful start-up of a Beloit twin-wire forming machine with speeds over 5,000 feet per minute and full computer control. My specific responsibility was for the wet end of the machine including both headbox and formers.

Salary requirements are in the high $65K range plus moving cost reimbursement. I am free to travel extensively and open to the prospect of future relocation.

I can be reached at the project site, on a confidential basis, during the day at (301) 742-0978. Additionally, I can be reached at my motel room during evening hours at (301) 742-7749, Room 32.

I would welcome the opportunity to further discuss your requirements in greater detail and am hopeful that I will be hearing from you shortly. Thank you for your consideration.

Sincerely,

Scott M. Criswell

Scott M. Criswell, PE

Enclosure

948 Elm Avenue
Stouffer, CA 99735
January 15, 2001

Box J-9487
The Philadelphia Inquirer
P.O. Box 8956
Philadelphia, PA 19101

Dear Sir or Madam:

Enclosed please find my resume in response to your recent advertisement in *The Philadelphia Inquirer* for a Director of Operations. This position sounds very interesting, and I think that you will find my background closely parallels your requirements.

Your ad states that you are looking for a "seasoned manufacturing manager with over ten years experience in the manufacture of sheet metal fabricated assemblies." As my resume will attest, I have over 15 years experience in the fabrication of residential and commercial air conditioning and heating units, making extensive use of sheet metal assembly.

Additionally, your ad states that you require "a mature individual who has had P&L responsibilities for a multi-location operation employing at least 1,000 employees and accounting for at least $100 million in annual sales volume." As Operations Manager for Trefton Manufacturing, I currently have P&L responsibilities for four manufacturing facilities totaling 1,500 employees and sales volume of $128 million. I also have a B.S. degree in Mechanical Engineering as called for in your advertisement.

If you agree that my background is a close match for your requirements, I would welcome the opportunity to meet with you personally for the purpose of further exploring the prospects of employment with your company.

Salary requirements are in the mid $90K range with some flexibility for negotiation dependent upon details of the total compensation and benefits package.

I can be reached during the day, on a confidential basis, at my office. My office phone number is (714) 375-8945.

Thank you for your consideration, and I look forward to hearing from you.

Sincerely,

Robert S. Peterson

Robert S. Peterson

Enclosure

85 Country Club Lane
Shaker Heights
Cleveland, OH 45382
February 18, 2001

Ms. Sandra B. Perkins
Employment Manager
Basker & Jardell, Inc.
801 Riley Square
Ridley Hills, MA 02356

Dear Ms. Perkins:

Enclosed please find my resume in response to Basker & Jardell's ad for a Senior Cost Accountant in this Sunday's *Boston Globe*. This position is very much in line with my current career objective, and I would appreciate the opportunity of discussing it further with you during a personal interview.

The following professional highlights from my background appear to be in keeping with your position requirements:

- B.A. Degree in Accounting from Cornell University
- Five years cost accounting experience in manufacturing
- Understanding and ability to apply modern cost theory
- Excellent oral and written communications ability (Editor of College Newspaper)
- Excellent rapport with manufacturing personnel
- High energy level and volume producer
- Not afraid to work long hours to get the job done

Since Boston is my home, I would welcome the opportunity to return to my native state. Future relocation, however, is not objectionable. Salary requirements are in the low $70K range.

I can be reached, on a confidential basis, at my office during the day – (312) 376-4400. Evening calls to my home are preferable, however. My home phone is (312) 376-3422.

I appreciate your consideration and look forward to hearing from you shortly.

Sincerely,

Stephen H. Ralston

Enclosure

Sample Cover Letter—Response to Advertisement

Apartment 10A
Ridgewood Arms Apts.
25 Rawley Aenue
Bakersville, ME 02235
June 14, 2001

Mr. Martin D. Smith
Vice President Human Resources
Delray Manufacturing Company
668 Parker Street
Springfield, MA 07727

Dear Mr. Smith:

Wednesday's edition of *The Springfield Newspaper* was a pleasant surprise. Your ad for a Human Resources Assistant brightened my day and gave me reason to hope that one can enter the field of Human Resources without prior experience. Hurrah for Delray Manufacturing Company!

Please consider my credentials carefully since they appear to be a close match for your job requirements. Consider the following highlights:

- M.S., Human Resources Management, Michigan State, 2001
- Honors Graduate, G.P.A. 3.3/4.0
- President of Student Government Association
- Editor-in-Chief, Student Newspaper
- Vice President, Delta Sorority
- Captain, Women's Swim and Tennis Teams

As you can see, I appear to have the academic and leadership credentials called for in your ad. Beyond these, however, I have a high energy level, am very results-oriented and have a strong desire for a career in Human Resources.

I would welcome the opportunity for a personal interview to further discuss my qualifications. I am sure that I can convince you of my potential for a bright career in Human Resources if given the chance!

Please call me at my home – (315) 744-5234. I look forward to hearing from you shortly.

Sincerely,

Mary Anne King

Enclosure

35 Cranberry Road
Green Forest Subdivision
Montgomery, AL 57556
December 12, 2001

Box R-334
The Atlanta Journal
304 West Peachtree Street
Atlanta, GA 33403

Dear Sir or Madam:

I read with great interest your ad in this Sunday's edition of *The Atlanta Journal* calling for a Research Engineer, Injection Molding. I would like to be considered for this position and feel that I have sufficient qualifications to warrant your serious interest.

Consider the following as they relate to your requirements:

- M.S. Degree in Mechanical Design Engineering
- B.S. Degree in Plastics Technology
- Five years with Hilton Plastics as a Research Design Engineer
- Eight patents for injection molded packages

I have enclosed a resume, which provides a fairly complete summary of my education and experience. I would be pleased to answer additional questions concerning my background and would welcome the opportunity of discussing this position with you during a personal interview.

Salary requirements are in the $80-85K range subject to negotiation depending upon specifics of the opportunity in question. Although open to relocation, I must confess to a preference for the Southeast.

Since I am not actively on the job market, I request that my application be handled in strictest confidence. I prefer not being contacted at the office and would appreciate all calls being directed to my home during evening hours. My home phone is (917) 374-0956.

Thank you for your consideration, and I look forward to hearing from you shortly.

Sincerely,

John B. Duncan

John B. Duncan

Enclosure

818 Kimberly Lane
Shillington, PA 19432
June 22, 2000

Mr. B. David Carter
Vice President of Marketing
Jarzan International, Inc.
35 Europe Avenue
Philadelphia, PA 19830

Dear Mr. Carter:

John Bristol, a close friend of mine, suggested that I contact you. John and I worked together in sales and marketing for the Mittinger Company. This was our first job following college, and we went through the Sales Training Program together. From there, we both went on to blaze new sales records for the Company!

I ran into John last week at the Electronics Convention in Atlanta. After explaining my current situation to him, he suggested that I contact you directly and feel free to use him as a reference as well.

Mr. Carter, my current contract with Tollerston Marketing Consultants expires next month. Since long-range growth opportunities appear rather limited, I don't plan to renew this relationship. I am thus on the market in search of a senior sales management position.

John advises me that you are searching for a National Sales Manager and, from what he describes, it appears that I could well be the person you are looking for. Additionally, your position sounds like a close match for my immediate career objectives. Perhaps there is sufficient reason for us to explore this possibility during a personal meeting.

I am enclosing my resume for your review and consideration. Of course, this is only a thumbnail sketch of my background and experience. I would appreciate the opportunity to more fully discuss my qualifications with you personally.

I will be in the Philadelphia area next week and plan to give you a call. Perhaps we can get together for a brief meeting over lunch.

Thank you for your consideration, Mr. Carter, and I look forward to talking with you.

Sincerely,

Rodney B. Smith

Enclosure

418 Butternut Lane
Burnt Hills, OK 43225
January 25, 2001

Ms. Katherine Marcus
Director of Human Resources
Holstetter Manufacturing Company
497 Dry Gulch Road
Tulsa, OK 74321

Dear Katherine:

It appears that we have a close mutual friend. John Carlson and I go back a few years. We have done quite a bit of sailing together including one three-week charter out of Norfolk to Bermuda. I understand that you have done your share of sailing as well. John tells me that the two of you are planning a charter trip out of St. Thomas in October. Sounds like a challenging and interesting trip. Wish I could join you.

While sailing with John last weekend, he mentioned that he knew you quite well and suggested that I contact you for some assistance on a personal matter to see if you could be of some help. I would very sincerely welcome any thoughts, ideas or suggestions you might have.

After 13 years as Human Resources Manager for Houston Minerals, the company has decided to close its doors on June 1st of this year. This unfortunate circumstance places me in the position of needing to locate a new position.

Although I know that it is highly unlikely that your company has an appropriate opening at this time, I would very much welcome your assistance and guidance in my job search. As a respected leader in the human resources community, perhaps some of your professional acquaintances may have a suitable opening or may know of one who does. Katherine, if it wouldn't be too much of an imposition, I would appreciate if you could provide me with the names of other professionals who you feel might be of possible assistance in helping me to identify an appropriate opportunity.

I am enclosing a copy of my resume for your use. Please feel free to use it as you may see fit.

I will plan to call you within the next couple of days to see if we can arrange a meeting. Thank you, Katherine, for your help.

Sincerely,

Lee Briton

Enclosure

8 Pickering Way
Hawthorne, PA 19372
May 15, 2000

Mr. Jeffrey R. Davis
Director of Operations
The Boston Carvinger Company
18 Bay Bridge Road
Boston, MA 02342

Dear Mr. Davis:

I understand that you are a close personal friend of David Thatcher. Dave and I grew up together in Wyomissing Hills and were co-captains of the high school football team. During our 20th class reunion last week, I mentioned a personal matter to Dave and he suggested that I might contact you for some guidance and assistance.

After a challenging and rewarding career in manufacturing with the Davidson Company, it appears that I will be seeking a new career opportunity closer to the Boston area. My wife's parents live near Framingham and Sally has been wanting to move back to the area. Although I have thoroughly enjoyed my career with Davidson, I must admit to a desire to return as well. In any event, we have made the decision and are in the process of seeking a new career opportunity in the Boston area. In this regard, I would appreciate your assistance.

I know that it is highly unlikely that The Boston Carvinger Company has an appropriate opportunity at this time, and I am not contacting you for that purpose. Instead, as a member of the greater Boston manufacturing community, I felt that you might be in a position to provide me with the names of a few good contacts who might be of assistance in my job search. Even if they do not have immediate openings within their own companies, perhaps they could refer me to others who do.

Mr. Davis, I will be in Boston next week and would appreciate the opportunity to meet with you. Perhaps we could get together over lunch or dinner. I will call you to see if we can arrange a convenient time.

In the meantime, I am enclosing a copy of my resume to give you a better understanding of my background. As a manufacturing executive, I would value your thoughts on the effectiveness of this resume. Perhaps you could give me some pointers during our meeting.

Thank you very much for your assistance, and I look forward to meeting with you personally. Dave speaks very highly of you.

Sincerely,

David B. Johnson

Enclosure

82 Fulton Street
Jamesville, NY 13779
March 22, 2001

Ms. Susan B. Harrison
Director of Engineering
Berrington Engineering Associates
857 North Arlington Drive
Syracuse, NY 17741

Dear Ms. Harrison:

A close personal friend and past sorority sister from Syracuse University, Joan Mattersby, suggested that I contact you. Joan and I were in many of the same engineering classes together at Syracuse and managed to keep one another afloat. Joan tells me that the two of you have been doing some interesting project work together for the Women in Business Association in the greater Syracuse area. I understand that your membership drive has gone tremendously well and that Association membership has more than tripled in the past year alone. Quite an accomplishment! Joan is quite excited with the potential for future impact of this organization on the business community.

Joan felt that, as a fellow woman engineer and successful engineering executive, you might be willing to help me with a personal situation. I would certainly welcome your advice and support.

Following completion of my M.S. degree in Mechanical Engineering in 1991, I accepted a position as Research Engineer with Hunter Laboratories here in Jamesville. Although the position was described as heavily research-oriented initially, it has not turned out that way. I find that I am spending 80% or better of my time in reduction-to-practice work, with less than 20% on true research and development projects. I have thus decided to seek other employment where there is greater opportunity to do conceptual, creative work.

Although I know that it is unlikely that Berrington has an appropriate position available, I would still appreciate if you could review my credentials. I have enclosed a copy of my resume for this purpose. More importantly, however, perhaps you could provide me with a list of personal contacts who might know of someone currently in search of a creative, young research engineer. If you could, I would be most appreciative.

If your busy schedule permits, it would be nice if we could have lunch together sometime during the next few weeks. I will give you a call early next week to see if we can work out an appropriate time to get together.

Thank you, Ms. Harrison, for your help.

Sincerely,

Regina A. Schweiz

Enclosure

935 Jefferson Avenue
Washington, DC 20202
April 22, 2001

Mr. J. Perrington Russell
Senior Vice President & Partner
Smith, Brennen & Russell Associates
Financial Consultants
300 Franklin Place, Suite 100
Washington, DC 20201

Dear Mr. Russell:

At Friday's meeting of the Darlington Investors Club, I was speaking to a friend of mine, Donald G. Crystal, President of the District of Columbia National Bank. He mentioned that you are currently searching for a Director of Taxes and suggested that I contact you.

I have an MBA in Finance from the University of Pennsylvania's Wharton School and over 20 years experience in taxes. I understand, by the way, that you are also a Wharton School graduate.

Mr. Russell, as my enclosed resume will attest, I have held a wide variety of positions of increasing responsibility in the field of taxes, starting as a Tax Accountant and ending with my current position as Manager of Corporate Taxes with Scherling Corporation. In my current position, I manage a staff of eight tax accountants in the preparation of all federal, state and local returns. Annual returns are valued at $85 million.

In the last three years, through creative and innovative approaches, I have saved Scherling $1.8 million in tax reductions. Through a new, creative approach in the area of foreign leasing, I expect to realize another $1 million in tax savings by year end.

From what Donald describes as your requirements, it would appear that my background is a fairly good match. If you agree, perhaps we could meet to explore this matter in greater detail on a more personal basis.

I will plan to call you next week to see if you are interested in arranging a meeting. I would very much appreciate this opportunity to talk with you.

Thank you for your consideration, and I look forward to the possibility of meeting with you personally.

Sincerely,

R. Samuel Gothing

Enclosure

17

THE
TOP 50
EXECUTIVE
SEARCH FIRMS

For those uninitiated in the ways of the employment market, there has long been a lot of confusion about the difference between the employment agency and the executive search firm. It is important for those in search of a new position to be knowledgeable of employment sources so that they have a good understanding of the roles of each and know what to expect. Further, without a clear understanding of these employment sources and how they function, you will end up frustrated and disillusioned and will not know how to capitalize on the individual expertise of each.

It is important that you understand the difference between the executive search firm and the employment agency. After conveying this understanding, we will take a detailed look at each of these services in an effort to distinguish the overall role of each in the employment process as well as how each functions. Let's start first with the employment agency.

There are thousands of employment agencies across the United States. Many are independent agencies working solely on their own except for an informal, loosely defined affiliation with a few other independent agencies. Others are part of a large franchise organization in which, although the agency is owned by an individual or autonomous group, the manner in which the agency functions is governed by a contract with the franchisor. This contract may stipulate certain constraints on the franchise, such as limiting the geographical territory in which the franchise may operate, restricting the franchisee's business to certain career disciplines (marketing, sales, engineering, etc.), or limiting the franchisee to certain industries.

The main distinction between the executive search firm and the employment agency lies in three principal areas.

1. Who is represented by the firm?
2. Who pays the firm's fee?
3. How does the firm operate?

EMPLOYMENT AGENCIES

The employment agency represents the individual who is in search of a job. With the employment agency, therefore, you are frequently required to sign a contract authorizing the agency to act in your behalf in search of a position for you. As with any contract, in order to be binding the contract must provide for "valuable consideration." In the case of the employment agency contract, the valuable consideration is the agent's fee that you must pay to the agency upon acceptance of a position with a company with whom the agency has placed you in contact. These employment agency fees can be substantial and are charged on the basis of a percentage of first year's anticipated income (salary plus all incentive payments).

Although there is some variation in employment agency fees, the industry standard appears to be based on a formula of 1 percent per $1,000 of annual income. Thus, under the terms of the normal agency contract, an anticipated first year's income of $20,000 would yield an employment agency fee of $4,000. Likewise, an income of $25,000 would result in an employment agency fee of $6,250. Most employment agencies with this type of standard contract have a cutoff or maximum fee of 30 percent on incomes of $30,000 and above. Thus an annual income of $50,000 would yield, under the terms of such a contract, an employment agency fee of $15,000.

The fee schedule below is representative of those employment agencies now charging an agency fee of 1 percent per $1,000 of first year's income with a maximum cap on fees of 30 percent. This should enable you to get a fairly close estimate of what your obligation would be under such an agency contract.

There are some variations between these firms. One common variation to the standard schedule is one that calls for 1 percent plus 1 percent for every $1,000 of the first year's estimated income. The fee schedule below is representative of firms falling into this category.

I am sure that after reviewing these fee schedules you will come to have a lot of respect for the size of the typical employment agency fee. Many people would shudder at the

Normal Agency Fee Schedule*

First Year's Income ($)	Agency Fee (%)	Range of Fees ($)
20,000–20,999	20	4,000–4,200
21,000–21,999	21	4,410–4,620
22,000–22,999	22	4,840–5,060
23,000–23,999	23	5,290–5,520
24,000–24,999	24	5,760–6,000
25,000–25,999	25	6,250–6,500
26,000–26,999	26	6,760–7,020
27,000–27,999	27	7,290–7,560
28,000–28,999	28	7,840–8,120
29,000–29,999	29	8,410–8,700
30,000 & Over	30	9,000 & Up

*Based on 1% per $1,000 for the first year's income, with a maximum of 30%.

thought of having to pay an agency fee in the range of $9,000 or more. Yet such fees are not uncommon for those whose annual salaries fall into the over $30,000 range. You should therefore approach the signing of an employment agency contract with a great deal of respect and caution.

This does not mean that you should shy away from working with employment agencies. You should simply be well aware of the obligation that you create when you sign the agency contract. Don't despair, however, since most of the better employers will agree to pay the employment agency fee on behalf of the professionals they hire. To be sure that this is the case, though, ask the employment agency, prior to agreeing to an interview, whether the prospective employer with whom you will be interviewing is willing to pay the agent's fee. Should the prospective employer be unwilling to do so, you may want to think twice before agreeing to an employment interview.

One way of safeguarding yourself against the payment of an employment agency fee is to write across the face of the employment agency contract—"Will interview for fee paid positions only." This places the responsibility for assuring that you are directed to "fee paid only" interviews on the

Agency Fee Schedule*

First Year's Income ($)	Agency Fee (%)	Range of Fees ($)
19,000–19,999	20	3,800–4,000
20,000–20,999	21	4,200–4,410
21,000–21,999	22	4,620–4,840
22,000–22,999	23	5,060–5,290
23,000–23,999	24	5,520–5,760
24,000–24,999	25	6,000–6,250
25,000–25,999	26	6,500–6,760
26,000–26,999	27	7,020–7,290
27,000–27,999	28	7,560–7,840
28,000–28,999	29	8,120–8,410
29,000 & Over	30	8,700 & Up

*Based on 1%+1% per $1,000 of the first year's income, with a maximum of 30%.

agency. Although I'm not an attorney, it would appear to me that you have shifted the bulk of the responsibility to the agency. In any event, however, you have certainly alerted the employment agency that you are unwilling to pay an agency fee. Even though you may have taken this action, I would still advise you to ask in advance of any interview whether the prospective employer has agreed to pay the agency fee if you are hired. In this way, you are absolutely certain that you will never find yourself in the position of having to pay a sizable fee.

For the inexperienced job seeker, one of the most confusing and bewildering aspects of any job-hunting campaign is the selection of a good employment agency. This task is complicated by the fact that there are literally thousands of employment agencies in the United States. Some have poor reputations from the professional standpoint and have conducted themselves in less than commendable fashion. There are many agencies that are good and handle themselves professionally. Unfortunately, however, the few that do not have accounted for some employment "horror stories," several of which I am sure you have heard.

It is important that you have some good advice regarding the selection of an agency that will truly represent your best interests and do a thoroughly professional job in helping you to find the position and employer that you seek. Let's first, however, examine the dangers of making a poor selection—some of the unnecessary experiences that you may encounter in utilizing a source that does not have your best personal and professional interests in mind.

Agencies who conduct themselves in an unprofessional manner are known among employment professionals as "body shops." These agencies operate on the premise that they are in business simply to make money. The more people that they are able to place, the more agency fees, or placement fees, will come rolling into their coffers. They care little about the individual employment candidate they represent; they are concerned only with making a placement and earning an agency commission. These are the agencies described by the professional employment community as the ones who attempt to "place a square peg in a round hole." Having received the employment candidate's resume, their typical

mode of operation is to pick up the telephone and call numerous employers in an effort to "pitch" their candidate. They
care little whether the company with whom they are speaking has an appropriate opening or whether such openings are
in line with the qualifications and interest of the employment
candidates they represent.

Such agencies are looked upon by the professional employment community with disdain. The experienced employment
professional has usually trained his or her administrative
assistant to screen out phone calls from such firms and will
refuse to even talk to them. The reason for such action is
simple. Too many times in the past the employment professional has experienced a situation where the agency has
grossly misrepresented the qualifications and/or the experience of the candidate they are representing. The result has
been that the employer agrees to an interview with the candidate only to discover, during the course of the interview,
that the candidate does not possess the skills and qualifications as presented by the agency. This proves to be both em-
barrassing and expensive to the employment manager.
First, the employment manager is embarrassed to discover
that the candidate is not qualified for the employment opening. Second, he or she is embarrassed by having to tell the
candidate that he or she does not have the qualifications
sought. If told at the beginning of the interview, the employment manager may terminate the interview early and the
job candidate is frequently both hurt and angered. Much of
this anger and hostility is directed toward the employer
rather than the agency who has made the referral. Unfortunately, the candidate has not been present when his or her
qualifications have been discussed with the employer and
thus may be left with the impression that the employment
manager is careless or incompetent. Should the employment
manager elect to proceed with the interview schedule and
use the valuable time of busy managers to interview an individual who is clearly unqualified for the position, he or she
will likely incur the wrath of these managers and risk earning a reputation for carelessness or incompetence.

In addition to the embarrassment and hard feelings
caused by this situation, there may be considerable expense
involved. There can be travel expenses reimbursed by the

company up to several hundred dollars (plane fare, meals, lodging, etc.). In addition, there is the time lost by the employment manager as well as the managers who interviewed the candidate. In salaries alone (not considering the lost production), this could easily result in costs of $100 or $200 (depending on the levels of the managers involved).

These "body shop" agencies earn an extremely unsatisfactory reputation in the employment community. The effect is that knowledgeable candidates with good qualifications, who have taken the time to research agencies, avoid these firms. These agencies thus frequently end up representing those employment candidates who have poor qualifications and are hard to place. This further renders such agencies useless as far as the employment professional is concerned.

From the employment candidate's standpoint, there is much at risk when selecting such an agency to represent you. One great danger, if you are currently employed, is that such firms may not use proper discretion in handling your resume. Many mass mail your resume to numerous employers. In such cases it is not entirely uncommon for the resume of an unknowing candidate to be sent to the candidate's current employer. In the case of better employers this may simply result in some embarrassment; in other cases, however, it may result in termination of the employee's employment.

On the other side of the employment equation, these agencies may grossly misrepresent a job to the employment applicant, indicating that the position pays considerably more than it in fact does, that the position has considerably more scope and authority than it really does, or that promotional opportunities are substantially greater than they really are. Such employment agencies appear to be substantially more motivated by receiving commissions than they are in deriving professional satisfaction from helping people locate a position that will satisfy their career objectives.

By contrast, there are also some excellent agencies out there. It is simply a matter of finding out who they are and how to make contact with them. There are techniques I would like to suggest to you in accomplishing this. First, if you know someone who is a human resources manager or employment manager in a major corporation, you might inquire of them which agencies they utilize and which they feel conduct themselves in a professional manner. This alone may not be a significant help since companies tend to gravitate toward those better employment agencies who specialize in their industries. Thus they may refer to you agencies that are proficient in finding people in the steel and automotive industries, but if you are in the chemical industry, this would be of little or no help to you. Where possible, therefore, it would be a good practice to attempt to make contact with human resource managers or professional employment individuals within your own industry. This is particularly true if your background is only marketable to the industry in which you currently work. Thus, if you are an engineer with considerable experience in the steel industry, the likelihood is that your background is far less marketable in other industries. Conversely, if your background is in a more generic function (e.g., accounting, finance, or human resources), there is a high likelihood that you will be able to cross industry lines with little or no effort.

Another good technique to use in identifying the better employment agencies is to check for advertisement in professional publications related to your career or field. After identifying a number of these agencies, call some of these firms on the phone without disclosing your name. Generally describe your background to them and tell them that you do not wish to disclose your name until you have had an opportunity to find out more about their firm. Request the names and telephone numbers of some employment candidates with whom they have recently worked. Having done this, call these individuals and introduce yourself. The following are some questions you might use:

1. Did the agency appear to have a good understanding of your background and qualifications such that they did a good job of representing you to prospective employers?

2. Did the agency appear to have contact with the better employers within your industry?

3. Did the agency do a reasonably thorough job of explaining to you the job opportunities of prospective

employers? Was the agency able to be factual in describing the reporting relationships of the position, job scope and accountability, promotional prospects, compensation levels, company benefits, and relocation expense reimbursement policy?

4. Did the agency do a good job in representing your interests during the negotiation phase with the prospective employer? Were the terms of the employment offer totally satisfactory?

5. If you were to be back in the labor market at some future point in time, would you consider using this agency again?

6. In your opinion, during the course of your relationship with the agency, did anything happen that caused you to feel that the agency was less than professional or ethical?

7. Who were you dealing with at the agency?

Having received answers to these questions from four or five employment candidates with whom the agency has worked, you are in a good position to judge whether the agency is the type of firm with whom you would like to deal.

EXECUTIVE SEARCH FIRMS

Unlike the employment agency, the executive search firm does not represent the individual. Instead, these firms are retained by the employer to search out qualified individuals to fill key positions within their client company. All fees are charged directly to the employer, with no fee charged to the successful candidate found by the search firm to fill the position.

The better executive search firms are highly respected within the employment community. They frequently belong to an association that requires them to operate in accordance with an extremely rigid code of ethics and conduct. Inappropriate behavior would cause a member firm to be immediately dismissed from the association. Member firms are very protective of their professional reputation and will not tolerate devious or unethical behavior on the part of other association members.

Perhaps the best known of these associations is the Association of Executive Search Consultants, Inc., headquartered in Stamford, Connecticut. This association is comprised of some 50 member firms and subscribes to a very tightly enforced code of ethics. The membership of this organization is believed to represent the top 50 executive search firms in the United States. A select listing of the association's membership appears at the end of this chapter, along with a few other select firms who are also well known in the executive search field.

Generally speaking, these search firms handle management and executive searches only (with salaries in the over $90,000 per year range). On occasion, however, they may agree to handle client searches for some technical or professional positions in the under $90,000 range that are particularly difficult to fill.

When writing to an executive search firm, it is important to remember that they may not be working on a compatible search at the time that your resume arrives. Additionally, they will make no attempt to help you find employment unless they coincidentally have a compatible opening with one of their client firms. It is important, therefore, that you acknowledge this fact in your cover letter. See Chapter 15 for guidance in the preparation of effective cover letters when writing to executive search firms.

If you are in search of a management or executive position, it is recommended that you write to some of the more reputable executive search firms as part of your overall job-hunting strategy. Should they not have an immediate search assignment that is compatible with your qualifications and interests, provided you have reasonable credentials, they will likely file your resume for future reference. There is always the possibility that an appropriate search assignment may be just around the corner and that you will be hearing from them.

The following listing of the top 50 executive search firms is provided for your convenience. They are listed by geographical region for ease in focusing on those geographical areas that are in line with your preference.

Top Executive Search Firms

Northeast

AST PARTNERS
One Atlantic Street
Stamford, CT 06901
(203) 975-7188

BARGER & SARGEANT, INC.
22 Windermere Road
Center Harbor, NH 03226
(603) 253-4700

**BATTALIA WINSTON
INTERNATIONAL, INC.**
555 Madison Avenue
New York, NY 10022
(212) 308-8080

379 Thronall Street, 10th Floor
Edison, NJ 08837
(732) 549-8200

65 William Street, Suite 240
Wellesley Hills, MA 02481
(781) 239-1400

**MARTIN H. BAUMAN
ASSOCIATES, INC.**
375 Park Avenue, Suite 2002
New York, NY 10152
(212) 752-6580

BOYDEN
364 Elmwood Avenue
Hawthorne, NY 10532-1239
(914) 747-0093

33 Union Place
Summit, NJ 07901
(908) 598-0331

221 Seventh Street
Pittsburgh, PA 15222-1423
(412) 391-3020

**BRANDYWINE CONSULTING
GROUP**
5 Great Valley Parkway,
Suite 213
Malvern, PA 19355
(610) 407-4600

CHRISTIAN & TIMBERS, INC.
24 New England Executive Park
Burlington, MA 01803
(781) 229-9515

750 Washington Boulevard,
5th Floor
Stamford, CT 06901
(203) 352-6000

570 Lexington Avenue, 19th Floor
New York, NY 10022
(212) 588-3500

**COLUMBIA CONSULTING GROUP,
INC.**
767 Third Avenue, 29th Floor
New York, NY 10017-2023
(212) 832-2525

EMA PARTNERS INTERNATIONAL
230 Park Avenue, 10th Floor
New York, NY 10017
(212) 808-3076

466 Southern Boulevard
Chatham, NJ 07928-1462
(973) 966-1600

**THE DIVERSIFIED SEARCH
COMPANIES**
One Commerce Square
2005 Market Street, Suite 3300
Philadelphia, PA 19103
(215) 732-6666

Two Penn Plaza, Suite 1920
New York, NY 10121
(212) 594-8340

35 Corporate Drive, Suite 210
Burlington, MA 01803
(781) 270-2318

**GILBERT TWEED
    ASSOCIATES, INC.**
415 Madison Avenue
New York, NY 10017
(212) 758-3000

**GOODRICH & SHERWOOD
    ASSOC., INC.**
521 Fifth Avenue
New York, NY 10175
(212) 697-4131

535 Connecticut Avenue,
    1st Floor
Norwalk, CT 06851
(203) 899-7900

4 Armstrong Road
Building #2, 3rd Floor
Shelton, CT 06484
(203) 944-2828

6 Century Drive
Parsippany, NJ 07054
(973) 455-7100

One Independence Way
Princeton, NJ 08540
(609) 452-0202

400 Andrews Street,
    Suite 400
Rochester, NY 14604
(585) 262-4277

HEIDRICK & STRUGGLES
150 Federal Street, 27th Floor
Boston, MA 02110
(617) 737-6300

Three Greenwich Office Park
Greenwich, CT 06831-5150
(203) 862-4600

245 Park Avenue, Suite 4300
New York, NY 10167-0152
(212) 867-9876

40 Wall Street, 48th Floor
New York, NY 10005
(212) 699-3000

One Logan Square
18th & Cherry Street, Suite 3075
Philadelphia, PA 19103
(215) 988-1000

HORTON INTERNATIONAL, LLC
Corporate Center West, Suite 327
433 South Main Street
West Hartford, CT 06110
(860) 521-0101

HUNT HOWE PARTNERS, LLC
One Dag Hammarskjold Plaza,
    34th Floor
New York, NY 10017
(212) 758-2800

HVS INTERNATIONAL
372 Willis Avenue
Mineola, NY 11501
(516) 248-8828

Riversbend
262 Lyons Plain Road
Weston, CT 06883
(203) 226-6000

KAZAN INTERNATIONAL, INC.
5 Cold Hill Road South, Suite 26
Mendham, NJ 07945
(973) 543-0300

**A.T. KEARNEY EXECUTIVE
    SEARCH**
153 East 53rd Street
New York, NY 10022
(212) 751-7040

One Landmark Square,
    Suite 2001
Stamford, CT 06901-2502
(203) 969-2222

KORN/FERRY INTERNATIONAL
265 Franklin Street, 17th Floor
Boston, MA 02110
(617) 345-0200

200 Park Avenue, 37th Floor
New York, NY 10166
(212) 687-1834

11 Penn Center, Suite 2626
Philadelphia, PA 19103
(215) 496-6666

7 Roszel Road, 5th Floor
Princeton, NJ 08540
(609) 452-8848

Financial Center
695 East Main Street
Stamford, CT 06901-2679
(203) 359-3350

THE JOHN LUCHT
    CONSULTANCY, INC.
The Olympic Tower
641 Fifth Avenue
New York, NY 10022-5908
(212) 935-4660

THE ONSTOTT GROUP, INC.
60 William Street, Suite 250
Wellesley, MA 02481-3803
(781) 235-3050

RAY & BERNDTSON
230 Park Avenue, Suite 1000
New York, NY 10169
(212) 309-8710

RUSSELL REYNOLDS
    ASSOC., INC.
200 Park Avenue, Suite 2300
New York, NY 10166-0002
(212) 370-0896

Old City Hall
45 School Street
Boston, MA 02108-3296
(617) 523-1111

ERIC SALMON & PARTNERS
245 Park Avenue
New York, NY 10167
(212) 372-8800

SKOTT/EDWARDS
    CONSULTANTS
1776 On the Green
Morristown, NJ 07960
(973) 644-0900

SPENCERSTUART
24 Federal Street, 10th Floor
Boston, MA 02110
(617) 531-5731

277 Park Avenue, 29th Floor
New York, NY 10172-2998
(212) 336-0200

One Commerce Square
2005 Market Street, Suite 2350
Philadelphia, PA 19103-7042
(215) 814-1600

Financial Center
695 E. Main Street
Stamford, CT 06901-2148
(203) 324-6333

TMP WORLDWIDE EXECUTIVE
    SEARCH
5 Clock Tower Place, Suite 500
Maynard, MA 01754
(978) 823-2600

622 Third Avenue
New York, NY 10017
(212) 351-7100

Metro Center
One Station Place
Stamford, CT 06902-6800
(203) 324-4445

WHITEHEAD MANN
One International Place,
    Suite 1100
Boston, MA 02110-2600
(617) 598-1200

280 Park Avenue
East Tower, 25th Floor
New York, NY 10017
(212) 894-8300

WHITNEY GROUP
101 Federal Street,
    Suite 1900
Boston, MA 02110
(617) 342-7332

860 Third Avenue
New York, NY 10022
(212) 508-3600

Southeast

ANDERSON & ASSOCIATES
112 South Tryon Street, # 800
Charlotte, NC 28284
(704) 347-0900

1595 Peachtree Parkway,
    Suite 204, # 200
Cummings, GA 30041
(770) 886-9705

BARTHOLDI & COMPANY, INC.
12020 Sunrise Valley Road,
    Suite 160
Reston, VA 20191-3429
(703) 476-5519

BOYDEN
3525 Piedmont Road
Five Piedmont Center, Suite 202
Atlanta, GA 30305
(404) 995-1700

217 East Redwood Street
16th Floor
Baltimore, MD 21202
(410) 625-3800

CHRISTIAN & TIMBERS, INC.
10211 Wincopin Circle, Suite 200
Columbia, MD 21044
(410) 393-0001

1750 Tysons Boulevard, Suite 540
McLean, VA 22102
(703) 448-1740

**COLUMBIA CONSULTING
    GROUP, INC.**
1 Southgate Drive
Annapolis, MD 21401
(410) 280-8858

The Sun Life Building
20 South Charles Street, 9th Floor
Baltimore, MD 21201
(410) 385-2525

185 Helios Drive
Jupiter, FL 33477
(561) 748-0232

**EMA PARTNERS
    INTERNATIONAL**
3040 Universal Boulevard,
    Suite 190
Weston, FL 33331
(954) 385-8595

**GOODRICH & SHERWOOD
    ASSOCIATES**
Overlook 3, Suite 1520
2859 Paces Ferry
Atlanta, GA 30339
(404) 872-7600

HEIDRICK & STRUGGLES
303 Peachtree NE, Suite 3100
Atlanta, GA 30308-3201
(404) 577-2410

Carillon Building
227 W. Trade Street,
   Suite 1600
Charlotte, NC 28202
(704) 333-1953

76 S. Laura Street,
   Suite 2110
Jacksonville, FL 32202-5448
(904) 355-6674

5301 Blue Lagoon Drive,
   Suite 590
Miami, FL 33126
(305) 262-2606

1001 Winstead Drive,
   Suite 355
Cary, NC 27513
(919) 380-6800

1750 Tysons Boulevard,
   Suite 300
McLean, VA 22102
(703) 848-2500

HVS INTERNATIONAL
Treman Center, Suite 216
8925 SW 148th Street
Miami, FL 33176

1300 Piccard Drive,
   Suite 100
Rockville, MD 20850
(301) 670-1635

KAZAN INTERNATIONAL, INC.
1135 Lafayette Drive
Eldersburg, MD 21784
(410) 552-1352

**A.T. KEARNEY EXECUTIVE
   SEARCH**
333 Carlyle Street
Alexandria, VA 22314
(703) 836-6210

3455 Peachtree Road,
   Suite 1600
Atlanta, GA 30326
(404) 760-6600

First Union Financial Center
200 S. Biscayne Boulevard,
   Suite 3500
Miami, FL 33131
(305) 577-0046

KINCANNON & REED
2106-C Gallows Road
Vienna, VA 22182
(703) 761-4046

KORN/FERRY INTERNATIONAL
303 Peachtree Street NE,
   Suite 1600
Atlanta, GA 30308
(404) 577-7542

200 South Biscayne Boulevard,
   Suite 4450
Miami, FL 33131
(305) 377-4121

8270 Greensboro Drive,
   Suite 850
McLean, VA 22102
(703) 761-7020

Presidential Plaza
900 19th Street NW, Suite 800
Washington, DC 20006-2183
(202) 822-9444

LEMMING/LEVAN, INC.
1040 Crown Pointe Parkway,
   Suite 1055
Atlanta, GA 30338
(770) 551-6979

**LLOYD PRESCOTT &
   CHURCHILL, INC.**
Presidential Plaza, Suite 360
4803 George Road
Tampa, FL 33634
(813) 881-1110

LOCKE & ASSOCIATES
2410 NationsBank Plaza
Charlotte, NC 28280
(704) 372-6600

4144 Carmichael Road, Suite 20
Montgomery, AL 36106-3614
(334) 272-7400

**NORMAN BROADBENT
INTERNATIONAL**
2859 Paces Ferry Road,
    Suite 1400
Atlanta, GA 30339
(770) 955-9550

RAY & BERNDTSON
191 Peachtree Tower,
    Suite 3800
Atlanta, GA 30303-1757
(404) 215-4600

**RUSSELL REYNOLDS
ASSOCIATES, INC.**
The Hurt Building
50 Hurt Plaza, Suite 600
Atlanta, GA 30303-2914
(404) 577-3000

1701 Pennsylvania Avenue NW,
    Suite 400
Washington, DC 20006-5805
(202) 654-7800

**SEELIGER Y CONDE
INTERNATIONAL—MIAMI, LLC**
95 Merrick Way, Suite 518
Coral Gables, FL 33134
(305) 442-1160

SOCKWELL ASSOCIATES
227 West Trade Street, Suite 1930
Charlotte, NC 28202
(704) 372-1865

2530 Meridian Parkway, 3rd Floor
Research Triangle Park, NC 27612
(919) 806-4450

SPENCERSTUART
2600 Resurgens Plaza
945 East Paces Ferry Road
Atlanta, GA 30326
(404) 504-4400

355 Alhambra Circle,
    Suite 1300
Miami, FL 33134
(305) 443-9911

1101 Pennsylvania Avenue, NW,
    Suite 600
Washington, DC 20004
(202) 756-3793

**STANTON CHASE
INTERNATIONAL**
100 East Pratt Street,
    Suite 2530
Baltimore, MD 21202
(410) 528-8400

**TMP WORLDWIDE EXECUTIVE
SEARCH**
191 Peachtree Street, NE,
    Suite 800
Atlanta, GA 30303-1747
(404) 688-0800

Midwest

BATTALIA WINSTON INT'L., INC.
150 South Wacker Drive,
    Suite 1220
Chicago, IL 60606
(312) 704-0050

EFL ASSOCIATES
7101 College Boulevard,
    Suite 550
Overland Park, KS 66210-1891
(913) 451-8866

BOYDEN
300 East Long Lake, Suite 375
Bloomfield Hills, MI 48304
(248) 647-4201

Two Prudential Plaza
180 North Stetson Avenue,
   Suite 2500
Chicago, IL 60601
(312) 565-1300

3012 Fairmount Boulevard
Cleveland, OH 44118
(216) 932-4164

1390 Timberlake Manor Parkway,
   Suite 260
Chesterfield, MO 63017
(636) 519-7400

CHRISTIAN & TIMBERS, INC.
One Corporate Exchange
25825 Science Park Drive,
   Suite 400
Cleveland, OH 44122
(216) 464-8710

One South Wacker Drive,
   Suite 1990
Chicago, IL 60606
(312) 281-1160

COMPASS GROUP LTD.
401 South Old Woodward,
   Suite 460
Birmingham, MI 48009-6613
(248) 540-9110

2021 Spring Road, Suite 750
Oak Brook, IL 60523-1880
(248) 540-9110

**DIECKMANN & ASSOCIATES,
   LTD.**
180 North Stetson Avenue,
   Suite 5555
Chicago, IL 60601
(312) 819-5900

**EMA PARTNERS
   INTERNATIONAL**
Lauer, Sbarbaro Associates/
   EMA Partners International
30 N. LaSalle Street, Suite 4030
Chicago, IL 60602-2588
(312) 372-7050

HEIDRICK & STRUGGLES
233 South Wacker Drive,
   Suite 7000
Chicago, IL 60606-6402
(312) 496-1000

600 Superior Avenue East,
   Suite 2500
Cleveland, OH 44114-2650
(216) 241-7410

HVS INTERNATIONAL
4405 West Erie Street
Chicago, IL 60610
(312) 587-9900

**A.T. KEARNEY EXECUTIVE
   SEARCH**
222 West Adams Street
Chicago, IL 60606
(312) 648-0111

8500 Normandale Lake
   Boulevard, Suite 1630
Minneapolis, MN 55437-3829
(952) 921-8436

1200 Bank One Center
600 Superior Avenue East
Cleveland, OH 44114-2650
(216) 241-6880

KORN/FERRY INTERNATIONAL
Sears Tower
233 South Wacker Drive,
   Suite 3300
Chicago, IL 60606
(312) 466-1834

4816 IDS Center
80 S. 8th Street
Minneapolis, MN 55402-2229
(612) 333-1834

RAY & BERNDTSON
Sears Tower
233 Wacker Drive, Suite 4020
Chicago, IL 60606-6310
(312) 876-0730

**RUSSELL REYNOLDS
ASSOCIATES, INC.**
200 South Wacker Drive,
  Suite 2900
Chicago, IL 60606-5802
(312) 993-9696

3050 Wells Fargo Center
90 South Seventh Street
Minneapolis, MN 55402-3900
(612) 332-6966

SPENCERSTUART
401 N. Michigan Avenue,
  Suite 3400
Chicago, IL 60611-4244
(312) 822-0080

225 South Sixth Street,
  Suite 4141
Minneapolis, MN 55402
(612) 313-2000

**TMP WORLDWIDE EXECUTIVE
  SEARCH**
225 West Wacker Drive,
  Suite 2100
Chicago, IL 60606-1229
(312) 782-3113

The Claxton Building,
  Suite 450
812 Huron Road
Cleveland, OH 44115
(216) 694-3052

7825 Washington Avenue South,
  Suite 725
Minneapolis, MN 55439
(952) 833-9245

**WITT/KIEFFER, FORD,
  HADELMAN & LLOYD**
2015 Spring Road, Suite 510
Oak Brook, IL 60523
(630) 990-1370

8000 Maryland Avenue,
  Suite 1080
St. Louis, MO 63105
(314) 862-1370

WHITNEY GROUP
625 N. Michigan Avenue
Chicago, IL 60611
(312) 587-3030

Southwest

BARTHOLDI & COMPANY, INC.
10040 E. Happy Valley Road,
  Suite 244
Scottsdale, AZ 85255
(602) 502-2178

BOYDEN
5847 San Felipe, Suite 3940
Houston, TX 77057
(713) 655-0123

248 East Vera Lane
Tempe, AZ 85284
(480) 705-7269

**DIECKMANN &
  ASSOCIATES**
8450 East Crescent
  Parkway
Greenwood Village, CO 80111
(303) 904-4852

**ROBERT W. DINGMAN
COMPANY**
8125 Wildridge Road
Black Forest, CO 80908
(719) 495-7898

EFL ASSOCIATES
Transearch International
7120 East Orchard,
   Suite 240
Englewood, CO 80112

CHRISTIAN & TIMBERS
2435 N. Central Expressway,
   Suite 1200
Richardson, TX 75080
(214) 712-7380

**EMA PARTNERS
INTERNATIONAL**
333 N. Sam Houston Pkwy. E,
   Suite 400
Houston, TX 77060-2403
(281) 999-7209

**GILBERT TWEED
ASSOCIATES, INC.**
8920 Upper Lando Lane
Park City, Utah 84098
(801) 264-6697

HEIDRICK & STRUGGLES
7000 N. Mopac Expressway,
   2nd Floor
Austin, TX 78731
(512) 514-6313

5950 Sherry Lane,
   Suite 400
Dallas, TX 75225
(214) 706-7700

16th Market Square
1400 Sixteenth Street,
   Suite 300
Denver, CO 80202
(720) 932-3800

One Houston Center, Suite 3050
1221 McKinney Street
Houston, TX 77010
(713) 237-9000

HVS INTERNATIONAL
2229 Broadway
Boulder, CO 80210
(303) 443-3933

1777 South Harrison Street,
   Suite 906
Denver, CO 80210
(303) 512-1222

2601 Sagebrush Drive
Flower Mound, TX 75028
(972) 410-2002

3209 East Missouri Avenue
Phoenix, AZ 85018
(602) 667-6655

**A.T. KEARNEY EXECUTIVE
SEARCH**
5400 Legacy Drive
B1-1A-01
Plano, TX 75024
(972) 543-7500

500 N. Akard Street,
   Suite 4170
Dallas, TX 75201-3385
(214) 969-0010

KORN/FERRY INTERNATIONAL
2100 McKinney Avenue,
   Suite 1800
Dallas, TX 75201
(214) 954-1834

1600 Broadway, Suite 2400
Denver, CO 80202
(303) 542-1880

1100 Louisiana, Suite 2850
Houston, TX 77002-5482
(713) 651-1834

PRENG & ASSOCIATES
2925 Briarpark, Suite 1111
Houston, TX 77042-3734
(713) 266-2600

**RUSSELL REYNOLDS
    ASSOCIATES, INC.**
Lincoln Park
8401 North Central Expressway,
    Suite 650
Dallas, TX 75225-4404
(214) 220-2033

500 Dallas Street, Suite 2840
Houston, TX 77002-4708
(713) 658-1776

SPENCERSTUART
1717 Main Street, Suite 5600
Dallas, TX 75201-4605
(214) 672-5200

1111 Bagby, Suite 1616
Houston, TX 77002-2594
(713) 225-1621

TASA INTERNATIONAL
5420 LBJ Freeway, Suite 1475
Dallas, TX 75240
(972) 458-1212

**TMP WORLDWIDE EXECUTIVE
    SEARCH**
5956 Sherry Lane, Suite 1800
Dallas, TX 75225
(214) 754-0019

One City Center, Suite 1050
1021 Main Street
Houston, TX 77002-6602
(713) 843-8600

**WITT/KIEFFER, FORD,
    HADELMAN & LLOYD**
Two Lincoln Center
5420 LBJ Freeway, Suite 460
Dallas, TX 75240
(972) 490-1370

10375 Richmond Avenue,
    Suite 1625
Houston, TX 77042
(713) 266-6779

432 North 44th Street, Suite 360
Phoenix, AZ 85008
(602) 267-1370

West Coast

BRYANT GROUP
4676 Admiralty Way, Suite 430
Marina Del Ray, CA 90292
(310) 827-8383

**BATTALIA WINSTON
    INTERNATIONAL, INC./
    EURAM**
1888 Century Park East,
    Suite 1150
Los Angeles, CA 90067
(310) 284-8080

One Sansome Street
Citicorp Center
San Francisco, CA 94104
(415) 984-3180

BOYDEN
Embarcadero Center,
    West Tower
275 Battery Street,
    Suite 420
San Francisco, CA 94111-3331
(415) 981-7900

Busch International
5150 El Camino Real, Suite A-30
Los Altos, CA 94022
(650) 623-0090

CHRISTIAN & TIMBERS, INC.
114 Pacifica, Suite 150
Irvine, CA 92618-3326
(949) 727-3400

2180 Sand Hill Road, Suite 300
Menlo Park, CA 94025
(650) 798-0980

ROBERT W. DINGMAN COMPANY
650 Hampshire Road, #116
Westlake Village, CA 91361
(805) 778-1777

THE DOMANN ORGANIZATION
Waterfall Towers, B107
2455 Bennett Valley Road
Santa Rosa, CA 95404
(800) 923-6626

City Front Terrace
500 W. Harbor Drive, Suite 1204
San Diego, CA 92101
(619) 525-7615

200 First Avenue West, Suite 400
Seattle, WA 98119
(206) 505-7955

**EMA PARTNERS
INTERNATIONAL**
363 San Miguel Drive, Suite 200
Newport Beach, CA 92660
(949) 720-9070

577 Airport Boulevard, Suite 130
Burlingame, CA 94010
(650) 343-2660

LEON A. FARLEY ASSOCIATES
31 Laderman Lane
Greenbrae, CA 94904
(415) 989-0989

HEIDRICK & STRUGGLES
18101 Von Karman Avenue,
    Suite 1050
Irvine, CA 92612
(949) 475-6500

633 West Fifth Street, Suite 3300
Los Angeles, CA 90071-2017
(213) 625-8811

10877 Wilshire Blvd., Suite 1802
West Los Angeles, CA 90024
(310) 209-9600

12760 High Bluff Drive,
    Suite 240
San Diego, CA 92130
(858) 794-1970

2740 Sand Hill Road
Menlo Park, CA 94025-7096
(650) 234-1500

One California Street, Suite 2400
San Francisco, CA 94111
(415) 981-2854

HVS INTERNATIONAL
116 New Montgomery Street,
    Suite 620
San Francisco, CA 94105
(415) 896-0868

KAZAN INTERNATIONAL, INC.
601 108th Ave., NE, 19th Floor
Bellevue, WA 98004
(425) 943-7709

**A.T. KEARNEY EXECUTIVE
    SEARCH**
Plaza Tower
600 Anton Boulevard, Suite 1000
Costa Mesa, CA 92626
(714) 445-6819

Biltmore Tower
500 S. Grand Avenue, Suite 1780
Los Angeles, CA 90071-2609
(213) 689-6800

Three Lagoon Drive, Suite 160
Redwood Shores, CA 94065
(650) 637-6600

KINCANNON & REED
111 Chestnut Street, Suite 603
San Francisco, CA 94111
(415) 834-0828

KORN/FERRY INTERNATIONAL
1800 Century Park East,
   Suite 900
Los Angeles, CA 90067
(310) 552-1834

2600 Michelson Drive, Suite 720
Irvine, CA 92612
(949) 851-1834

Three Lagoon Drive, Suite 280
Redwood City, CA 94065
(650) 632-1834

One Embarcadero Center,
   Suite 2101
San Francisco, CA 94111
(415) 956-1834

999 Third Avenue, Suite 4760
Seattle, WA 98104
(206) 447-1834

NORMAN BROADBENT
100 Pine Street, Suite 1750
San Francisco, CA 94111
(415) 274-8333

**RUSSELL REYNOLDS
   ASSOCIATES, INC.**
333 South Grand Avenue,
   Suite 3500
Los Angeles, CA 90071-1539
(213) 253-4400

2500 Sand Hill Road, Suite 105
Menlo Park, CA 94025-7015
(650) 233-2400

101 California Street, Suite 3140
San Francisco, CA 94111-5829
(415) 352-3300

SPENCERSTUART
10900 Wilshire Boulevard,
   Suite 800
Los Angeles, CA 90024-6524
(310) 209-0610

2020 Main Street, Suite 350
Irvine, CA 92614
(949) 930-8000

525 Market Street, Suite 3700
San Francisco, CA 94105
(415) 495-4141

2988 Campus Drive, 3rd Floor
San Mateo, CA 94403
(650) 356-5500

**TMP WORLDWIDE EXECUTIVE
   SEARCH**
16255 Ventura Boulevard,
   Suite 400
Encino, CA 91436-2394
(818) 905-6010

222 North Sepulveda Boulevard,
   Suite 1780
El Segundo, CA 90245
(310) 321-3220

595 Market Street, Suite 1100
San Francisco, CA 94105
(415) 356-3600

**WITT/KIEFFER, FORD,
   HADELMAN & LLOYD**
2200 Powell Street, Suite 890
Emeryville, CA 94608
(510) 420-1370

1920 Main Street, Suite 310
Irvine, CA 92614
(949) 851-5070

Canada

THE CALDWELL PARTNERS
   INTERNATIONAL
64 Prince Arthur Avenue
Toronto, Ontario M5R 1B4
Canada
(416) 920-7702

400 3rd Avenue SW, Suite 3450
Calgary, Alberta T2P 4H2
Canada
(403) 265-8780

1840 Sherbrooke Street West
Montreal, Quebec H3H 1E4
Canada
(514) 935-6969

1095 West Pender Street,
   Suite 850
Vancouver, British Columbia
   V6E 2M6
Canada
(604) 669-3550

EMA PARTNERS
   INTERNATIONAL
1100 de la Gauchetiere, Suite
   1100
Montreal, Quebec H3B 2S2
Canada
(514) 849-2333

350 Bay Street, Suite 1000,
   10th Floor
Canada Trust Tower
Toronto, Ontario M5H 2S6
Canada
(647) 777-3111

Guinness Tower, Suite 2020
1055 Hastings Street
Vancouver, British Columbia V6E
   2E9
Canada
(800) 664-9970

HVS INTERNATIONAL
4235 Prospect Road
N. Vancouver, British Columbia
   V7N 3L6
Canada
(604) 988-9743

Hammersmith House
2120 Queen Street East
Toronto, Ontario M4E 1E2
Canada
(416) 686-2260

KORN/FERRY INTERNATIONAL
520 5th Avenue, SW, Suite 2500
Calgary, Alberta T2P 3R7
Canada
(403) 269-3277

420 McGill Street, Suite 400
Montreal, Quebec H2Y 2G1
Canada
(514) 397-9655

BCE Place
Bay Wellington Tower, Box 763
181 Bay Street, Suite 3320
Toronto, Ontario M5J 2T3
Canada
(416) 365-1841

Four Bentall Center, Suite 3300
1055 Dunsmuir Street
P.O. Box 49206
Vancouver, British Columbia V7X
   1K8
Canada
(604) 684-1834

RAY & BERNDTSON
1250 W. Rene Levesque
   Boulevard, Suite 3925
Montreal, Quebec H3B 4W8
Canada
(514) 937-1000

200-29 Beechwood Avenue
Ottawa, Ontario K1M 1M2
Canada
(613) 749-9909

Royal Bank Plaza
200 Bay Street
South Tower, Suite 3150
Toronto, Ontario M5J 2J3
Canada
(416) 366-1990

710-1050 West Pender Street
Vancouver, British Columbia V6E
  3S7
Canada
(604) 685-0261

SPENCERSTUART
1002, rue Sherbrooke Quest,
  Suite 2500
Montreal, Quebec H3A 3L6
Canada
(514) 288-3377

One University Avenue, Suite 801
Toronto, Ontario M5J 2P1
Canada
(416) 361-0311

International

ACCORD GROUP
Hanssens & Partners
Clos du Chemin Creux 6c / Box 3
Holleweggaarde 6c / Box 3
B-1030 Brussels
Belgium
+32 2 242 73 80
(Australia, Belgium, Brazil, Czech
  Republic, Finland, France,
  Germany, Hong Kong,
  Hungary, India, Italy, The
  Netherlands, New Zealand,
  Poland, Portugal, Romania,
  Russia, South Africa, Spain,
  Sweden, United Kingdom)

THE AMROP HEVER GROUP
Klein Fontenay 1
20354 Hamburg
Germany
+49 40 413-2350
(Argentina, Australia, Austria,
  Belgium, Brazil, Chile, China,
  Colombia, Czech Republic,
  Denmark, Estonia, Finland,
  France, Germany, Greece,
  Hungary, India, Indonesia,
  Ireland, Italy, Japan, Korea,

Latvia, Lebanon, Mexico, The
  Netherlands, New Zealand,
  Norway, Peru, Philippines,
  Poland, Portugal, Romania,
  Russia, Saudi Arabia,
  Singapore, Slovakia, Spain,
  Sweden, Switzerland, Taiwan,
  Thailand, Turkey, United
  Kingdom, Venezuela)

BOYDEN
364 Elmwood Avenue
Hawthorne, NY 10532-1239
(914) 747-0093
(Argentina, Australia, Belgium,
  Brazil, Chile, China, Colombia,
  Czech Republic, Denmark,
  England, Finland, France,
  Germany, Greece, Hong Kong,
  Hungary, India, Indonesia,
  Italy, Japan, Korea, Luxemburg,
  Malaysia, New Zealand,
  Norway, Philippines, Poland,
  Portugal, Russia, Singapore,
  South Africa, Spain, Sweden,
  Switzerland, Taiwan, Thailand,
  Turkey, Venezuela)

EUROMEDICA PLC
8 Enterprise House
Vision Park
Histon, Cambridge CB4 4ZR
United Kingdom
(011) 44 1223 235333
(Belgium, Denmark, France,
  Germany, India, Italy, Spain,
  United Kingdom)

HEIDRICK & STRUGGLES
Corporate Office
Sears Tower, Suite 4200
233 South Wacker Drive
Chicago, IL 60606-6402
(312) 496-1200
(Argentina, Australia, Belgium,
  Brazil, Chile, China, Colombia,
  Denmark, Finland, France,
  Germany, Hong Kong, India,
  Italy, Japan, Korea, Mexico,
  The Netherlands, Norway,
  Peru, Poland, Portugal,
  Singapore, South Africa,
  Spain, Sweden, Switzerland,
  Taiwan, Turkey, United
  Kingdom, Venezuela)

HORTON INTERNATIONAL, LLC
Corporate Center West, Suite 327
433 South Main Street
West Hartford, CT 06110
(860) 521-0101
(Argentina, Australia, Belgium,
  Brazil, China, Czech Republic,
  Denmark, Finland, France,
  Germany, Greece, Hungary,
  Indonesia, Italy, Japan, Korea,
  The Netherlands, Norway,
  Portugal, Singapore, Spain,
  Sweden, Switzerland,
  Thailand, United Kingdom)

HVS INTERNATIONAL
1300 Piccard Drive, Suite 100
Rockville, MD 20850
(301) 670-1635

(Argentina, Brazil, Hong Kong,
  India, Singapore, Spain, United
  Kingdom)

**A.T. KEARNEY EXECUTIVE
SEARCH**
153 East 53rd Street
New York, NY 10022
(212) 751-7040
(Australia, Belgium, France,
  Germany, Hong Kong, Italy,
  Japan, The Netherlands,
  Norway, Singapore, Spain,
  Switzerland, United Kingdom)

KORN/FERRY INTERNATIONAL
1800 Century Park East,
  Suite 900
Los Angeles, CA 90067
(310) 552-1834
(Australia, Austria, Belgium,
  Chile, China, Colombia,
  Denmark, Ecuador, India,
  Indonesia, Finland, France,
  Germany, Greece, Hungary,
  Italy, Japan, Korea, Luxemburg,
  Malaysia, Mexico, New Zealand,
  Norway, Peru, Poland,
  Romania, Russia, Singapore,
  Spain, Sweden, Switzerland,
  Thailand, Turkey, United
  Kingdom, Venezuela)

H. NEUMANN INTERNATIONAL
Gunthergasse 3
A-1090 Vienna
Austria
+43 1 40 140 0
(Argentina, Australia, Austria,
  Belgium, Croatia, Czech
  Republic, France, Germany,
  Hungary, Italy, The
  Netherlands, Poland, Portugal,
  Russia, Slovakia, Slovenia,
  Spain, Turkey, United
  Kingdom, Yugoslavia)

PENRHYN INTERNATIONAL
Hansar International
Rue Belliard, 205
1040 Brussels
Belgium
+ 32 2 231 0635
(Argentina, Australia, Belgium,
    France, Germany, Japan,
    Spain, Sweden, Switzerland,
    United Kingdom)

RAY & BERNDTSON
230 Park Avenue, Suite 1000
New York, NY 10169
(212) 309-8710
(Argentina, Australia, Austria,
    Belgium, Brazil, Colombia,
    Czech Republic, Denmark,
    Finland, France, Germany,
    Hungary, India, Italy, Japan,
    Mexico, The Netherlands,
    Norway, Poland, Portugal,
    Russia, Scotland, Singapore,
    Spain, Sweden, Switzerland,
    Turkey, United Kingdom,
    Venezuela)

RUSSELL REYNOLDS
    ASSOCIATES, INC.
200 Park Avenue, Suite 2300
New York, NY 10166-0002
(212) 351-2000
(Australia, Belgium, Brazil,
    China, Denmark, France,
    Germany, Italy, Japan, Mexico,
    The Netherlands, Poland,
    Singapore, Spain, United
    Kingdom)

ERIC SALMON & PARTNERS
95 avenue des Champs-Elysees
75008 Paris
France
(011) 33 1 53 23 88 88
(Germany, Italy, United Kingdom)

SPENCERSTUART
401 N. Michigan Avenue,
    Suite 3400
Chicago, IL 60611-4244
(312) 822-0080
(Argentina, Australia, Austria,
    Belgium, Brazil, Chile, China,
    Colombia, Czech Republic,
    France, Germany, Hong Kong,
    Hungary, Italy, Japan, Mexico,
    The Netherlands, Poland,
    Singapore, South Africa,
    Spain, Sweden, Switzerland,
    United Kingdom)

STANTON CHASE
    INTERNATIONAL
100 East Pratt Street, Suite 2530
Baltimore, MD 21202
(410) 528-8400
(Argentina, Australia, Brazil,
    Chile, Denmark, France,
    Germany, Italy, Japan, Korea,
    Mexico, Mumbai, The
    Netherlands, Norway, Spain,
    South Africa, Sweden, United
    Kingdom, Uruguay, Venezuela)

TMP WORLDWIDE EXECUTIVE
    SEARCH
622 Third Avenue
New York, NY 10017
(212) 351-7100
(Argentina, Australia, Belgium,
    Brazil, France, Germany, Hong
    Kong, Hungary, Italy, The
    Netherlands, New Zealand,
    Poland, Spain, Switzerland,
    United Kingdom)

18

THE TOP 20 INTERNET CAREER SITES

U se of the Internet is virtually exploding. More and more Web sites and portals emerge almost daily, as the world of e-commerce rapidly takes root on the global economic stage. This great engine of change has touched almost every facet of human existence. The employment and job-search process is caught right in the middle of this awesome technological revolution that is radically and forever changing the way we conduct business.

To convey the magnitude of this change from the employment perspective, consider this remarkable forecast. In 1998, employment spending for job listings on the Internet stood at $446 million. By the year 2005, it is expected that such expenditure will reach or exceed $13.5 billion. According to a 2002 survey by iLogos Research, use of corporate Web sites for recruiting purposes by the Fortune

500 companies has already gone from 29 percent to 91 percent, and is now approaching saturation.

These eye-opening statistics are a clear indication of the wide, universal acceptance of the Internet as a valuable recruiting tool by employers. Key reasons for the explosive growth of the Internet as a recruiting powerhouse include the following:

- *It's cheap.* The average cost of a single job listing on the Internet is in the range of $150 to $200. Compare this to the average $4,000 to $5,000 cost-per-hire typically experienced by employers when using other traditional recruiting sources!
- *It's faster.* Often, within minutes of posting a job, employers can receive several resume submissions via e-mail or fax.
- *It's better.* Many companies report that the quality of candidates responding to electronic job postings is a "cut above" those responding from other sources (i.e., those using snail mail).
- *It offers large market exposure.* The employer's job listing on the Internet reaches global masses rather than the smaller, restricted audience reached by other traditional recruiting sources.
- *It reaches "passive" job seekers.* Those not actively on the market.
- *It increases efficiency and reduces costs.* When combined with resume management systems, employers can use computer technology to rapidly process huge volumes of electronically submitted resumes, increasing department efficiency and simultaneously decreasing administrative costs.

The motivations for employers to increasingly shift much of their recruiting to the Internet are many, and compelling. If this is where employers are shifting their recruiting focus, then this is where you need to be in order to enhance job-hunting success. If you're not already there, it's time to take your resume to the Web.

INTERNET RESUME DATABASES

In addition to using the job-posting features of today's Internet career sites to advertise employment openings to the global community, experienced Internet recruiters also make extensive use of the searchable resume databases offered by many of these commercial Web sites to discover qualified candidates who are a good fit for their staffing requirements. Often containing several thousand and even over a million resumes, employers can quickly search these databases electronically, using keywords and concept-based inquiries, for early candidate identification. Savvy employers often subscribe to several of these resume database sites, and constantly explore new ones to discover which sites are most effective in consistently yielding well-qualified candidates.

Today there are literally several thousand career-focused Web sites where you can post your resume at no cost in hopes of being discovered by that one ideal employer for whom you would dearly love to work. These sites come in many shapes and sizes, and the choices become more complex and numerous as each day passes. How does the average employment candidate cut through this morass and select those job search sites that are most beneficial? With the virtual explosion of job search sites now flooding the Internet, this is not an easy task!

THE TOP 20 CAREER WEB SITES

The sheer number of career-related Web sites now saturating the Internet is mind-boggling! Some experts estimate the number at 40,000 and growing rapidly. Those sites with job postings are believed to number about 25,000. Imagine the time it would take to visit and evaluate each of these sites? By the time you completed the process, you could well be qualified for Social Security benefits.

How can you narrow the field to a select few that are well-known, proven sites? Fortunately, much of the hard work has already been done for you. This information can be gleaned, as I have done here, by comparing the results of several highly regarded survey and research organizations known for their thorough, professional job of Web site evaluation. These are:

- IBN (Interbiznet.com): IBN, located in Mill Valley, California, annually publishes the *Electronic Recruiting Index,* an exhaustive study derived from survey of several thousand Internet recruiters which measures their level of satisfaction with various career sites.

  A copy of the most recent study can be ordered directly from their Web site.

- TrafficRanking (TrafficRanking.com): TrafficRanking is a research firm that ranks the popularity of some 720,000 Internet Web sites based on the number of Internet surfers who visit that site.

  The firm uses a statistically-based process that ranks sites based on the number of unique visitors, visits, and page views. I used the firm's search engine to prepare a targeted ranking of only Internet career sites to determine which are the most popular and frequently used. You can generate your own ranking by visiting their Web site at the URL shown above.

- Media Metrix: Media Metrix is a provider of Internet and Digital Media measurement. Data is compiled by taking a nationwide sampling of some 50,000 home and business Internet users, monitoring their usage, and then aggregating their data.

- *CareerXRoads: CareerXRoads* is an annual directory of job, resume and career management sites on the Web. In preparing this directory the authors, Gerry Crispin and Mark Mehler, carefully evaluate over 4,000 annually and provide a brief description of the 500 best sites using their evaluation criteria. They also designate a group of 50 sites as the "best of the Best." A copy of this directory can be ordered from their Web site at careerxroads.com or by phone at (732) 821-6652.

By carefully reviewing and comparing the data presented by these highly respected research sources, coupled with my own independent research, I have distilled my findings to what I believe are the top 20 career Web sites on the Internet. A listing of these top sites, along with their respective URLs follows:

Top 20 Internet Career Sites

1.	4Work	www.4work.com
2.	6FigureJobs	www.6figureJobs.com
3.	Abracat	www.Abracat.com
4.	AfterCollege	www.AfterCollege.com
5.	America's Job Bank	www.ajb.dni.us
6.	BlueSteps	www.BlueSteps.com
7.	BrassRing	www.BrassRing.com
8.	CareerBuilder (Head Hunter)	www.CareerBuilder.com
9.	CareerJournal	www.CareerJournal.com
10.	ComputerJobs	www.ComputerJobs.com
11.	DICE	www.DICE.com
12.	DirectEmployers	www.DirectEmployers.com
13.	ExecuNet	www.ExecuNet.com
14.	FlipDog	www.FlipDog.com
15.	HotJobs (Yahoo! Careers)	www.HotJobs.com
16.	Monster	www.Monster.com
17.	NationJob Network	www.NationJob.com
18.	Net-Temps	www.Net-Temps.com
19.	Recruiters Online Network	www.RecruitersOnline.com
20.	TrueCareers (Career City)	www.TrueCareers.com

To facilitate selection of the career Web sites best suited to your specific resume posting and job-search needs, the remainder of this chapter provides a brief summary of the features of these 20 top sites. The site descriptions and the specific data presented in these summaries are based on the information available on the Web site at the time of this writing and may not totally reflect what exists at the moment you read this chapter.

In particular, database size and specific site content are likely to change with time, especially considering the current rate of change on the Internet. These appear to be well-developed, mature sites, however, so I don't expect to see the kind of dramatic change one might expect of a newly developed career site. These are clearly today's career Internet site market leaders, and I expect them to continue at "the head of the class" for the foreseeable future.

As a side note, although these are the major large volume sites and you should definitely consider posting your resume on them as a key part of your job-search strategy, you need to be aware that there are thousands of other smaller, specialty sites now emerging which focus on specific industries and/or occupations. These are far too numerous to cover here, however, the annual *CareerXroads* directory (described earlier) does an excellent job of covering many of the most significant ones. Several indices at the rear of this directory should prove particularly helpful in helping you to zero in on those most related to your job-search objectives. You should seriously consider acquiring a copy of this book for the purpose of identifying other career sites, beyond those presented below, to which you will want to post your resume.

The following is a full description of each of the top 20 career sites that I recommend for resume posting.

4Work (www.4work.com)

Consistently rated one of the top Internet job-hunting sites, this free site contains over 40,000 job postings. As of December 2002, the site also reports over 308,000 job seekers now using Job Alert, the site's personal career agent. Job Alert provides instant e-mail alerts of any new job postings matching the job seeker's requirements. Additionally, it allows you to set up one or more individual job search profiles, each tailored to specific job interests.

Setting up a Job Alert profile is simple. After registering and inputting required personal contact information, you choose the type of work you seek (i.e., full-time permanent position, internship, youth/part-time/seasonal, or volunteer). Then enter up to five keywords to describe the kind of work you wish to find. Next, choose the specific location you want to target (i.e., nationwide, state and/or city). Finally, by clicking "finish," your Job Alert is activated, and you will begin receiving e-mail alerts for positions meeting your search criteria.

As an alternative to Job Alert, you can elect to use the "Find a Job Now" option. This feature allows use of a single keyword as the basis for finding job matches.

4Work does not maintain a searchable resume database for use by employers. Instead, it relies on the Job Alert feature as the basis for matching the individual job seeker with a job. When the match is made, an e-mail alert allows you to preview the job and then, if interested, apply using the specific instructions provided by the employer in the job posting.

According to the Web site, 4Work believes its approach, using Job Alert, protects your privacy and allows you to control who does or does not receive your resume. Only those firms you choose to contact have the opportunity to review your credentials. So, it puts you completely in control of the process, and your privacy is protected.

6FigureJobs (www.6FigureJobs.com)

6FigureJobs is fast becoming a premiere career site for those looking for senior management or executive positions. A company spokesperson advises that the site's job board daily contains about 2,500 searchable positions, representing approximately 1,200 employers. Average salary of those using the site for job search purposes is approximately $150,000. Searching this internal database and posting your resume on the site is free.

However, for a modest fee, you can also use the site's meta job search feature to expand your search considerably. According to the Web site, this feature allows you to search a database of some 4.5 million jobs, 2.8 million from other job boards and 650,000 from corporate career centers.

Anyone can search and apply for positions listed on the Web site's internal database, however, registration and membership is recommended. Once inside, members can store and forward resumes to employers, access unadvertised opportunities, obtain a biweekly newsletter, and receive automatic e-mail notification of new positions matching their job search requirements.

A trial, nationwide search for Director of Human Resources instantly turned up some 20 job opportunities that appeared to be reasonable matchs. The easy-to-use search feature allows you to search by keyword, industry, function, and location. It also allows you to specify your job preference as full time, contract, or startup. Also, when reviewing job-listing details on those jobs you select, you can also activate "Hoover's Company Capsules," which appears at the bottom of each job posting, and instantly receive an overview of the company, its products, markets, and financials.

Abracat (www.Abracat.com)

Abracat's Web site boasts over 200,000 positions in its job database. Serving as the classified advertising Web site for over 700 smaller U.S. and Canadian newspapers, this site allows the job seeker to thoroughly search the smaller targeted job markets laying outside of the urban areas serviced by mass-circulation media. Resume/profile posting and job database search services are free to the job seeker.

After registering on the site, you can choose to use either the "Quick Job Search" or "Power Search" to scan the database for appropriate openings. The quick search option allows you to search using only location and occupational preference. Power Search, on the other hand, is more refined and provides the ability to search by occupation, desired location, and skill requirements.

If elected, the personal career agent, AdHound, continuously searches the ad database each day and automatically provides you with e-mail notification of jobs meeting your criteria. You can create as many AdHounds as you like, customizing each to your job preferences. You can also search for several types of positions—full time, consulting, contract, part-time, temporary, co-op, or intern.

Additionally, you can choose to post a full resume with name and contact information, or just a brief anonymous profile citing your qualifications. You can also elect to withhold your resume or profile, submitting them only to those employers in whom you have interest. In this way, your confidentiality is assured.

AfterCollege (www.AfterCollege.com)

Founded by two Stanford students in 1996, and recently rated as the number 1 college career center by Lycos. This site, as suggested by its name, caters to college students, recent grads, and recent alumni. Site usage is somewhat seasonal, reflecting the college recruiting season. A site spokesperson stated the site averaged about 5,000 to 5,500 job postings on any given day, but during the height of the recruiting season can reach levels of 8,000 to 10,000 jobs daily. Likewise, the range of employers advertising on a given day can swing from a low of about 150 to a high of 400 or better. Students are not charged a fee for either posting their resume or searching job listings.

The job search feature allows you to search the job database by occupational specialty, industry, work type (i.e., full time, part time, or internship/co-op), location (by state), and keyword. You resume can easily be uploaded, in MS Word format, for viewing by employers, however, your confidentiality is protected through elimination of your name and contact information. Interested employers will then contact you via e-mail, and, if interested in the position, you can opt to release your name and contact information at that time.

When browsing the Web for job opportunities in general, a nifty feature, AfterCollege Agent™, enables you to automatically send your resume to *any* e-mail address on the Web with a single click of the mouse. When activated, this feature allows you to say goodbye to attaching, copying, pasting, and even opening an e-mail application in order to send your resume—a huge time-saver! Also, the AfterCollege Alumni Network™ feature provides you with the opportunity to locate other registered alumni from your school, and is an excellent vehicle for job search networking!

America's Job Bank (www.ajb.dni.us)

America's Job Bank was developed as a partnership between the U.S. Department of Labor and some fifty states and four territories. It links employment services of these entities together in a common jobs database allowing the job seeker to search a huge number of job openings for the right employment opportunity. At the time of this writing, for example, the Web site was showing 867,153 positions posted on its job database and 476,012 resumes on its re-sume database. The cost of using this service is limited only the time that it takes you to register and establish a user-name and password. All services are absolutely free to the job seeker.

Following online registration, you initiate your job search by simply selecting an occupational area from a prescribed list. The selected category is then automatically expanded, allowing you to fine-tune your selection to a more specific area of occupational focus. As an alternate to this approach, you can choose to initiate your online search by entering keywords that most appropriately describe your area of oc-cupational interest.

Once search criteria have been finalized and entered, you can then specify the geographical focus of your job search by selecting national/international, state or specific city and zip code. This is then followed by selection of desired com-pensation range.

Should you wish to automate your search, you can choose the "Job Scout" feature simply by clicking on this option immediately following input of the above search criteria. In activating this feature, the system continuously checks all new employer job postings, automatically adding those matching your criteria to the Scout List. The program per-mits creation of up to 10 distinct Job Scouts, each reflect-ing totally different job search criteria.

As individual jobs are automatically added to your Job Scout list, simply click on a selected job title and review de-tails of the position, including company and position de-scriptions as well as directions on how to apply. Jobs in which you have specific interest can then be saved in the "My Account" section of the Web site for immediate action or further review at a later date.

The "My Account" feature allows you to manage your job search from a single location on the Web site. Here you can not only save jobs in which you have interest, but you can also create and store up to 5 different resumes and cover let-ters for instant use as needed.

BlueSteps (www.bluesteps.com)

Launched by the Association of Executive Search Consultants (AESC) in January 2001, this site has created a searchable resume database for use by some of the most prestigious global executive search firms. As of this writing, AESC has 144 member firms with offices in over 70 countries throughout the world, and includes such well-known member firms as Heidrick & Struggles, Korn/Ferry International, Russell Reynolds Associates, SpencerStuart, and Boyden. These are the firms to whom most major corporations look when filling top executive positions.

If you are a senior level executive earning over $100,000 per year, registration on this site is a must. According to BlueStep, the typical registrant earns $220,000, has 10+ years experience, and holds a postgraduate degree. The current registration fee of $99 would appear to be well worth the expenditure for those meeting the above criteria.

Upon registration, AESC member firms, through thousands of offices and consultants throughout the world, will have exclusive and confidential access to your personal profile and resume. According to the Web site, "Nonmember firms and other companies will not be able to view your career data. Furthermore, your information will not be disclosed to any third party without your express permission."

Once registered, the site states that your personal data will remain accessible to AESC members indefinitely, so your registration fee is a one-time investment.

BrassRing (www.BrassRing.com)

Claiming 1.7 million site visits per month and a database of some half-million resumes, BrassRing is a major destination job site for the job seeker and employer alike. Recipient of numerous awards, this site is a standout in the world of Internet job search and recruiting. For the job seeker the site is rich with relevant articles and career resources, and job search and resume posting services are provided at no cost.

After registering on the site and providing basic contact information, you first upload your resume, and are then asked to fill out a fairly detailed profile for use by employers in identifying you for their job openings. This profile includes years of experience, degree level, industry experience, salary requirements, willingness to relocate and travel, and citizenship status. An enhanced confidentiality feature allows you to block as many companies as you want from viewing your resume or profile. Additionally, you can choose to declare both your resume and profile as confidential, in which case they are not available to employers unless you elect to apply for a given position and manually send forward you resume document.

The Web site allows you to post and store up to five different resumes and cover letters. Additionally, the job search engine enables you to search the vast job database by date of job posting, keywords, industry, location, company, and so on. Individual searches can also be saved as a search agent, automatically scanning new job postings, and e-mailing results to you.

Other site features include the ability to research companies through use of the employer search functionality, the ability to get up-to-date career advice and job-hunting tips, and the opportunity to use the Salary Wizard to obtain job-relevant compensation data. You may also want to check BrassRing's calendar of career events for specific events, such as career fairs and seminars, that will be held in your area.

CareerBuilder (www.CareerBuilder.com)

The CareerBuilder Web site is another of the premiere online career sites. It is widely recognized as one of the Web's largest career sites, containing over 400,000 job listings and, according to the Web site, providing employers with access to over 3.9 million resumes. Purchase of Headhunter.net, another top career site, in 2001, further enhanced both the site's size and variety of career-related offerings. Use of both the job search and resume posting services of the site are free to the job seeker.

CareerBuilder's parent companies, Knight-Ridder Tribune and Gannett, own and operate 135 major metropolitan newspapers. These newspapers have renamed their Sunday career section CareerBuilder, offering a seamless transition from offline to online job seeker. Through its 375+ online partners, the site has over 6.5 million unique visitors per month and a resume database of over 6 million—both major attractions for employers who wish their job postings to receive maximum visibility on the Web.

A quick job search feature allows you to rapidly search job postings using keywords, city and state, occupation, field of interest, and Web ID. Additional search options include company, industry, Canadian, En Espanol, and International. You can also use this feature to automatically set up a personal search agent by clicking on the "E-mail me jobs like these" appearing on the search results page. By activating this feature, your search agent will automatically search new job postings and e-mail you those positions matching your search criteria.

As an option to "quick search," CareerBuilder offers its "smart choice" feature. Electing this choice requires you to register with the site and complete a very extensive personal profile and job requirement form as well as uploading or pasting your resume in the space provided for this purpose. When posting your resume, the site offers three privacy options: standard posting (highest visibility), anonymous posting (no contact info provided), or private posting (for applying online only).

The CareerBuilder Web site also offers a huge array of career-related resources and offerings, both directly and through its large network of affiliate partners.

CareerJournal (www.CareerJournal.com)

On the average day, according to a company spokesperson, you will find 50,000 to 75,000 jobs posted on the Career-Journal Web site. Average number of employers represented by these postings is about 10,000. Site content comes from the editorial resources of the *Wall Street Journal*, published by Dow Jones & Company, and the CareerJournal editorial team. Job seeker use of this site is free, it should be an obvious choice for those seeking senior management and executive positions.

When choosing to use the CareerJournal resume database, you can choose to use a resume or create a confidential profile. The confidential profile can be searched by corporate and executive recruiters and, where there is a match, recruiters will forward an e-mail to CareerJournal, which will then, in turn, be forwarded to you. Then, you decide whether or not to respond. CareerJournal states it will not share your contact information with recruiters. Optionally, you can create and store multiple resumes in your account, however, employers will not be able to view these unless you personally send them.

When using the job search feature to scan the job database for suitable opportunities, you can search by job title or full text, by keyword (any words or all words), and by location (city, state, zip code, and country). You can also search by occupational area and company, using drop-down menus for this purpose.

Other features offered by this Web site will enable you to:

- Create multiple resumes (tailored to multiple job search objectives).
- Receive job seek agents (automatic e-mails of new jobs matching your search criteria).
- Define job folders (save and organize jobs you find).
- Create cover letters (save multiple letters for use as needed).

ComputerJobs (www.ComputerJobs.com)

Founded in 1995, ComputerJobs.com is a leading IT employment Web site. Catering to information technology professionals, the site provides job seekers with high quality computer-related job opportunities and career-related content organized into 18 vertical skill sets and 20 major metropolitan markets. It is reported that more than 4,000 companies post jobs to the Web site. The site also reports over 190,000 IT resumes in its database and has some 1.2 million registered users.

At the time of this writing, the Web site showed a grand total of 5,348 job postings, including 840 new jobs posted within the past week. It also lists the number of job openings in each of the 20 cities covered, giving the job seeker a good idea of where to focus their job search.

Search for positions is easy and highly intuitive. You can search by location (city or state), by industry or by one of the 18 IT skill sets. By clicking on Detroit, for example, the Detroit page pops up, showing 133 current job listings. The Detroit page then shows the 18 skill set categories, with specific hot link job listings for each. By clicking on a link, you are immediately whisked to a description of the position and company, from which you can then apply by e-mailing a copy of your resume. Both search criteria and selected jobs can be saved for future reference or use.

Additionally, you can elect to post your resume to the Web site's huge resume database so that you can be easily identified by the many companies who use the site in search of qualified IT professionals.

DICE (www.DICE.com)

For over a decade, DICE, Inc. has been a leading provider of online recruiting services for technology professionals. Among several awards received by DICE since its inception, the 2002 Weddle's User's Choice Awards (a highly coveted award within the online recruiting industry) recognized this career Web site as the best specialty board for both recruiters and for job seekers. A call to a company spokesperson, at the time of this writing, indicated that job postings typically average approximately 30,000 positions daily, and represent about 3,000+ employers. Actual postings on the day of my call were 20,568. Both resume posting and job search are free services offered to site users.

When searching the site's job board for your next opportunity, you are offered three options: advanced search, metro search, and search by company. The advanced search feature provides full text search capability using all words, any words or Boolean expression. Additionally, this feature allows you to menu select type of position sought (i.e., full time, part time, contract), location preference (state and country), acceptable travel percentage, and whether you wish to limit your search to telecommuting only. Further, you can also search by telephone area code and specify formatting options, including the number of days you wish the search to go back as well as the number of positions to be displayed in search results.

The metro search feature offers the opportunity to search jobs by some 28 major cities, while the "search by company" feature, which uses a color-coded map, allows you to search for companies by geographical region or by alpha search. All search features are extremely user friendly and produce results quickly.

Once you have registered with DICE and set up an account, you have access to the Web site's many other functions and features. First, you can customize up to five separate profiles and, using the Job Alert feature, be automatically notified when a matching job is posted. Second, by filling out and posting a skills profile, you enable employers seeking this same skill set to identify and contact you. Additionally, you can create a new resume or paste an existing resume for use on the Web site.

Should confidentiality be an issue, the relatively new passive candidate database may be the way to go. This feature allows you to post a profile of your background without providing contact information or copy of your resume to an interested employer. Once you have been notified of an employer's interest, via a unique URL, you have the option to either disclose your identity and contact information or withhold it.

DirectEmployers (www.DirectEmployers.com)

Exploding onto the Internet job search scene in early 2002, DirectEmployer's employment search engine is owned and managed by employers through DirectEmployers Association, Inc., a nonprofit employer association. This search engine was developed by employers in response to the increasing costs employers have experienced in posting their job listings on the commercial job boards. Its popularity among companies is evidenced by the fact that, as of this date (January 6, 2003) employers already have 209,021 positions currently posted on the Web site—an incredible achievement!

Job seeker benefits are numerous and, best of all, the site's features cost nothing to use. A prime benefit realized by site users is participating companies list *all* jobs appearing on their Web site, rather than just the few typically advertised on commercial job boards. This is estimated to be more than three times the number of positions now found on the commercial boards. Second, you may establish ongoing relationships with employers leading to other opportunities for which they are not actively recruiting. Third, direct employer application eliminates the need to register with third-party job sites, thus ensuring greater privacy and faster decision making. Fourth, since you actually "visit" the company's Web site, you can use this opportunity to learn more about the company and view other opportunities described there. And finally, direct application to employers usually means that your resume will be stored in their resume management/applicant tracking system for review against future opportunities, in the event your initial application is unsuccessful.

The site's search engine is robust but, at the same time, is simple and easy-to-use. Using keyword search and a series of convenient drop-down menus, you can search job listings by industry, company, state, metro area, U.S. region, or International. You can elect to limit your search to employers only, or may also elect to include staffing firms— your choice.

Establishing an account allows you create and post a searchable resume, store and use your resume when applying for jobs, and create scheduled searches that automatically notify you if a company posts your dream job. You can also use the forums to network with fellow job seekers— sharing information, job leads, advice, and experiences.

ExecuNet (www.ExecuNet.com)

Founded in 1988, ExecuNet operates from a different business model than the traditional commercial job board. Targeting executives whose earnings are $100,000 and above, this organization operates much like a club, but with one of its benefits being online job search. New members currently pay a $150 membership fee for the first calendar quarter, and then $139 per quarter each subsequent quarterly membership renewal.

According to site literature, since 1988, ExecuNet has helped over 100,000 executives find new positions. In addition to its job listings and many online job-search related resources, the company sponsors over 70 informative networking meetings throughout the United States each month. Here members gather to hear knowledgeable experts speak on a variety of career and job-search related topics, as well as to mingle and network among meeting attendees. Membership includes access to ExecuNet's job listings and other online services.

Interestingly, companies and executive recruiters pay nothing to post job opportunities on the ExecuNet site, a major advantage of this Internet site. A company spokesperson indicated that some 15,000 companies and search firms make use of the site, and typical daily job postings number approximately 2,000 to 2,500 positions.

When searching the job database, you simply use a drop-down menu to select your target business function, then click on the search button. A listing of jobs then appears, showing job title, industry type, compensation level, and location. By clicking on one or more of the job listings, a screen then appears showing complete job details including position title, industry, location, compensation level, contact, job description, and qualifications required. You can try the search engine to see how it works; however, search results will exclude contact information unless you are an ExecuNet member.

FlipDog (www.FlipDog.com)

FlipDog delivers one of the Internet's largest job collections, all direct from their original source—employer Web sites, and use of the Web site by job seekers is free. Using proprietary web-crawling technology, FlipDog continuously combs the Web, pulling thousands of jobs off company Web sites and posting them to its own jobs directory. According to a company spokesperson, on a typical day, job listings total between 300,000 to 400,000 positions, and represent about

57,000 employers. This is one of the Internet's mega sites when it comes to career job boards and is well worth a try.

The Web site's job search engine is uncomplicated and easy to use. Using a map, you first click on a state, and then a list of cities appears. After choosing a city from the drop-down menu, you then choose a job category from a second menu. A list of companies, having openings in your designated job category then appears. By clicking on the names of selected companies, you are transported to their Web site, where you can apply for positions in which you have interest. Searches can be augmented and further refined by entering keywords in the keyword window provided for this purpose.

By registering and setting up a free account, job seekers can use the account feature to create and store both resumes and cover letters, instantly apply for selected positions, post their resume on the resume database for search by employers, and create multiple personal search agents that will e-mail matching jobs to them automatically. Also, the privacy setting feature allows the job seeker to select one of three privacy options (active, passive, or private) dependent on the degree of confidentiality they wish to maintain.

HotJobs (www.HotJobs.com)

HotJobs, a subsidiary of Yahoo!, is one of the leading career domains on the Web, and was voted "best general purpose job board" in a survey of job seekers by Weddle's, the noted research firm that evaluates Web-based employment resources. With over 100,000 job listings, posted by 20,000+ employers, it is considered one of the top Internet job boards and career sites. Use of its extensive site features and resources by the job seeker is free.

Job seekers can search the vast job database using either the quick search feature or the advanced job search option. Augmented by keyword search, the jobs database is searchable by job categories, company, staffing firm, U.S. location (city and state), and international location, and is very easy to use.

By registering for a my HotJobs account, you have immediate access to a number of neat features. This includes a resume manager that allows you to create, store, and use up to 10 different resume versions. You can either create your resume from scratch, using one of several resume templates provided, or paste a copy of an existing resume from your word processing files.

Privacy options include making your resume available for search by employers and staffing firms, employers only, staffing firms only, or classifying it as "all private," in which case it is searchable by neither. An additional privacy option, HotBlock, allows you to completely block designated companies from accessing and viewing your resume document at all.

Another site feature, enhanced career agent, allows you to create multiple personal search agents that will continuously screen new job postings against your search profile and automatically notify you of matching job opportunities.

Monster (www.Monster.com)

For sheer size and volume, as far as job seekers and recruiters are concerned, Monster.com continues to be the "Monster of the Midway"! According to its Web site, there are over one million job postings each month—that's 12 million per year! Since job seeker services are free, it would appear that registration on Monster.com should be standard operating procedure for anyone engaged in a serious job search.

Monster's search engine enables you to search its vast job database by location (U.S. city and state), industry, job category, company, and international location. Individual searches (maximum of five) can be saved in your My Monster account as search agents, automatically searching new job postings and listing matching opportunities in your account for periodic review, as your schedule permits.

Once site registration is complete and an account has been established, you can create and store up to five versions of your resume. Only one resume version, however, may be active and searchable by employers at a time. Should you wish to restrict resume access, this can be accomplished by simply "deactivating" all stored resumes, thus prohibiting access by all parties searching the resume database. Additionally, you can create and store up to five different cover letters for use as needed. When you elect to send a letter, you will be automatically prompted to insert the appropriate e-mail address.

Monster.com is loaded with job-search resources including over 3,000 pages of employment advice, resume help, salary data, industry information, and so on. It even has its own travel center, offering savings on airfare, hotels, and auto rentals.

NationJob Network (www.NationJob.com)

One of the pioneers of online job search, NationJob Network, is still among the top career sites on the Web and continues to win awards for excellence. Rated highly by such publications as *Fortune, BusinessWeek, PC World,* and others. Recently named by *Forbes* as *Best of the Web,* NationJob currently boasts over 850,000 job seeker subscribers, and has over 35 specialty sites attracting job seekers to specific categories of interest. According to *Forbes,* the "large number of postings, especially in the Midwest," and "jobs in small to medium-sized cities" are among NationJob's best features. According to a site spokesperson, typical daily job listings number about 25,000 to 30,000 positions, representing approximately 2,000 to 2,500 employers on average. There is no charge to job seekers for using the site.

Interestingly, NationJob has teamed up with a number of chambers-of-commerce throughout the United States, offering chamber members discounted pricing for job postings, with no fees charged to employers of less than 100 employees. This strategy has attracted a lot of job postings and accounts for NationJob's penetration in a many of the smaller markets not typically reached by the larger commercial job boards. The company, however, has its fair share of the large metro markets as well.

The search engine for use in scanning the job listings is one of the best out there. It consists of a number of drop-down menus making it truly simple to use. It also receives high marks for accuracy, delivering to the job seeker positions that are a close match to their requirements, something that is not true of many of the commercial job boards.

Searches can be accomplished by selecting a field/position (28 categories), geographical region (7 regions), degree level (none, Associates, Bachelor, or Post-Graduate), duration (full time, part time, contract/temporary), and salary range.

Using drop-down menus, the software then automatically breaks down these categories more definitively. For example, if you chose Human Resources as your field/position, you are now asked to choose (one or more categories) from a subset menu that includes all Human Resources, Benefits/Compensation, Employee/Labor Relations, Human Resources Management, Recruiting, and Training and Development. You are then asked to further narrow your search by choosing specific states within your targeted geographical region. This then leads to a menu requiring you to select specific cities and towns within these states. If you wish to further refine your search, you may enter appropriate keywords in the window provided and then click on the search button. Search results are then displayed as a list of positions and companies fitting your criteria. Clicking on each position listed then produces a complete description of that position along with contact information and instructions on how to apply.

Search criteria can then be saved on P.J. Scout, the site's personal search agent. P.J. will then continuously check each new job posting, automatically e-mailing a weekly listing of new positions meeting your search requirements.

NationJob also provides the job seeker with the opportunity to post their resume on the P.J. Resume Database Service, where it can be searched and reviewed by employers against their hiring requirements. This confidential service, according to the Web site, lets employers read your resume (though not your contact information) and contact you via e-mail with job openings. You then have the opportunity to contact the employer, if you choose to do so.

Net-Temps (www.Net-Temps.com)

Founded in 1996, Net-Temps is a privately held online recruiting portal principally serving the contract and temporary staffing industry, but more recently expanded to include direct employer job posting as well. This site has consistently ranked in the top ten job-posting sites, based on traffic, by Media Metrix and Nielsen Net Ratings. As of this writing, the Web site has a total of 37,398 job postings (21,316 contract jobs and 16,082 direct jobs). If you are considering the possibility of working as a temporary or contract worker, this is clearly the site you will want to use in finding employment. Both online search of the site's job postings and resume posting are free services offered to the job seeker. So, you have nothing to lose.

When searching the job listings, you have two choices. The first, quick search, allows you to search by location and keyword only. The expanded search feature allows you to search by career channel (16 categories), job type (*contract*— temporary/consulting, *direct*—full-time positions, or both *contract and direct*), location (state and city/town), and key words. From the search results page you can either click on a specific job listing or save the job to a clipboard for later review. When clicking on an opening, you are automatically transported to a position and candidate description from which you can apply directly for the job, store it on your clipboard, or forward it to a friend.

To post your resume on the site, you have two choices. You can either create a resume from scratch, using the online template provided, or simply copy and paste an existing resume from one of your stored word-processing documents files. Depending on your privacy needs, you can then click on the "activate" button, enabling companies to search and review your resume, or click on the "nonactive" button, in which case it cannot be viewed by others.

A nifty Job Seekers Desktop feature acts as a dashboard for managing your job search. From here you can create, store, send, edit, and post your resume (up to three different versions); create, edit, or delete up to five job search agents that will automatically e-mail matching positions to you; review your clipboard of saved job opportunities; check on the number of times your resume has been reviewed; track all job applications you have made (including specific notes on each); and track results of these applications.

The site also provides a Salary Wizard to help you determine what you are worth in the marketplace, and hundreds of articles offering career and job-hunting tips.

Recruiters Online Network
(www.RecruitersOnline.com)

Recruiters Online Network, as the name suggests, is a network of 11,000 employment agencies and search firms who subscribe to a common resume database, which they can search to find qualified candidates for their client companies. They also list client job openings on the Web site to attract candidates and encourage them to e-mail their resumes in response to theses opportunity listings. According to a site spokesperson, on a typical day there are about 17,000 to 18,000 searchable job postings on the site and about a half-million resumes in the resume database. Employers do not have direct access to the site or the resumes posted there.

As a job seeker, you can search the job database and post your resume in the resume database (searchable by the 11,000 member recruiters) free of charge. The job search engine is fairly simplistic, but adequate. You can search by keywords, industry, city, sate/providence, and country. There are international headhunters who post their jobs on the Web site, so it is possible to find jobs in various countries as well. Search results show up as a list of job titles within the geographical target you established as part of your search parameters. By clicking on a title, you are provided with a position and candidate description as well as contact information for reaching the employment agency who posted the position on the Web site.

A unique feature that might prove helpful to job seekers is the ability to search the 11,000 member database for employment agencies and search firms which specialize in the occupations and industries of interest to that job seeker. Searches can be conducted using occupational field, location, and keywords as the basis. Searches result in a list of recruiters meeting the job seeker's requirements. By clicking on the name of a specific recruiter, you can then get a detailed description of the recruiting firm and their specialties. You can also view all of the current search assignments on which these firms are working, and secure contact information to discuss specific opportunities that appear interesting.

TrueCareers (www.TrueCareers.com)

With the July 2002, acquisition of Career City, TrueCareers is fast emerging as a major job board/career site on the Internet. According to a company press release, the Web site, in just over one year of operation, has amassed a resume database of over one million resumes, which is sure to create increased interest on the part of employers looking for qualified candidates to fill their job openings. During this same period, daily job postings have gone from about 2,000 to approximately 25,000 (over a 1,000 percent increase). Web site information indicates the site is primarily focused on professional degreed candidates with experience, and draws heavily from the over seven million students now on the Sallie Mae student loan database. (It should be noted that True-Careers ia a subsidiary of Sallie Mae.) Both resume posting and search of the site's job listings are free to the job seeker.

There is a quick search feature that allows you to rapidly search the job database by keywords, field of interest (13 categories), and state. You can also find a specific company's list of openings by using the company alpha search capability. Additionally, you can view the site's job listings by either occupational category or by state.

The advanced job search feature is more comprehensive. Here you can search the job posting database by a combination of keywords, occupational category, employment type (full time, part time, contract, or intern), city, state, postal code, country, and radius (in mileage) from a specific postal code.

The TrueCareers Web site enables you to create, store, edit, and e-mail multiple resume documents. These can be developed using the site's resume builder, or may be pasted as a word document from your word processing documents file. When copying and pasting your resume in the resume section, you are asked to exclude contact information. Contact information, according to site instructions, is taken from the Contact page. As part of the resume posting process, you are asked to use drop-down menus to furnish additional information including job title, job function, and industry (best matching your background), citizenship status, and type employment sought (full time, part time, contract, or intern). You are then asked to choose one of the following three resume privacy selection: public (can see full resume and contact information), confidential (can see full resume excluding contact information—contact made via confidential e-mail through TrueCareers), or private (employers unable to see resume and contact information unless sent to them by you).

The Web site also allows you to create, store, edit, and send multiple cover letters from your account as needed. Additionally, you can create multiple search agents that will use your job requirements to automatically search new job postings and e-mail any matching your criteria to your account. Other features include "my job in-box where you will find jobs to which you have applied as well as those sent to you by your job search agents. Finally, the "my saved job searches" feature allows you to temporarily park jobs that you are planning to review at a later time.

The "career resources" area contains profiles of almost 50 common occupations for review by the job seeker. These provide insight into both the type of work as well as the skill profiles of those who would likely do well in each. These should prove helpful to those attempting to select and appropriate occupational fit.

GET ON THE NET!

As you can see from a review of these top 20 Internet career sites, there is a major revolution taking place in the world of job search. Take full advantage of the free offerings of these outstanding career sites, and your job search will get airborne in a hurry. The opportunity to use technology to rapidly search millions of jobs and market yourself to hundreds-of-thousands of employers, greatly increases the chances of finding that one dream job you are looking for. Don't hesitate, get on the "net" now. Post your resume so the world can discover you!

INDEX

C

D

E